# THE IMPLICATIONS OF CHINA-TAIWAN ECONOMIC LIBERALIZATION

Daniel H. Rosen & Zhi Wang

PETERSON INSTITUTE FOR INTERNATIONAL ECONOMICS
Washington, DC

January 2011

Daniel H. Rosen, visiting fellow at the Peterson Institute for International Economics, is a principal at the Rhodium Group, a New York-based research firm. He is also an adjunct professor at Columbia University's School of International and Public Affairs (2001–present). Rosen was a member of the National Economic Council staff (2000–01), where he served as senior adviser for international economic policy. His work has focused on the economic development of East Asia, particularly greater China, and US economic relations with the region. Other areas of research include energy, agriculture and commodities, trade and environment linkages, and economic transitions and competitiveness. He is author or coauthor of *Prospects for a US–Taiwan Free Trade Agreement* (2004), *Roots of Competitiveness: China's Evolving Agriculture Interests* (2004), *APEC and the New Economy* (2002), *Behind the Open Door: Foreign Enterprises in the Chinese Marketplace* (1998), and *Powering China* (1995).

Zhi Wang has been a senior international economist at the Research Division, Office of Economics, US International Trade Commission (USITC) since 2005. Before joining the USITC, he worked as an economist at Purdue University, the Economic Research Service of the US Department of Agriculture, and Bureau of Economic Analysis of the US Department of Commerce and as a senior research scientist at the School of Computational Sciences, George Mason University. He was a research fellow at the Chinese Academy of Agricultural Sciences before coming to the United States and served on the board of directors of the Chinese Economists Society in 1992–93. Wang's major fields of expertise include computable general equilibrium modeling, value chain in global production network, data reconciliation methods, economic integration in the Greater China area, Chinese economies, and international trade.

**PETER G. PETERSON INSTITUTE FOR INTERNATIONAL ECONOMICS**
1750 Massachusetts Avenue, NW
Washington, DC 20036-1903
(202) 328-9000   FAX: (202) 659-3225
www.piie.com

C. Fred Bergsten, *Director*
Edward Tureen, *Director of Publications, Marketing, and Web Development*
*Typesetting by BMWW*
*Printing by United Book Press, Inc.*

Printed in the United States of America
13 12 11    5 4 3 2 1

**Library of Congress Cataloging-in-Publication Data**

Rosen, Daniel H.
The implications of China-Taiwan economic liberalization / Daniel H. Rosen & Zhi Wang.
    p.  cm.
Includes bibliographical references and index.
  ISBN 978-0-88132-501-0
  1. China—Foreign economic relations—Taiwan.  2. Taiwan—Foreign economic relations—China.  3. China—Economic conditions—21st century.  4. Taiwan—Economic conditions—21st century.  5. United States—Commerce.  6. United States—Foreign economic relations.  7. International trade.  I. Wang, Zhi. II. Title.

  HF1604.Z4T286 2011
  337.5105124'9—dc22
                                2010046034

# Contents

**Boxes**

# Preface

China and Taiwan have each played important roles in the world economy over the past quarter century, and the Institute has devoted considerable attention to both. We have in particular assessed China's emergence since the early 1990s with a long list of studies, briefs and testimony on topics including rebalancing of the economy, exchange rate policy, the costs of trade protection, agriculture, foreign investment in China, energy-sector dynamics, the environment, and global and regional regime participation. Our work on Taiwan has covered the prospects for US-Taiwan trade deepening, exchange rates, industrial policy, regional trade regimes, electronic commerce and other topics. This volume adds an important facet to this body of work: assessing the implications of economic deepening between these Chinese economies themselves.

While the combined volume of trade and investment flowing across the Taiwan Strait has grown enormously over the past decades, it has done so in an asymmetric manner. Trade and investment has been flowing much more unimpeded from Taiwan to China than the other way. Taiwan maintained limitations to inflows from China ostensibly to mitigate security risks arising from China's insistence that Taiwan is a part of China even while its own outflows became ever more focused on the mainland. While this system has permitted Taiwan to benefit from China's development, it also gave rise to serious concerns about the longer-term prospects for the Taiwan economy as other economies in the region move concretely to lower barriers to economic integration with China, threatening Taiwan with trade diversion and marginalization. And the tone of ambiguity if not outright hostility in Taiwan toward China is hard to reconcile with the centrality of China to the Asian growth outlook (and to the world growth outlook for that matter).

Taiwan and China have therefore committed to normalizing and liberalizing their economic relationship. However, the scope of that opening, the bilateral effects and the global welfare effects are as yet poorly understood. This volume attempts to remedy that uncertainty with careful modeling combined with a qualitative assessment of the implications of the cross-strait economic opening now agreed in an Economic Cooperation Framework Agreement (ECFA). While all economic opening agreements are inherently political, the China-Taiwan undertaking is particularly fraught with political and geosecurity concerns since the Taiwan Strait remains one of the world's potential flashpoints for great power confrontation. This volume must therefore examine the security implications of cross-strait deepening in addition to the usual economic variables considered in trade deepening assessments.

Daniel Rosen's 2004 study for the Institute, *Prospects for a US-Taiwan Free Trade Agreement* (coauthored with Nicholas Lardy), was prescient in recommending that Taiwan focus on the larger benefits of cross-strait normalization, which he and Zhi Wang now catalogue in this volume, rather than the modest gains to be found in a US agreement at that time. As he and Wang point out, however, the cross-strait agreement now does make the prospect of deeper US-Taiwan economic relations more attractive. They conclude that the United States should consider the increased value of Taiwan as a gateway to China's domestic economy and respond strategically to the reality that even long-time geopolitical rivals are setting aside history to build economic relations. By attending to relations with Beijing, Taiwan appears to have increased the probability that additional undertakings will happen, and in fact Taiwan and Singapore are already in open consultations over a bilateral accord. This study continues a long tradition of Institute analysis of the implications and political economy of bilateral and plurilateral free trade agreements and similar undertakings including *Sustaining Reform with a US-Pakistan Free Trade Agreement* (2006), *Anchoring Reform with a US-Egypt Free Trade Agreement* (2005), *Free Trade Between Korea and the United States?* (2001), *New Regional Trading Arrangements in the Asia Pacific?* (2001), and *North American Free Trade: Issues and Recommendations* (1992).

The Peter G. Peterson Institute for International Economics is a private, nonprofit institution for the study and discussion of international economic policy. Its purpose is to analyze important issues in that area and to develop and communicate practical new approaches for dealing with them. The Institute is completely nonpartisan.

The Institute is funded by a highly diversified group of philanthropic foundations, private corporations, and interested individuals. About 35 percent of the Institute's resources in our latest fiscal year was provided by contributors outside the United States. This study was undertaken with support from the Smith Richardson Foundation and the Starr Foundation.

The Institute's Board of Directors bears overall responsibilities for the Institute and gives general guidance and approval to its research program, including the identification of topics that are likely to become important over the medium run (one to three years) and that should be addressed by the Institute. The director, working closely with the staff and outside Advisory Committee, is responsible for the development of particular projects and makes the final decision to publish an individual study.

The Institute hopes that its studies and other activities will contribute to building a stronger foundation for international economic policy around the world. We invite readers of these publications to let us know how they think we can best accomplish this objective.

C. FRED BERGSTEN
Director
December 2010

# Acknowledgments

Daniel Rosen and Zhi Wang are grateful for the assistance and support of many people in the course of preparing this study. Research assistance was provided by a number of Rosen's Rhodium Group colleagues based in New York. Nin-Hai Tseng was responsible for collecting and organizing the initial statistics for the study, which she undertook with typical independence and perseverance. Pan Hua helped manage final preparations of the text, as well as helping to organize review sessions in Beijing to critique the manuscript. Particular credit is due to two other members of the Rhodium team. Shashank Mohan coordinated the economic modeling work under Zhi Wang's supervision, bringing enormous creativity and energy to the task of tweaking the model to reflect rapidly changing assumptions about the parameters for cross-strait opening, collecting data for the baseline calibration, and pulling model results into tables and graphs from the policy simulations. Thilo Hanemann worked tirelessly to integrate the quantitative analysis with the authors' qualitative assessments.

The authors benefited from two study groups held to review the quantitative results, one at the Peterson Institute for International Economics in September 2009 and the other in Beijing in November 2009. Daniel Rosen benefited from meetings organized by Taiwan's Board of Foreign Trade and National Security Council in April 2009, which were critical for their ability to design model scenarios, and corresponding meetings at China's Taiwan Affairs Office. Susan Shirk at the University of San Diego and Steve Orlins at the National Committee for US-China Relations made key introductions on both sides of the Taiwan Strait. Xu Shiquan of China's National Society for Taiwan Studies was essential in helping us clarify China's position on key matters. In Hong Kong, Ronnie Chan convened senior policy professionals with perspective on both deepening economic relations with the mainland and with regard to Taiwan affairs.

Participants in study groups made valuable comments. Extensive written feedback from Nick Lardy at the Peterson Institute—Rosen's coauthor on an earlier Institute study on Taiwan and the originator of the grant behind the current volume—was invaluable, as were written comments from Drew Thomson of the Nixon Center and Ellen Frost. Lawrence Shao-liang Liu at China Development Financial Holding Corporation in Taipei was extremely helpful. The American Chamber of Commerce in Taipei was also very helpful.

On security dynamics the authors have benefited from advice (imperfectly followed) from Bonnie Glaser, Don Keyser, Michael Green, Alan Romberg, Derek Mitchell, Mark Stokes, Randy Schriver, and of course Richard Bush. Rupert Hammond-Chambers of the US-Taiwan Business Council has been helpful for many years, on politics and security but on commercial and economic matters as well.

The final manuscript benefited from careful review and suggestions from four outstanding outside reviewers: John Gilbert of Utah State University, Doug Paal of the Carnegie Endowment, Eric Ramstetter of International Centre for the Study of East Asian Development, and Tung Chen-yuan of Taiwan's National Chengchi University. The authors are especially grateful for their contributions. The Peterson Institute's publications department is the envy of think tanks around the world, and for good reason: The authors are grateful for the department's ability to process their manuscript into this volume with such alacrity.

The authors regret omitting a long list of individuals currently serving in government in Taipei, Beijing, Washington, and elsewhere. They have adopted this convention due to the preference of the majority to remain unrecognized. Without question, these public officials were the most essential contributors to the authors' understanding of the topic, and without them this study would not be possible.

This study was supported by a generous grant from the Smith Richardson Foundation. Allan Song at the Foundation has been more than patient in awaiting this publication. Suffice it to say that the Smith Richardson Foundation had extraordinary foresight and timing in backing this volume on the implications of closer China-Taiwan economic relations, as this publication and that eventuality are so closely set in time. The authors are grateful for that support and thank them for their tolerance on the time-table.

Finally, Dan Rosen wishes to thank the Peterson Institute for inviting him to maintain a productive, not-in-residence relationship with the Institute for the past decade. This is his fourth book completed as a visiting fellow. He would like to dedicate this book to his daughters, Annabelle and Josephine, in the hope that they will grow up knowing Asia more an economic miracle and less as a security dilemma.

Zhi Wang wishes to thank Robert Koopman and Hugh Arce at the US International Trade Commission for their strong support of his China-related research since joining the commission. His greatest debt is to his wife, Zhonghua Yan, for her tolerance of endless evenings conducting the modeling and simulation exercises for this study and her willingness to endure with him the vicissitudes of his endeavors to promote economic integration in the greater China area.

# Acronyms

| | |
|---|---|
| ADB | Asian Development Bank |
| APEC | Asia Pacific Economic Cooperation Forum |
| ARATS | Association for Relations across the Taiwan Strait, China |
| ASEAN | Association of Southeast Asian Nations |
| ASEAN+3 | Association of Southeast Asian Nations plus China, Japan, and South Korea |
| CEPA | Closer Economic Partnership Agreement, Hong Kong |
| CES | constant elasticity of substitution |
| CET | constant elasticity of transformation |
| cif | cost, insurance, and freight |
| CGE | computable general equilibrium |
| DPP | Democratic Progressive Party, Taiwan |
| ECCT | European Chamber of Commerce in Taipei |
| ECFA | Economic Cooperation Framework Agreement |
| EIU | Economist Intelligence Unit |
| ELES | Extended Linear Expenditure System |
| FDI | foreign direct investment |
| fob | free on board |
| FTA | free trade agreement |
| GTAP | Global Trade Analysis Project |
| IIP | international investment position |
| ISIC | International Standard Industrial Classification |
| IMF | International Monetary Fund |
| ITA | Information Technology Agreement |
| ITRI | Industrial Technology Research Institute, Taiwan |
| KORUS | Korea–United States Free Trade Agreement |
| LCD | liquid crystal display |
| M&A | merger and acquisition |

| | |
|---|---|
| MAC | Mainland Affairs Council, Taiwan |
| MFN | most favored nation |
| MOEA | Ministry of Economic Affairs, Taiwan |
| MOFCOM | Ministry of Commerce, China |
| MOU | memorandum of understanding |
| NAFTA | North American Free Trade Agreement |
| OECD | Organization for Economic Cooperation and Development |
| QDII | qualified domestic institutional investor |
| QFII | qualified foreign institutional investor |
| SAM | social accounting matrix |
| SEF | Straits Exchange Foundation, Taiwan |
| TFP | total factor productivity |
| TFT | thin film transistor |
| TIFA | US-Taiwan Trade and Investment Framework Agreement |
| TPPA | Trans-Pacific Strategic Economic Partnership Agreement |
| WTO | World Trade Organization |

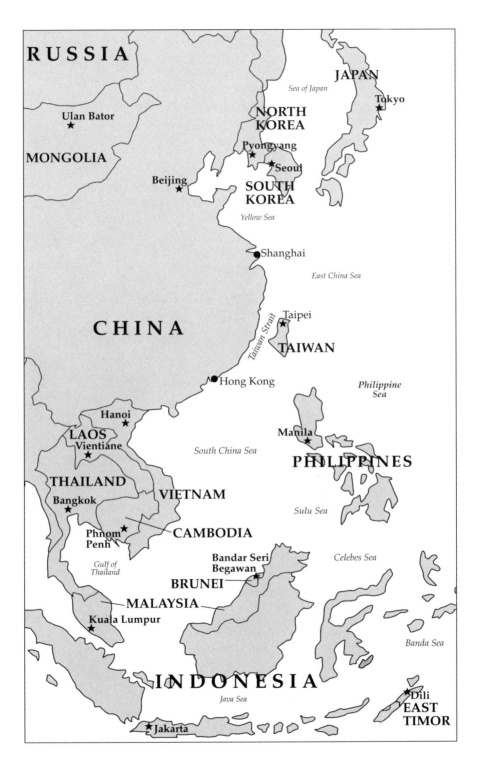

# Introduction

On June 29, 2010, representatives of China and Taiwan signed an Economic Cooperation Framework Agreement (ECFA) in Chongqing, China. The agreement is a road map to a comprehensive free trade agreement (FTA) covering most aspects of economic relations across the Taiwan Strait. Whether that map will be followed faithfully is not a given, but the initial "early harvest" terms are a strong down payment.[1] It is a significant undertaking in economic terms, although in the Asia-Pacific neighborhood such integration is increasingly the norm rather than the exception. But the significance of the ECFA is more than economic. China regards Taiwan as a renegade province, while Taiwan sees itself as either de facto or de jure independent of the mainland, depending on whom you ask. The legacy of 20th century Chinese history has kept the sides apart in many ways, even while one of the most interdependent commercial relationships in the world has grown up between them. The ECFA foretells a shared economic destiny with a heavy political subtext, not just a normal trade-deepening arrangement.

The agreement was negotiated during the most tumultuous years in global economic affairs since China's republican era. But despite the global maelstrom, officials in Beijing and Taipei delivered an agreement on the schedule they had set out to achieve. China sees the agreement as drawing Taiwan closer in sociological terms, and thus has a logic independent of commercial considerations. For Taiwan, China's relative strength through the financial crisis of 2008–09 and beyond made it even clearer that deepening cross-strait relations was imperative.

---

1. An early harvest agreement refers to a reduction in tariffs on selected products prior to entering into a full-fledged FTA.

The cross-strait gambit is significant for the bilateral economic outlook and for the regional outlook as well. China-Taiwan economic rapprochement unlocks the prospect of including Taiwan in a broader array of liberalization agreements in Asia. Moreover, it lends momentum to the regionwide integration train. It moderately displaces those economies that had served as entrepôts for China-Taiwan trade and transport flows in the past, especially Hong Kong. And it gives Taiwan additional advantages—if only for a brief moment—over rival South Korea (short-lived because South Korea starts FTA consultations with China in 2011).

The implications do not stop with the economics, and they do not stop with Asia. The Taiwan Strait is commonly referred to as the most serious potential security flashpoint in Asia—meaning the most likely to tangle global powers in a confrontation. Therefore if the economic significance of the ECFA were not enough to get the attention of the United States, which is committed to serve as security guarantor for a peaceful resolution of China-Taiwan differences, then the geosecurity implications of closer cross-strait economic relations certainly are. The United States will experience a modest direct trade diversion impact from a fully implemented ECFA, a more significant impact in terms of Asia-Pacific economic leadership and momentum, and a very important but difficult-to-calculate impact on the security scene from altered political dynamics between Taipei and Beijing.

Myriad political, political economy, security, and commercial and economic questions arise from the policy development of closer cross-strait economic relations. This study attempts to make it easier to analyze and answer many of those questions by clarifying the long-term economic implications of cross-strait liberalization. Our goal is to combine a narrow but thorough assessment of the immediate economic implications of cross-strait deepening with a richer exploration of the strategic significance for the parties directly involved and for interested third parties, most importantly the United States.

Chapter 1 sets the scene for a forward-looking assessment by reviewing current China-Taiwan economic relations. We highlight trade, investment, and the movement of people in the context of growth and the relationship of these economies to the rest of the world. From this review of the status quo, we draw observations about abnormalities at present and their implications.

Building on this foundation, chapter 2 introduces an economic model to examine the likely effects of normalizing and liberalizing cross-strait economics. These effects will require some time to accrue, and we project effects out to 2020 to capture that.

Chapter 3 looks beyond China and Taiwan in several ways. First, we ask whether cross-strait economic deepening will significantly affect other economies in terms of trade creation or diversion. We also ask the critical Taiwan-specific question of how much more significant the effects would be if Taiwan were able to use normal cross-strait ties as a spring-board toward inclusion in regionwide economic liberalization under way. This has been a cherished ambition in Taiwan, and will continue to be a priority.

Chapter 4 addresses these questions in terms of the United States. But it also goes further to consider the geoeconomic significance of China-Taiwan economic deepening for the United States. Finally, it follows the analysis to the logical endpoint of security and political considerations, which loom at least as large in Washington as trade and investment flows.

Finally, chapter 5 rounds up the observations, implications, and conclusions flowing from this analysis for policymaking audiences. We believe that there are important policy implications worthy of attention in Taipei, Beijing, and Washington and that, given the importance of that triptych for the international economy generally, officials in other capitals may also take note. The commercial effects of the policy shocks we explore are complex and in some cases surprising, and so we will not be surprised if the business decision-making audience takes an interest in our projections as well.

As a point of departure, we highlight a common thread that runs through all three sets of conclusions. Whatever policy initiative is begun to deepen cross-strait economic relations will not mark the resolution of the six decades of history that have defined China-Taiwan-US relations so much as it will mark the beginning of the most dramatic decade of that evolution. We hope this study can help clarify some of the commercial and economic uncertainties about the implications of China-Taiwan economic deepening so that attention can be redirected toward achieving mutually beneficial outcomes to the competitiveness, geopolitical, and geostrategic questions we identify but cannot answer.

# China-Taiwan Economic Relations

Both China and Taiwan have sustained rapid economic growth for more than three decades, and this growth has become ever more symbiotic over the years, despite political ups and downs.[1] By 2009 China's GDP was reported at $4.9 trillion, or $3,680 per capita, while Taiwan's GDP was $370 billion—much smaller in absolute terms, but an impressive $16,442 on a per capita basis given its modest population of 23 million (fewer than greater Chongqing alone).[2] For a decade and a half, Taiwan and China have ridden the same wave of globalization, a wave that has drawn them increasingly closer to one another. Since early in China's post-1978 reform period, Taiwanese entrepreneurs and capital, along with outsourcing by Taiwanese firms, have played an important role in seeding coastal China with manufacturing capabilities. Today, those early investments in China anchor powerful, global production chains stretching from Taiwan's Hsinchu Technology Park to Chinese factories in the south, east, and, increasingly, inland, to the retail electronics giants of North America and Europe.

This growing interdependence is manifest in all economic indicators, though not symmetrically. China is generally open to Taiwanese trade, in-

---

1. Authorities in Taiwan and Beijing have incompatible preferences with regard to the proper nomenclature for their respective polities, especially in discussions of cross–Taiwan Strait matters. The authors of the present volume are economists with insufficient expertise to comment on these toponymic concerns, and we therefore employ the vernacular terminology for these distinct economic entities most commonly understood by the American reading audience, without prejudice to political interpretations.

2. Measured in purchasing power parity terms, Taiwan's and China's respective per capita GDPs were $29,829 and $6,546 in 2009, according to the International Monetary Fund (IMF).

vestment, and labor, while Taiwan has been far more restrictive toward reciprocal flows from China. Two-way trade as a share of all trade and GDP had grown almost continuously since the 1980s from Taiwan to China, and since 2000 from China to Taiwan, before hitting the global financial crisis wall in 2008, from which trade is now recovering sharply. Direct investment from Taiwan to China has driven China's redevelopment since the early days of reform, though most of it was routed through Hong Kong and other locations. Direct investment from China to Taiwan, by contrast, has been severely limited by the unreadiness of both parties. But these limitations are under revision, and genuine two-way investment will likely grow significantly (though the balance of openness will favor Taiwanese outflows for some time). This is true for portfolio investment restrictions as well, giving investors from both sides the opportunity to invest in stocks, bonds, and other securities issued by the other. The movement of people across the Taiwan Strait has also expanded rapidly, though with a pronounced asymmetry: the number of Taiwanese citizens visiting or working in China dramatically surpasses the number of visitors and permanent residents from China in Taiwan. Normalization of long-stymied direct transportation links and tourism policies is broadening the base of two-way exchanges beyond business interests to civic groups and individuals.

The organic, bottom-up growth of economic interaction for more than 20 years occurred despite political tensions and obstacles to commerce. Recently, stepped-up ad hoc negotiations have accelerated the pace of economic integration and begun to formalize quasi-official mechanisms to undergird bilateral commerce. Arguably, the effectiveness of the ad hoc approach is already on the decline, and a more comprehensive approach to cross-strait economics is past due.

Such an approach is being undertaken in the form of an Economic Cooperation Framework Agreement that will soon lead to FTA-type talks. Chapter 2 of this study explores the ECFA and its likely economic implications. To set the scene for that analysis of the economic consequences of closer China-Taiwan economic relations, this chapter examines the status quo in terms of the flow of trade, investment, and people.

## Trade: Data Problems, Economic Drivers, and Political Barriers

### Trade in Goods

Taiwan-China trade in goods has swelled over the past decade as China assumed the leading role in final assembly in regional manufacturing production networks, foremost in information and communications technology. The exact values are obscured by politicized trade regimes that complicate statistical recordkeeping, unilateral Taiwanese import bans on basic products from China, and the fact that Taiwan's exports to China largely consist of intermediate products then assembled and reexported to consumers in North America, Europe, and elsewhere. In other words, China runs a large trade deficit with Taiwan that is more than offset by a trade surplus with the United States and Europe, but, nonetheless, China's trade deficit with Taiwan would be smaller if it were not for protectionist Taiwanese policies.

The starting point for an analysis of cross-strait trade patterns is the aggregate direct trade numbers issued by statistical authorities, which illustrate the complicated trade relationship between China and Taiwan (figure 1.1). China's exports to Taiwan remained relatively low during the 1990s and gradually grew to around $5 billion annually in the years preceding China's accession in 2001 to the World Trade Organization (WTO). Since then, annual exports have grown fivefold to around $25 billion to $30 billion in recent years despite import restrictions on the Taiwan side (see discussion on trade barriers below). The difference between Taiwan's reported imports and China's reported exports was 21 percent on average over 2000–2009. Whereas a certain variance in bilateral trade statistics is natural because of the use of different valuation concepts,[3] this discrepancy is much more pronounced due to indirect trading through third locations. In the case of China and Taiwan, Hong Kong has evolved as a major transshipment location as a result of historical restrictions on direct trade, but also because of its status as the largest reexport hub in the region and as a doorway to the south China economy, where many Taiwanese manufacturing operations are located. These indirect flows inflate the natural discrepancy between cost, insurance, and freight (cif) and free on board (fob) shipping, as import numbers are tracked on a country-of-origin basis (which includes indirect flows) whereas export numbers often capture only the first and not the final destination of goods. Valuation effects related to indirect trade flows—such as reexport markups (the "value added" by the third location) or mispricing to evade taxes or circumvent quotas and other trade restrictions—can further increase these discrepancies.[4]

Whereas the discrepancy for China's exports to Taiwan is in the same range as with other trading partners,[5] the discrepancy for trade flows in the other direction is more extreme. In the second half of the 1990s,

3. Export data are usually valued in fob prices (which means the price at which the exporter delivers a product past the ship's rails at the port of shipment), whereas import data are valued in cif prices (which is the fob price plus costs, freight, and insurance, or total costs associated with transport of the goods to the named port at destination).

4. For further elaboration on discrepancies in bilateral trade statistics, see Ferrantino and Wang (2008).

5. For example, the differential over the period between China's figures and partner data in the United States and Japan ranges from 20 to 29 percent.

**Figure 1.1  Cross-strait merchandise trade, nominal and adjusted flows, 1991–2009**

billions of US dollars

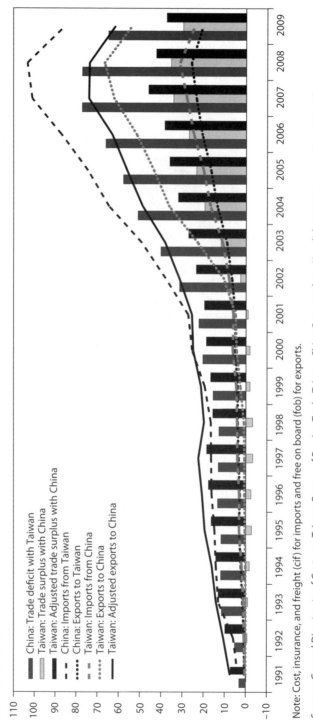

Note: Cost, insurance, and freight (cif) for imports and free on board (fob) for exports.

*Sources:* General Directorate of Customs, Taiwan; Bureau of Foreign Trade, Taiwan; China Customs, http://english.customs.gov.cn; Hong Kong Customs.

## Box 1.1    Estimating Taiwan's exports to China

Taiwan's Mainland Affairs Council (MAC) and Board of Foreign Trade use the following formula to estimate the value of Taiwan's exports to China:

$$A + (B1 - B2)*80\% + C - r*A.$$

The variety of different trade flows built into this formula demonstrates the complicated nature of China-Taiwan economic relations. The first item is straightforward: explicit direct exports to China from Taiwan ($A$). Second, MAC takes what Taiwan says it exports to Hong Kong and subtracts what Hong Kong says it imports from Taiwan—the difference (less shipping) being Taiwan's exports being transshipped through Hong Kong to China ($B1 - B2$). The MAC formula actually just takes 80 percent of this amount, the remainder presumably being transshipped off somewhere else. To this is then added exports shipped indirectly but formally to China, so-called transit trade through Hong Kong ($C$). Finally, since the increase in explicit direct exports increasingly displaces that transit trade—except for shipments that go to Guangdong, for which Hong Kong is a natural first stop—a subtraction of 33 percent (the average ratio of Taiwanese exports to Guangdong to total exports to China) times explicit direct exports is made ($r*A$). The latter adjustment and the exclusion of one-fifth of the Hong Kong discrepancy are meant to avoid double counting.

Taiwan's direct shipments to China were prohibited, so recorded exports were virtually zero, whereas China's data recorded indirect imports through Hong Kong. Around 2000, the deviation between Taiwan's reported exports and China's reported imports was 500 percent and more. In the years that followed, direct shipping was gradually allowed, and in recent years the divergence has declined to around 60 percent. However, in 2009 the difference between China's reported imports and Taiwan's reported exports was still more than $25 billion. The reason for this large discrepancy is twofold. Taiwan's statistics are not capturing the real extent of exports to China, as they are omitting indirect flows. On the other hand, China's figures overcount imports from Taiwan, as they appear to cumulate all of Taiwan's direct exports and all transit trade through Hong Kong and other third countries such as Japan, and do not adjust for the above-mentioned valuation effects.[6] In order to approximate the real extent of Taiwan's exports to China, which lies somewhere in the middle of the two figures, we can use a formula from Taiwan's Mainland Affairs Council and Board of Foreign Trade (see box 1.1). The solid line and dark

---

6. According to estimates from the Hong Kong Census and Statistics Department, the average reexport markup rate for Taiwanese goods going to the mainland was about 8 to 11 percent during 2004–07, while the rate for Chinese goods to Taiwan was about 4 to 7 percent in the same period.

columns in figure 1.1 present these adjusted numbers for two-way trade between Taiwan and China alongside the nominal figures. Understandably, the discrepancies were quite significant in the 1990s but have since gradually narrowed.

Based on adjusted numbers, two-way trade has averaged 16 percent growth annually for the past decade, lifting the value of trade from $30 billion in 2000 to $105 billion in 2008, this after having roughly tripled in the preceding decade of the 1990s. In 2008, Taiwan's exports to China reached $74 billion, accounting for 8 percent of total Chinese imports that year.[7] In comparison, Taiwan's imports from China totaled $30 billion, leaving a $44 billion Taiwanese trade surplus. In 2009, bilateral trade crashed in line with the decline in global trade flows (to $87 billion), but was back on track to previous highs with $25 billion in the first quarter of 2010.[8] While the absolute value of Taiwan's trade surplus with China has grown increasingly large over time, the ratio of Taiwan-China cross-strait exports has come down since the advent of nontrivial Chinese exports to Taiwan beginning around the time of the two economies' WTO accession in December 2001. The ratio went from $5 of Taiwanese exports to China for each $1 of Chinese exports to Taiwan in 2001 to around $3 to $1 in 2008–09.

Although China's and Taiwan's trade statistics fall short of accurately capturing Taiwanese exports to China, we have to rely on these datasets for most of the following detailed analysis. The computable general equilibrium trade model we later use to compute various scenarios to assess the economic impact of cross-strait economic deepening adjusts for reexports via Hong Kong but no additional third countries, which has important implications for interpretation of the results.[9]

In the aggregate, is Taiwan's structural cross-strait trade surplus disadvantageous for China? From Taiwan's perspective, its exports to China reflect migration of final assembly that used to occur elsewhere—most notably in Taiwan itself—to China, which then generates reexports of final goods to other markets. Also, in the process of setting up the operations to facilitate those reexports, machinery and equipment exports have followed direct investment from Taiwan to China. And certainly given China's structural global trade surplus, Beijing should not be concerned about bilateral trade deficits. Figure 1.2 shows the net value of regional surpluses and deficits for China, and figure 1.3 shows the shift of US

---

7. Estimate based on adjusted Taiwanese fob exports to China plus a 25 percent upward adjustment for transportation-related costs to make the number comparable to Chinese cif import statistics.

8. Nominal number from China Customs, http://english.customs.gov.cn.

9. For details on the model and interpretation of results, see explanations and comments in chapters 2 and 3.

**Figure 1.2 China's trade balance by region, June 2003–June 2010** (monthly surplus or deficit; three-month moving average)

billions of US dollars

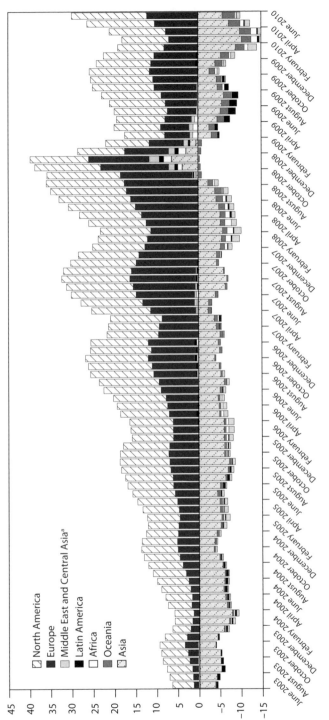

a. Includes Bahrain, Kuwait, Oman, Palestine, Israel, Qatar, Saudi Arabia, United Arab Emirates, Yemen, Iraq, Iran, Kazakhstan, Uzbekistan, Tajikistan, Kyrgyzstan, and Turkmenistan.

*Source:* China Customs, from CEIC.

**Figure 1.3   Composition of US merchandise trade deficit, 1994–2009**

percent of total deficit

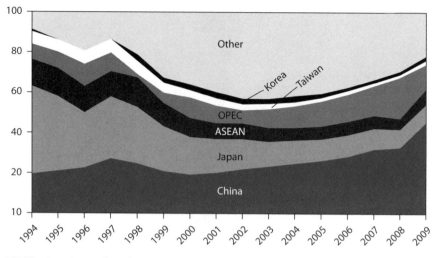

ASEAN = Association of Southeast Asian Nations; OPEC = Organization of Petroleum Exporting Countries.

*Source:* US import and export merchandise trade statistics via US Trade Online.

deficits from a range of Asian economies to a concentration in China over the past decade. However, China officially takes a different position. While acknowledging that direct investment from Taiwan and other origins benefits China and contributes to its export performance, officials have attributed this "serious imbalance" to restrictive trade policies and other measures taken by Taiwan exclusively against China. China further argues that these restrictions are not justifiable under WTO rules and norms and should be rescinded (WTO 2006). Notwithstanding this argument, China has (largely for political reasons) stopped short of formally challenging Taiwan's barriers through the WTO or other fora.

China's role as a final assembler in global manufacturing value chains became significant in the 1990s, with Taiwanese production of high-value intermediate goods going into those value chains. Indeed, Taiwanese firms in consumer electronics and other industries often were the pioneers in building China into this value chain role. Figure 1.4 shows that electrical machinery and optical equipment have dwarfed other Taiwanese exports such as chemicals, base metals, and plastics.[10] In fact, just

---

10. As discussed further below, we employ Taiwan direct trade data for a description of China-Taiwan trade for the sake of consistency unless indicated otherwise. Due to restrictions on direct trade, the value of these data before 2000 is very limited. Mirror data for earlier years are available from China Customs, http://english.customs.gov.cn.

**Figure 1.4  Taiwanese exports to China by category, 1993–2009**

billions of US dollars

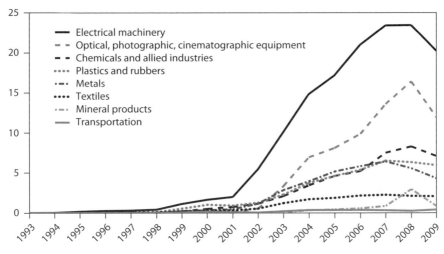

*Source:* Unadjusted flows, Bureau of Foreign Trade, Taiwan.

a handful of Taiwanese electronics-related manufacturers have a dominant role in Taiwan's relations with the mainland.[11]

By 2009, 8 percent of China's imports originated from Taiwan. In manufactured processing trade (which includes most of China's high-tech exports), 82 percent of Chinese product value by 2006 came from foreign value added, not value created in China (Koopman, Wang, and Wei 2008). For example, 99 percent of China's computer exports arise from processing trade. And given that Taiwanese brands control 80 percent of the world laptop computer market, it is apparent that a high share of Taiwan's exports to China is bound for other markets. Mirror data from China Customs presented in figure 1.5 show that about 70 percent of China's imports from Taiwan are processing goods.[12] According to Chinese data, wholly foreign-owned or joint venture firms accounted for about 80 percent of China's imports from Taiwan in 2008, and many of

---

11. The authors thank reviewer Eric Ramstetter for pointing this out, noting that "nine of Taiwan's 10 largest manufacturers in 2006 were in these categories [electrical and optical machinery]: Hon Hai Precision, Quanta Computer, Asustek Computer, Taiwan Semiconductor, Compal Electronics, AU Optronics, Inventec Corp., Winstron Corp., and Chi Mei Corp. These firms alone accounted for sales of NT$3.3 trillion in electronics-related industries or 24 percent of the sales of the largest 2,687 manufacturers in Taiwan."

12. While China's reported value of imports from Taiwan is likely overestimated (see our comments earlier in this section), the ratios shown in figures 1.5 and 1.7 should be close to reality, as both denominator and nominator are scaled up in the same way.

**Figure 1.5   Composition of China's imports from Taiwan, 1995–2008**

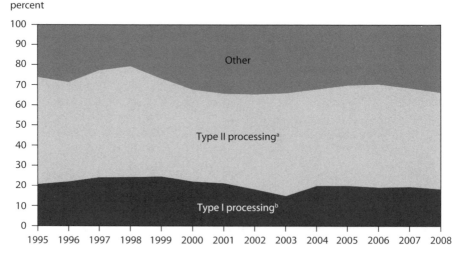

percent

a. Type II processing: ownership of traded components is transferred to a local firm.
b. Type I processing trade: traded components remain the property of the foreign supplier.

*Source:* China Customs, http://english.customs.gov.cn.

these are in fact Taiwanese firms.[13] Of course, the same integration that was profitable enough to lure Taiwanese manufacturers despite political risks inflicted severe pain on Taiwan as global demand for "China's" finished goods plummeted during the 2008–09 financial crisis, reducing Taiwanese exports by more than 40 percent year on year in December 2008 and January 2009 while Taiwanese imports from China fell by a much smaller percentage.

Taiwan's imports from China have also grown significantly in recent years, doubling in share terms from 7 percent of total Taiwanese imports in 2002 to 14 percent in 2009, notwithstanding the unilateral prohibitions on many imports from China that are not applied to other economies (discussed below). Figure 1.6 provides a breakdown of Taiwan's imports from China. Electrical machinery is the largest import category by value, by a considerable margin. A greater share of these imports is for final consumption in Taiwan and not for reexport, partly explaining why these imports have not grown at the rate that Taiwan's exports to China have. The data from China Customs shown in figure 1.7 support this point. The share of processing trade in China's exports to Taiwan is lower than in the other direction and declined from over 60 percent before China's WTO accession to less than half in 2008. The share of these Chinese exports going to

---

13. China Customs data; statistics on trade by firm ownership.

**Figure 1.6    Taiwanese imports from China by category, 2000–09**

billions of US dollars

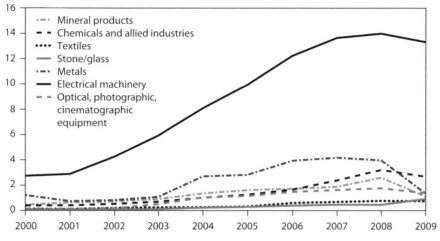

Source: UN Comtrade database, accessed through the World Bank's World Integrated Trade Solution (WITS) software.

**Figure 1.7    Composition of China's exports to Taiwan, 1995–2008**

percent

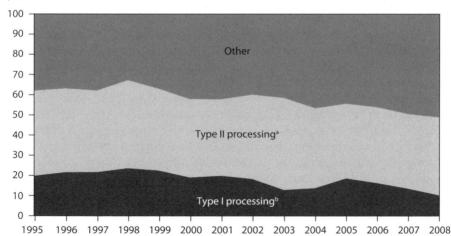

a. Type II processing: ownership of traded components is transferred to a local firm.
b. Type I processing trade: traded components remain the property of the foreign supplier.

Source: China Customs, http://english.customs.gov.cn.

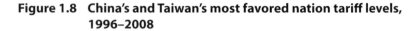

**Figure 1.8  China's and Taiwan's most favored nation tariff levels, 1996–2008**

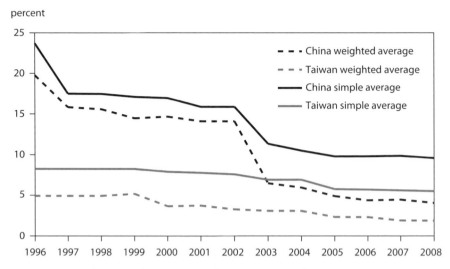

percent

Legend:
- China weighted average
- Taiwan weighted average
- China simple average
- Taiwan simple average

Notes: Missing values in single years were replaced with values of the previous year. For China, the value for 2002 is missing and the 2001 value is taken for that year. For Taiwan, the values for 1997, 1998, and 2004 are missing; the value for 1996 is used for 1997–98, and 2003 is used in lieu of 2004.

Source: UNCTAD, Trade Analysis and Information System (TRAINS) database, accessed through the World Bank's World Integrated Trade Solution (WITS) software.

wholly or partly foreign-owned firms was just 65 percent in 2008, compared to 80 percent for imports into China from Taiwan.

Cross-strait trade relations have not developed in a vacuum—over past decades both Taiwan and especially China have instituted broad economic policy reforms. This general liberalization has made the residual cross-strait abnormalities starker. Figure 1.8 shows the simple average and trade-weighted-average tariffs for the two since 1996, including the period of WTO accession. China's trade-weighted, most favored nation (MFN) tariff rate has come down from around 20 percent in 1996 to 4 percent today, and Taiwan's from 5 percent to 2 percent. Importantly, both economies are party to the WTO Information Technology Agreement, which stipulates free trade (zero tariffs) in components and products related to electronics, computing, and other industries central to the China-Taiwan trading relationship.[14] As noted above, these MFN-level tariffs are generally applied to Taiwan by China, but not by Taiwan to goods from China.

---

14. For details see www.wto.org/english/tratop_e/inftec_e/itaintro_e.htm (accessed on September 15, 2010).

Another important driver of higher cross-strait goods trade was the re-laxation of transportation sector controls. Until the late 1990s, Taiwan maintained a complete ban on direct transport and shipping links with China. Cargo had to go through third-party transshipment points such as Hong Kong, and shipping companies were not allowed to offer direct cross-strait services. These strict prohibitions were first relaxed in 1997, when Taiwan adopted "offshore shipping center" regulations that al-lowed limited direct shipping between Fujian province and Taiwan.[15] In October 2001, Taiwan further relaxed rules and allowed imports from China into special processing zones and industrial parks through Kaoh-siung port. In May 2004, two more ports in Taiwan and all ports in China were opened for direct shipping services.[16] This greater freedom for direct shipment of goods is evident in the convergence of direct and indirect ex-port statistics shown in figure 1.1. This convergence can be expected to further increase following an agreement in November 2008 allowing all ships from China and Taiwan to engage in direct shipping across the strait. Taiwan opened 11 ports under this accord, China 63.[17] In Novem-ber 2008 and April 2009, the parties signed agreements to normalize air transportation for passengers and goods, with daily fights. Taiwan com-mitted itself to open eight destinations and China 21. Air cargo will run on a regular basis with two or three designated operators.[18]

Despite the progress made in tariff reduction and better transportation links for trade in goods, much remains to be normalized, let alone liberal-ized, in cross-strait trade. There remain a host of nontariff barriers nega-tively impacting commerce, the bulk of these imposed unilaterally by Tai-wan. Most importantly, despite obligations under the WTO, Taiwan has a negative list in place that prohibits the import of more than 2,200 products from China. In 1993, Taiwan's Bureau of Foreign Trade developed regula-tions for trade relations allowing unlimited exports but restricted im-ports.[19] The bureau issued a "positive list" of goods allowed to be im-ported, which in 1996 was turned into a "negative list" of prohibited

---

15. "Offshore Shipping Centers" (境外航運中心), Ministry of Transportation and Commu-nication, Taiwan, April 1997. Available (in Chinese) at http://www.iot.gov.tw/public/data/ 7122111234871.pdf.

16. "Measures to Make Cross-Strait Shipping Convenient"(海運便捷化措施), Mainland Affairs Council, Taiwan Executive Yuan, May 2004. www.mac.gov.tw/ct.asp?xItem= 62187&ctNode=6227&mp=1 (accessed on September 15, 2010).

17. "Cross-Strait Sea Transport Agreement" (海峽兩岸海運協議), Association for Relations across the Taiwan Strait, November 4, 2008.

18. Ibid., footnote 17; and "Supplement to Cross-Strait Air Transport Agreement" (海峽兩岸空運協議補充協議), Association for Relations across the Taiwan Strait, April 2009.

19. "Regulations Governing the Permission of Trade between Taiwan Area and Mainland Area" (台灣地區與大陸地區貿易許可辦法), Bureau of Foreign Trade, Taiwan, April 26, 1993.

**Table 1.1    Taiwan's import prohibitions by category**

| Number | Taiwan commodity classification code | Code name | February 2009 | January 2010 | +/- |
|---|---|---|---|---|---|
| 1 | 50–63 | Textiles | 480 | 486 | 6 |
| 2 | 72–83 | Metals | 417 | 433 | 16 |
| 3 | 01–05 | Animal products | 284 | 316 | 32 |
| 4 | 06–15 | Vegetables | 282 | 282 | 0 |
| 5 | 16–24 | Foodstuff | 268 | 268 | 0 |
| 6 | 84–85 | Electrical machinery | 139 | 137 | -2 |
| 7 | 28–38 | Chemicals and allied industries | 116 | 120 | 4 |
| 8 | 86–89 | Transportation | 95 | 95 | 0 |
| 9 | 68–71 | Stone/glass | 54 | 49 | -5 |
| 10 | 90–97 | Miscellaneous | 29 | 29 | 0 |
| 11 | 39–40 | Plastics and rubbers | 15 | 15 | 0 |
| 12 | 25–27 | Mineral products | 9 | 9 | 0 |
| 13 | 44–49 | Wood and wood products | 6 | 5 | -1 |
| 14 | 41–43 | Raw hides, skins, etc. | 0 | 0 | 0 |
| 15 | 64–67 | Footwear | 0 | 0 | 0 |
| | | Total | 2,194 | 2,244 | 50 |

*Source:* Bureau of Foreign Trade, Taiwan, http://fbfh.trade.gov.tw (accessed on September 15, 2010).

items.[20] After its accession to the WTO, Taiwan reviewed its import regime and now has three lists to regulate imports from China: a positive list, a negative list, and a list with conditionally restricted goods, all of which are updated on a regular basis.[21] Table 1.1 gives an overview of the distribution of prohibited items by category. The comparison over time also illustrates that Taiwan keeps extending the list of banned goods despite recent relaxations and the ECFA undertaking. New restrictions were most recently issued in the categories of textiles, metals, and animal products. Other categories such as glass and stone products saw a modest reduction of restrictions, but on net the negative list was extended by 50 products. In the early harvest agreement signed alongside the ECFA text in 2010, none

---

20. In the case of a positive list, products are not tradable unless expressly listed; in the case of a negative list, products are tradable unless listed. The latter is much more permissive, generally, than the former.

21. "Overview of Managing Imported Goods from China" (大陸物品進口管理概況), WTO Center of Taiwan, November 2003. www.wtocenter.org.tw/SmartKMS/do/www/listDocs-ByCategory?isMenu=true&categoryId=118. The most updated import regulation list is available at http://fbfh.trade.gov.tw/rich/test/indexfhE.asp (both websites accessed on September 15, 2010).

of the 267 project categories for which Taiwan committed to remove tariffs for China were from this lengthy banned list.

Although importers are rumored to bypass the negative list often by reporting imports under categories that are not banned, the restrictions are not compatible with Taiwan's WTO commitments and have a clear negative impact on imports in many categories. China has chosen not to challenge these barriers formally at the WTO so as to avoid underscoring Taiwan's independent status and also to avoid raising anxiety in Taiwan about economic pressure. However, in 2006 China's WTO representatives did include pointed comments in the occasional *Trade Policy Review* of Taiwan (known as "Chinese Taipei" in the WTO). These comments included the following (as summarized by the Trade Policy Review Body chairperson):

> China was concerned over problems relating to the WTO nondiscrimination principle. Chinese Taipei practiced trade-restrictive policies against China in many areas, which had limited the potential for cross-strait trade and economic cooperation. Chinese Taipei had maintained import prohibitions on 2,237 [sic; accurate at the time] tariff lines of products from China without WTO-consistent justification. Access for China's services providers was virtually blocked in many ways, and Chinese companies found it impossible to invest in Chinese Taipei. This was not conducive to the development of cross-strait trade and economic relations; it was not only against the interests of businesses and consumers in Chinese Taipei, but also had a negative impact on business investment in China. As a result, the economic growth of Chinese Taipei had been greatly impaired. China urged Chinese Taipei to . . . take steps to correct these trade policies and practices, which were inconsistent with WTO rules, so as to promote trade liberalization (and facilitation) across the strait. (WTO 2006, 12, paragraph 59)

Taiwan has argued that its WTO obligations do not apply to China in the same way because China was not a WTO member when they were negotiated. (China and Taiwan negotiated accession and entered the WTO in parallel.) But WTO obligations, however arrived at, are multilateralized and applied to all members on an MFN basis, unless a specific exception is registered at accession, which Taiwan did not do. In addition to its list of prohibited imports from China and its residual restrictions on transport links, Taiwan has maintained special restrictions on Chinese investment, services, and the physical movement of people for employment and personal travel, as described below. The lack of normal government-to-government contact has further frustrated a variety of commercial activities dependent on consultation and communication between regulators and overseers.

For its part, China maintains a more limited set of restrictions on Taiwanese commerce. Beijing does not impose restrictions on Taiwanese goods imports different from those applied to other WTO members. However, it has declined to issue licenses for Taiwanese services sector firms to conduct business, most notably in the financial services industry, on the grounds that such firms could not be adequately regulated due to the lack of normal regulator-to-regulator communication between governments on each side of the strait. With the advent of WTO+ FTAs between China and other economies, China now applies lower rates of import duty to goods from some other WTO members than from Taiwan. While this is neither unusual in the world today nor necessarily noncompliant with WTO obligations, it adds an element of distortion for Taiwan and has been the main argument employed by President Ma Ying-jeou's government in making the case for a formal arrangement to achieve deeper economic integration.

## Trade in Services

Our description of China-Taiwan trade has thus far focused on trade in goods. However for an advanced economy like Taiwan, the opportunity for services trade with China is extremely important. Comprehensive data on trade in services between China and Taiwan are not available, but we can describe the aggregate services trade situation for the two and draw a general assessment of bilateral flows based on available and circumstantial information.

Taiwan's balance of payments data indicate a services trade deficit throughout 1984–2009. Services exports grew faster than imports in all these years, though starting from a very low base. As table 1.2 and figure 1.9 show, growth was highest in the late 1980s, with average annual rates at 24 percent for exports and 20.5 percent for imports. This growth has slowed over time, falling to 3.9 percent annually for exports and a negative number for imports in 2004–09. As a share of total exports and imports, services exports increased from 7.5 percent in 1984 to 13.3 percent in 2009, while services imports declined from 20 percent of all imports in 1984 to 14.8 percent in 2009 (figure 1.9).

Taiwan's balance of payments data break down trade in services, and figure 1.10 tracks the trade balance of subsectors over time. In business services, Taiwan has built a growing surplus over two decades, while for most other services Taiwan is near balance or in deficit (royalty and licensing fees being the biggest "import" for Taiwan today, a healthy reflection of the development of its high-tech industries). Looking forward, Taiwan considers the development of its services industries to be key to maintaining its prosperity and competitiveness. Sectors earmarked for strategic attention include finance, logistics/distribution, information and media, medical and healthcare services, education, tourism, research and development, environmental services, and engineering. Taiwan is thinking specifically about future demand from China for consumer and business services and Taiwan's ability to sustain comparative advantage in these industries, which do not rely on large-scale capital-intensive assets or abundant low-cost labor—two endowments Taiwan conspicuously lacks.

**Table 1.2    Growth of Taiwan's services exports and imports with the world**
(percent)

| Period | Exports | Imports |
|---|---|---|
| 1984–89 | 23.76 | 20.50 |
| 1989–94 | 13.10 | 9.20 |
| 1994–99 | 5.48 | 3.00 |
| 1999–2004 | 8.50 | 4.80 |
| 2004–09 | 3.90 | −0.50 |

*Source:* Balance of payments data from the Central Bank of Taiwan.

**Figure 1.9    Taiwan's trade in services with the world, 1984–2009**

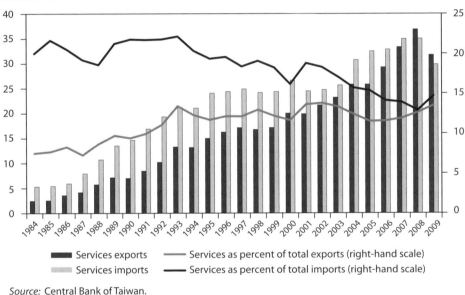

*Source:* Central Bank of Taiwan.

The development of China's trade in services reflects the different phases of the country's integration into the global economy. In the 1980s and first half of the 1990s, China's trade in services was generally low and mostly balanced, with a slight surplus in earlier years (figure 1.11). After 1995, the growth of services imports outpaced the export side and China turned into a net importer of services. This shift was mostly related to a strong growth in imports of services related to China's integration into regional production chains such as transport and various business services.

# Figure 1.10    Balance of Taiwan's services trade with the world by sector, 1984–2009

billions of US dollars

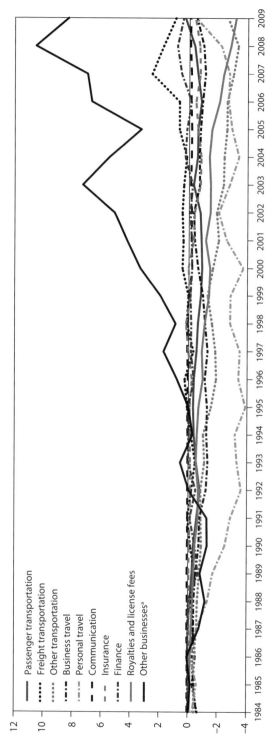

a. Other business services include accounting, advertising, legal services, agricultural processing, business consulting, merchant services, operating/leasing services, technical services, waste treatment, research and development, etc.

Note: The figure does not include all categories.

*Source:* Central Bank of Taiwan.

**Figure 1.11 China's trade in services with the world, 1982–2009**

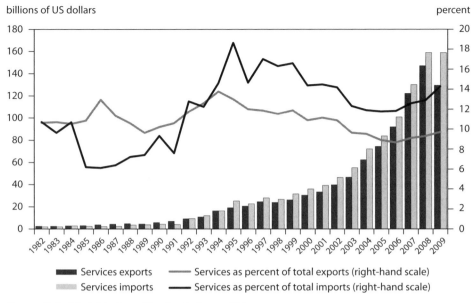

Source: State Administration of Foreign Exchange, China.

After 2001, the annual growth of services imports averaged 22 percent and services exports 24 percent, compared to 24 percent and 18 percent in the previous decade. However, this increase was not enough to keep pace with the growth in merchandise trade; hence the share of services in China's total trade fell. Since 2006, these patterns have been reversing again and services trade is expected to grow in importance to China in the years ahead. The services sector accounted for 43 percent of China's GDP in 2009 but has averaged 17 percent annual growth since 2005, faster than the other sectors of the economy. Efforts to rebalance the economy and shift investment away from polluting and capital-intensive manufacturing to labor-intensive activities is expected to further boost the role of the services sector in the economy (He and Kuijs 2007).

The services trade balance from China's balance of payments statistics (figure 1.12) reveals the most important sectoral trends. China has long been a major net importer of transportation services, a deficit that widened after WTO accession in 2001. Other major deficit items on the balance sheet are insurance services and fees related to intellectual property rights. On the net export side, China's strongest position has long been tourism. Since 2001, business services have also grown into a major net export category. In recent years, construction, consulting, and information technology services emerged as major net export sectors. In 2008, China's Ministry of Commerce (MOFCOM) issued a report that contains several data

**Figure 1.12  Balance of China's services trade with the world by sector, 1991–2009**

billions of US dollars

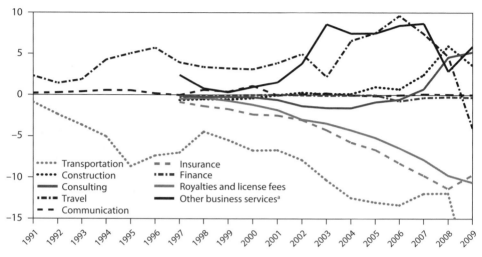

a. Other business services include accounting, advertising, legal services, agricultural processing, business consulting, merchant services, operating/leasing services, technical services, waste treatment, research and development, etc.

Note: The figure does not include all categories.

*Source:* State Administration of Foreign Exchange, China.

points on the regional distribution of China's services trade.[22] According to MOFCOM, Hong Kong, the United States, European Union (EU), Japan, and the countries of the Association of Southeast Asian Nations (ASEAN) account for around 70 percent of China's total services trade. Not surprisingly, Hong Kong alone accounted for around 20 percent of the total trade value. Hong Kong also was the trading partner with the largest surplus, whereas the largest deficits occurred with the European Union, Australia, and Japan.

While services make up more than 70 percent of Taiwan's GDP, Taiwan's weight in global services trade is relatively low. Services trade growth by local peers was strong enough to overshadow Taiwan (figure 1.13). China, on the other hand, already is an important market in global services trade given the overall size of the economy. In 2009, it ranked fifth in global services exports and fourth in imports, surpassed only by

22. MOFCOM, "An Overview of the Development of China's Trade in Services in 2007." http://tradeinservices.mofcom.gov.cn/en/c/2008-11-17/62284.shtml (accessed on September 15, 2010).

**Figure 1.13   Trade in services of countries in East Asia with the world, 1982–2008**

billions of US dollars

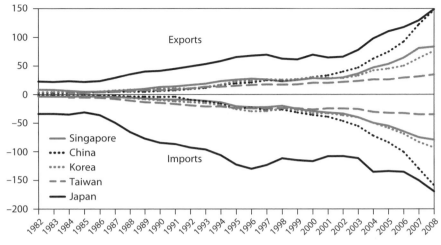

*Source:* International Monetary Fund.

the United States, Germany, and the United Kingdom.[23] In East Asia, Japan leads in global services exports and imports value, though China nearly passed that position in 2008. Given the size of its economy and the current growth trajectory of its services sector, China will most likely soon be the most important market for services trade in East Asia.

With regard to bilateral services trade, neither China nor Taiwan publishes reliable statistics.[24] However, we can surmise that China's services exports to Taiwan are extremely low, given that services trade often includes direct investment flows and movement of people, or direct shipping, and until recently Taiwan has been largely closed to investment and labor from China (discussed further below).[25] In fact in the WTO's *Trade Policy Review* of Taiwan, China complained that at most only one of 160 services subsectors had been opened by Taiwan to Chinese investment,

---

23. See the WTO's annual report on trade services via the Chung Hua Institution of Economic Research. http://taiwan.wtocenter.org.tw/WTOissueindex.asp?id=18 (accessed on September 15, 2010).

24. MOFCOM's 2008 services trade report (see footnote 22) mentions that China's services trade in 2006–07 was strongest with Taiwan in tourism, transportation, and insurance services, but does not provide specific data.

25. Establishment of such a commercial presence is not the only way to generate a services export: services can be sent abroad by phone or computer, consumed "for export" by visitors like tourists and business travelers, or delivered by a temporary visitor.

and that even that sector (real estate) was not practical due to restrictions on visitation by mainland citizens.[26] For other WTO members, meanwhile, Taiwan provided at least partial opening in 120 of these subsectors. But with the growth of direct trade links, tourism, and especially the recent opening of Taiwan to mainland investment generally, China's services exports to Taiwan are likely to grow, while the major impediment in Taiwan will continue to be national security concerns.[27]

Taiwan's services export offerings to China have also been curtailed by cross-strait abnormalities, but to a smaller degree. Some services sectors that Taiwan considers to be promising and important—notably financial services—have been restricted by Beijing out of reciprocity and also for want of direct channels for handling regulatory oversight. Taiwan had restricted transportation and shipping services exports to China unilaterally, although these were diverted to Hong Kong and Japan instead, and hence cross-strait normalization may not mean growth (though liberalization *would*, by fostering faster GDP growth). In a variety of nonfinancial business services including consulting, technical advisory, and technology licensing, Taiwan has enjoyed strong exports to China for some time, as these services exports have been necessary to support the Taiwanese firms that have migrated production to China.[28]

As of 2010, extensive Taiwan opening to inbound direct investment from China is taking place under memoranda of understanding (MOUs) signed in ad hoc cross-strait meetings since 2008. These agreements will open many Taiwanese sectors to investment from China, and address financial services in particular. Banking and the trust investment sector are in line for opening to investment from qualified Chinese institutional investors (as they have been to other foreign investors, like Standard Chartered Bank and Citibank). For example, two Chinese fund management services firms—China AMC and China International Fund Management—have completed registration procedures and are preparing to trade shares in Taiwan.[29]

---

26. Very significantly, this presents a real challenge to econometrically modeling the effects of deeper China-Taiwan trade integration in the years ahead, because zero values of past trade do not lend themselves to growth in economic models, and the nonquantitative (nontariff) barriers constraining services trade are more difficult to operationalize in a model. See chapter 2 and appendix A for further discussion.

27. In general, services imports are much more sensitive from a national security standpoint than goods imports as they require foreign direct investment and people on the ground, and reach into areas that are highly relevant for national security, such as finance, information technology, communication, infrastructure, and transportation.

28. See MOFCOM's 2008 services trade report (footnote 22).

29. Jingying Ma, "Finance Industry Is Not Included in the Second Round of ECFA Negotiation" (金融业未纳入ECFA第二轮协商), Caing News, March 31, 2010. http://finance.caing.com/2010-03-31/100130861.html (accessed on September 15, 2010).

# Direct Investment and Portfolio Holdings

The integration of production chains across the Taiwan Strait is also evident from the patterns of foreign direct investment (FDI) between the two sides. China has experienced growing inflows of direct investment from Taiwan since the 1980s, mostly for greenfield manufacturing facilities. China's direct investment in Taiwan was virtually zero until recently: except in a handful of cases since 2002, Taiwan did not permit investment from China, ostensibly on national security grounds. As with trade statistics, the real extent of FDI flows between China and Taiwan is obscured by the extensive use of third economies as intermediate jurisdictions. Recent changes in Taiwan's inward investment rules and the increasing motivation and readiness of China's firms to invest abroad will likely bolster the mainland's FDI flows to Taiwan in the near future. Compared to direct investment, levels of cross-border portfolio investment holdings have been very low on both sides until recently but are expected to grow rapidly on the back of regulatory changes for portfolio investment in general and cross-strait investment in particular.

## Direct Investment from Taiwan to China

Direct investment in China by Taiwanese firms was explicitly prohibited until 1992 and still is tightly controlled today by Taiwan, but the reality is that flows have mushroomed for more than two decades. As early as the late 1980s, Taiwanese firms started to shift manufacturing operations to China from Taiwan and elsewhere in Asia, as China had set up export processing zones with favorable conditions for foreign investors and had a natural comparative advantage for labor-intensive industries in which sparsely populated Taiwan was unable to maintain cost competitiveness.[30] While foreign exchange controls on capital account transactions were lifted in 1987, investment flows to China remained tightly restricted, while investment via third country locations such as Hong Kong was not.

In his study of China-Taiwan relations, *Untying the Knot: Making Peace in the Taiwan Strait*, Richard Bush points out that it was not just the attraction of production costs in China that motivated Taiwan's firms, but an upward inflection in Taiwanese production costs as well (Bush 2005, 24). Through the 1980s, real wages in Taiwan rose an average of 7 to 8 percent annually, and easy steps to stay ahead of the cost curve with productivity-enhancing investments in technology had already been taken.[31] By the mid-1980s

---

30. On the growing allure of China for manufacturers in this period, see Rosen (1998). The potential of the domestic Chinese market was the focus of many investors, but for the majority of Taiwanese firms the allure was China as an export platform to serve the rest of the world.

31. Authors' calculations based on data from Taiwan's General Directorate of Budget, Accounting and Statistics.

there were strong US perceptions that Taiwan was building an unnatural amount of US dollar foreign exchange reserves as a result of an intentional policy of currency undervaluation. At the time, Washington was coordinating with Japan to revalue the yen, and from 1985 onward Taiwan commenced to permit appreciation of its currency. Already in those years Taiwan had identified South Korea as a peer competitor, and while Taiwan conceded some adjustment on its exchange rates, Korea conceded less so, adding more competitive pressure that motivated Taiwanese firms to seek out cost structures less prone to competitive concerns abroad. In this way, exchange rate pressure from the United States helped to hasten the migration of Taiwanese firms to the mainland. Similarly, in the years ahead US pressure on Taiwan's shortcomings in the protection of intellectual property rights would impel movement across the strait in search of a "blind eye."

Thus, indirect Taiwanese investment in China grew bigger and in 1992 authorities responded to that reality and formalized oversight and administration through the *Act Governing Relations between Peoples of the Taiwan Area and China Area* (Article 35). New regulations virtually encouraged the indirect investment option, but required firms to register and seek approval from Taiwan's Ministry of Economic Affairs (MOEA) for any existing or new investment in China.[32] This change allowed Taiwanese firms to legally invest in China. However, the regulations also specified several conditional rules for outbound investment—for example, that a firm's investment in China not exceed 40 percent of its net worth—in order to prevent a "hollowing out" of economic activity in Taiwan. Taiwan's approval process for direct investing in China remain burdensome, while the regulatory requirements for investing in other countries are relatively simple—in most cases firms just need to register with the MOEA Investment Commission.[33] Because of these discrepancies, firms often circumvented the China approval process through the MOEA and registered their projects

---

32. *Act Governing Relations between Peoples of the Taiwan Area and China Area* (臺灣地區與大陸地區人民關係條例), Ministry of the Interior, Taiwan, April 2, 2002. www.mac.gov.tw/public/MMO/RPIR/book367.pdf (accessed on September 15, 2010).

33. Outbound investment is governed by multiple regulations. The most important rules for outbound FDI to the mainland are summarized in the "Regulations Governing the Approval of Investment or Technical Cooperation in Mainland China." http://law.moj.gov.tw/Law Class/LawContent.aspx?pcode=Q0040001 (accessed on September 15, 2010). Approval from the MOEA Investment Commission is needed for large investment and reporting is needed for small projects. A project will be suspended if it is not approved or reported. Investment into Hong Kong and Macau only requires approval from the MOEA (not its Investment Commission) for large projects and reporting for smaller projects. No sanctions for nonreporting are mentioned. www.moeaic.gov.tw/system_external/ctlr?PRO=LawsLoad&id=6 (accessed on September 15, 2010). Investment in other foreign countries only requires reporting to the MOEA's Investment Commission. Again, no sanctions are mentioned. www.moeaic.gov.tw/system_external/ctlr?PRO=LawsLoad&id=49 (accessed on September 15, 2010).

as FDI to Hong Kong, Singapore, and, later, Caribbean tax havens. As in goods trade, the role of these entrepôts complicates data assessment, obscures the true value of FDI flows, and makes analysis of disaggregated investment details more difficult.

The starting point for estimates of aggregate Taiwan FDI to China is the MOEA's data on approved outbound FDI (table 1.3, columns 2–4). These data are compiled by the MOEA based on reporting requirements for firms seeking investment approvals, and include a breakdown of approved outward FDI by country, including indirect flows to China (column 3). Since 2002, China has accounted for more than two-thirds of Taiwan's approved annual outbound FDI. However for a number of reasons these official approval figures are not accurately capturing the reality of FDI outflows. First, Taiwanese firms frequently shifted investment out of Taiwan without going through registration, especially in earlier years when outward FDI approval procedures were most burdensome and investment to China prohibited.[34] When the firms did report, they reported anticipated, not realized, values. As a result, these data show occasional spikes during periods of stricter enforcement by Taiwan, or when statisticians chose to adjust estimates to better reflect unregistered outflows (1993, 1997, and 2002).[35] Second, these data capture only the first destination of outward investment, and many firms used locations with lower regulatory barriers as switchyards for their China investments. The stark differences between Taiwan's approved numbers and data on contracted FDI from Taiwan as reported by Beijing (column 5) reinforce the evidence of underreporting by Taiwanese businesses to their home authorities. Taiwanese analysts typically assume that the majority of Taiwan investment flowing to Hong Kong, Singapore, and Caribbean tax havens (column 4) in reality went to China.[36] And of course this means reinvested earnings might not be captured in the data. And third, Taiwan's data on approved investment is not very useful for mapping out actual flows because the data consistently diverge from *utilized* FDI—frequently to an extreme degree, as many negotiated projects are not ultimately carried out for commercial or regulatory reasons.

Taiwanese authorities do not collect and report utilized outbound FDI as opposed to that which is approved, so one must determine an accurate

---

34. There is a wide variety of techniques used to surreptitiously shift money abroad for such purposes. For instance, firms can underinvoice for transactions overseas in order to leave cash abroad that would otherwise come home.

35. There are compounding factors for 1993 and 2002: 1993 saw an uptick in FDI to China generally as investor confidence redoubled after the political turmoil of the Tiananmen Square demonstrations and crackdowns around the country in 1989; 2002 saw a direct investment surge as a result of China's accession to the WTO in late 2001.

36. Chen (2004) reports that the Central Bank attributed 80 percent of the tax haven flows to China investment at that time.

**Table 1.3    Dimensions of Taiwanese outward foreign direct investment, 1988–2009** (annual flow in millions of US dollars)

| Year | Total approved outward FDI from Taiwan to world[a] | Approved indirect outward FDI to China[b] | Approved outward FDI to tax havens, Hong Kong, and Singapore[c] | Contracted inward FDI to China from Taiwan[d] | Actual total outward FDI from Taiwan to world[e] | Utilized inward FDI to China from Taiwan[f] | Actual equity investment in greenfield projects and M&A deals[g] |
|---|---|---|---|---|---|---|---|
| 1988 | 219 | — | 19 | — | 4,121 | — | — |
| 1989 | 931 | — | 87 | — | 6,951 | — | — |
| 1990 | 1,552 | — | 426 | — | 5,243 | — | — |
| 1991 | 1,830 | 174 | 523 | — | 2,055 | — | — |
| 1992 | 1,134 | 247 | 305 | — | 1,967 | — | — |
| 1993* | 4,829 | 3,168 | 425 | — | 2,611 | — | — |
| 1994 | 2,579 | 962 | 966 | — | 2,640 | — | — |
| 1995 | 2,450 | 1,093 | 614 | 5,849 | 2,983 | 3,162 | — |
| 1996 | 3,395 | 1,229 | 1,316 | 5,141 | 3,843 | 3,475 | — |
| 1997* | 7,228 | 4,334 | 1,552 | 2,814 | 5,243 | 3,289 | — |
| 1998* | 5,331 | 2,035 | 2,153 | 2,982 | 3,836 | 2,915 | — |
| 1999 | 4,522 | 1,253 | 1,926 | 3,374 | 4,420 | 2,599 | — |
| 2000 | 7,684 | 2,607 | 3,086 | 4,042 | 6,701 | 2,297 | — |
| 2001 | 7,176 | 2,784 | 2,550 | 6,914 | 5,480 | 2,980 | — |
| 2002* | 10,093 | 6,723 | 1,938 | 6,741 | 4,886 | 3,971 | — |
| 2003* | 11,667 | 7,699 | 2,694 | 8,558 | 5,682 | 3,377 | 8,172 |
| 2004 | 10,323 | 6,941 | 2,204 | 9,306 | 7,145 | 3,117 | 12,417 |
| 2005 | 8,454 | 6,007 | 1,471 | 10,358 | 6,028 | 2,152 | 7,559 |
| 2006 | 11,958 | 7,642 | 2,903 | 11,336 | 7,399 | 2,136 | 5,598 |
| 2007 | 16,441 | 9,971 | 3,082 | — | 11,107 | 1,774 | 6,791 |
| 2008 | 15,158 | 10,691 | 2,721 | — | 10,287 | 1,899 | 5,490 |
| 2009 | 10,148 | 7,143 | 1,075 | — | 5,876 | 1,881 | 8,058 |
| Cumulative | 145,102 | 82,703 | 34,037 | 77,415 | 116,504 | 41,023 | 54,086 |

* = years with adjusted volume

— = not available

FDI = foreign direct investment; M&A = merger and acquisition.

a. Taiwan Ministry of Economic Affairs (MOEA); sum of approved FDI to China and other countries.
b. Taiwan MOEA.
c. Taiwan MOEA.
d. Taiwan Ministry of Commerce.
e. Taiwan's central bank based on balance of payments data.
f. Taiwan Ministry of Commerce.
g. Authors' compilation based on Thomson ONE and fDiIntelligence.

figure for aggregate Taiwan-to-China FDI using other proxies. The Central Bank of China—Taiwan's central bank—provides an estimate of actual FDI outflows from Taiwan "to the world" in its annual balance of payments statistics, which have been compiled according to IMF standards in recent years (table 1.3, column 6).[37] There are a number of options for estimating the share of these global flows going to China. One can use the numbers for utilized FDI entering China with a stated Taiwan origin, as reported by China's Ministry of Commerce (MOFCOM, column 7). This number is significantly lower than the Taiwanese MOEA's *approved* outward FDI, and lower than MOFCOM's contracted inward FDI, and certainly underestimates actual Taiwan investment (for example, it does not capture all Taiwanese FDI fed through Hong Kong and other locations). In addition to these official numbers, the value of Taiwanese investment can be approximated from public announcements of greenfield projects and cross-border acquisitions (column 8). This methodology is also imperfect, since it describes equity capital only, omits reinvested earnings and other capital flows, and considers only the nationality of the investing company and not the origin of capital (which is probably why in some years it is higher than total outflows recorded in Taiwan's balance of payments figures).

We use these various data points to assemble a best guess for actual direct investment outflows from Taiwan to China. Due to the shortcomings of MOEA data, we start with Taiwan's balance of payments data as a reference point. From the late 1980s through the 1990s, outbound Taiwanese investment was overwhelmingly focused on China, and we assume that 80 to 90 percent of annual balance of payments outflows ended up in China. This is true for the years surrounding WTO accession and China's integration into regional manufacturing networks as well. More recently, Taiwanese firms have diversified into a greater range of markets and segments, for example in a downstream presence in US, Japanese, and EU consumer markets or other low-cost manufacturing locations in Asia such as Vietnam. Thus, the share of China-as-destination is likely to have come down to 60 to 80 percent of total outflows in recent years from 80 to 90 percent in earlier years, depending on the trends and larger-scale projects in each respective year.

In early 2003, Taiwan's central bank reported that firms had $67 billion invested in China—roughly 87 percent of Taiwan's year-end 2002 outbound FDI stock of $77 billion. Adding 60 to 80 percent of actual annual outflows recorded in the balance of payments in 2003–08, and applying the same ratio for asset revaluation as for all FDI stock in this period, we arrive at a range of $130 billion to $150 billion for total Taiwanese outward FDI stock in China at year-end 2008, or around 80 percent of Taiwan's total

---

37. Balance of payments data from Taiwan's central bank, www.cbc.gov.tw/ct.asp?xItem= 2070&ctNode=512&mp=2 (accessed on September 15, 2010).

overseas FDI stock of $175 billion. The imprecise nature of these projections notwithstanding, it is fair to say that Taiwan is far and away the largest foreign investor in China. According to our estimates, Taiwan accounted for around 15 to 17 percent of China's inward FDI stock in 2008. In 2009, this stock probably rose by at least $8 billion, which can be surmised from deal reports. According to Taiwanese government estimates, around 70,000 Taiwanese firms were invested in China by the end of 2009.[38] Looking forward, these flows are likely to remain large as additional restrictions on direct investment are removed.[39] In the first months of 2010, Taiwanese investments in China were running above past trends.[40]

These aggregate uncertainties cast a shadow on the breakdown of flows by industry and subregion, which can be approached using MOEA data. These approved numbers are not reliable in terms of value, for the reasons stated above, but taken together with commercial databases on greenfield and merger and acquisition (M&A) investments by industry, they can be used to get an idea of the patterns and inflections in investment.

The composition of approved Taiwanese FDI to China by sector clearly shows that manufacturing dominates Taiwan's investment activity in the mainland, accounting for around 90 percent of the total (figure 1.14), although this share has come down to 80 percent in more recent years as a result of expanding investment activity in services sectors. The evolution of manufacturing FDI by subsector echoes the evolving economic relationship as seen in the trade data (table 1.4). In the early 1990s, investment was well distributed across industries, with a focus on traditional labor-intensive sectors including food, electrical components, plastics, and apparel. In subsequent years, investment shifted to computers, optical equipment, and other electronics, reflecting China's integration into these manufacturing value chains as the final assembly point. As outbound Taiwanese investment moved further up the sophistication curve to semiconductors and other higher value-added manufacturing, capital intensity per project increased. This is evident in the sharp increase in average approved investment project value in the MOEA data (figure 1.15).

In the most recent period (2005–09), the strongest Taiwan-to-China investment growth momentum is seen in wholesale and retail trade (figure 1.16). Electronics and information technology remain the top investment sectors in the period by value, but with comparably modest growth rates, and computers and optical products see declining investment flows. Tai-

38. President Ma in an interview with the *Wall Street Journal* on December 15, 2009. http://online.wsj.com/article/SB10001424052748703514404574588863008012766.html (accessed on September 15, 2010).

39. On July 17, 2008, for instance, Taiwan's Executive Yuan increased the limit on China-bound investment for Taiwanese companies from 40 to 60 percent of net assets.

40. MOEA, "Statistics Summary," February 2010. www.moeaic.gov.tw/system_external/en_home.html (accessed on September 15, 2010).

**Figure 1.14   Taiwanese foreign direct investment into China by sector, 1997–2009**

percent

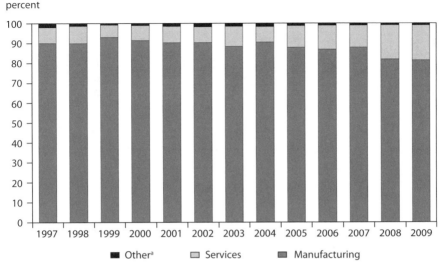

a. Includes agriculture, mining, utilities, and construction.

*Source:* Ministry of Economic Affairs, Taiwan, approved direct investment.

wan's China profile is evolving beyond high-tech assembly to consumer and business services, in pursuit of downstream market share instead of just manufacturing for reexport. This new emphasis on China as the consumer market of the near future rather than assembly point to serve traditional Organization for Economic Cooperation and Development (OECD) markets predated the global financial crisis of 2008–09, which brought so much attention to the rise of the Chinese consumer and the decline of US trend consumption growth. However, the crisis certainly amplified the sense of urgency for this investment-focus shift in Taiwan.

Figure 1.17 depicts the evolving 1991–2009 Taiwan-to-China investment pattern by province. In the early 1990s, Guangdong and Fujian dominated due to family ties, export processing zones, and other policies favorable to Taiwanese investors, as well as the suitability of these locales for Taiwan's small and medium-size light manufacturing (Guangdong and Fujian are both known as light manufacturing hubs). The rise of Taiwanese investment in Jiangsu Province since the 1990s has resulted from investments in the capital-intensive semiconductor industry and computer sector, both of which are clustered in the adjoining provinces of Shanghai—Zhejiang and Jiangsu. In 2008, the MOEA approved more Taiwanese investment to Jiangsu than the next three provinces—Guangdong, Shanghai, and Zhejiang—together. Shanghai's share has also grown rapidly since 2000, surpassing Guangdong in 2008.

**Table 1.4  Top 10 Chinese industries targeted by Taiwanese foreign direct investment, 1991–2009** (millions of US dollars)

| | 1991–95 | | 1996–2000 | | 2001–05 | | 2006–09 | |
|---|---|---|---|---|---|---|---|---|
| | Industry | Amount | Industry | Amount | Industry | Amount | Industry | Amount |
| 1 | Food | 546 | Computers, electronics, and optical products | 1,741 | Computers, electronics, and optical products | 4,916 | Electronic parts and components | 7,898 |
| 2 | Electrical equipment | 416 | Electronic parts and components | 1,220 | Electronic parts and components | 4,836 | Computers, electronics and optical products | 5,963 |
| 3 | Plastic products | 388 | Electrical equipment | 1,107 | Electrical equipment | 2,791 | Electrical equipment | 3,240 |
| 4 | Fabricated metal products | 384 | Fabricated metal products | 787 | Fabricated metal products | 2,418 | Wholesale and retail trade | 1,967 |
| 5 | Other manufacturing | 334 | Plastic products | 721 | Chemical material | 1,617 | Plastic products | 1,661 |
| 6 | Nonmetallic mineral products | 325 | Nonmetallic mineral products | 625 | Plastic products | 1,441 | Machinery and equipment | 1,587 |
| 7 | Leather, fur, and related products | 314 | Food | 506 | Nonmetallic mineral products | 1,374 | Basic metal | 1,518 |
| 8 | Textile mills | 282 | Machinery and equipment | 493 | Machinery and equipment | 1,311 | Fabricated metal products | 1,266 |
| 9 | Computers, electronics, and optical products | 269 | Textile mills | 461 | Wholesale and retail trade | 897 | Chemical material | 1,197 |
| 10 | Electronic parts and components | 260 | Chemical material | 425 | Textile mills | 822 | Nonmetallic mineral products | 1,036 |

*Source:* Ministry of Economic Affairs, Taiwan, approved direct investment.

**Figure 1.15    Average size of approved Taiwanese foreign direct investment into China, 1991–2009**

billions of US dollars

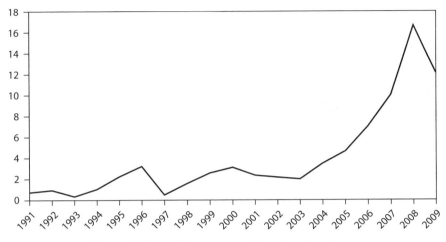

*Source:* Ministry of Economic Affairs, Taiwan, approved direct investment.

**Figure 1.16    Growth of approved Taiwanese outward foreign direct investment into China by industry, 2005–09**

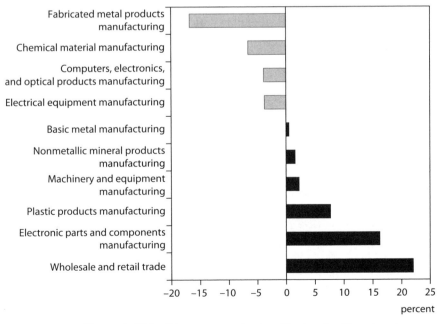

*Source:* Ministry of Economic Affairs, Taiwan, approved outward foreign direct investment.

**Figure 1.17  Taiwanese outbound foreign direct investment into China by province, 1991–2009**

percent of total

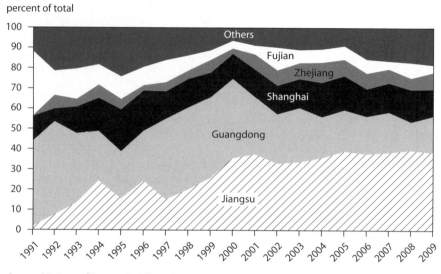

*Source:* Ministry of Economic Affairs, Taiwan, approved outbound foreign direct investment.

Figure 1.18 shows the leaders in approved Taiwanese investment to China through 2009 by industry, and within each industry the provincial distribution within China. Jiangsu was the major recipient of FDI in all of the key industries, most importantly electronic parts (43 percent of the total), computer electronics (34 percent), and electrical equipment (43 percent). With manufacturing bases including Kunshan and Suzhou, Jiangsu has a leading role in the computer and electronics clusters. The increasing importance of Shanghai, on the other hand, is related to services sector competence, as shown in figure 1.19. By 2009, Shanghai accounted for 32 percent of Taiwan's approved investment in wholesale and retail trade in China, 58 percent in financial and insurance services, and 56 percent in scientific and technical services.

## Direct Investment from China to Taiwan

Direct investment flows from China to Taiwan are easier to discuss—because so little has been permitted so far. Under Taiwan's 1992 *Act Governing Relations between Peoples of the Taiwan Area and China Area*, investment from China to Taiwan was treated more prohibitively than outbound investment to China.[41] The treatment of outbound investment

41. Op. cit. footnote 32.

**Figure 1.18  Regional breakdown of Taiwanese foreign direct investment to China, top manufacturing sectors, end 2009**

billions of US dollars

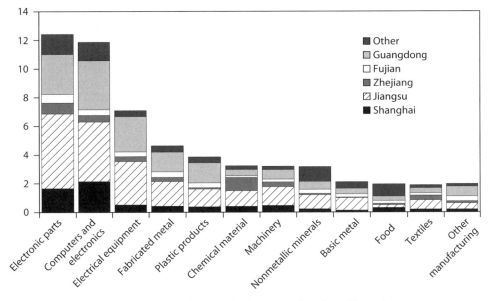

**Figure 1.19  Regional breakdown of Taiwanese foreign direct investment to China, top services sectors, end 2009**

billions of US dollars

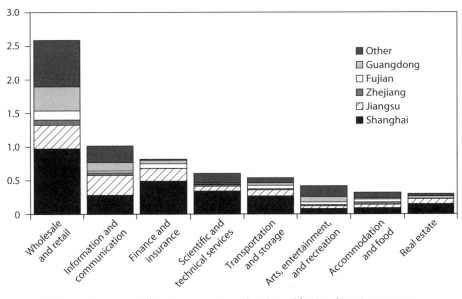

*Source:* Ministry of Economic Affairs, Taiwan, approved outbound foreign direct investment.

(Article 35) begins affirmatively: "Any individual, juristic person, organization, or other institution of the Taiwan Area permitted by the Ministry of Economic Affairs may make any investment or have any technology cooperation in [the] China Area," before restrictions and (somewhat onerous) procedures are elaborated. For inbound investment from China (Article 40–1), the presumption is negative: "Unless permitted by the competent authorities and having established in the Taiwan Area a branch or liaison office, no profit-seeking enterprise of [the] China Area may engage in any business activities in Taiwan." While Taiwan investment through third parties into China became the common practice and is also acknowledged by regulators, under Article 73 the use of third parties by Chinese firms to invest in Taiwan is explicitly included in the restrictions: "[A]ny individual, juristic person, organization, or other institution of [the] China Area, or any company it invests in [in] any third area may not engage in any investment activity in the Taiwan Area," unless expressly approved.

This lack of reciprocity imposed little on Beijing in 1992, because China's outbound FDI at the time was extremely limited and tightly controlled by Beijing administratively. Beijing sought to conserve foreign exchange reserves as a buffer against balance of payments pressures or other eventualities, and a closed capital account and strict licensing to convert renminbi for liquid currencies made it difficult to go abroad. Further, Taiwan was a less interesting target during the 1990s for firms from China that *did* go abroad, which were state-owned giants interested in natural resources.

By 2002 Taiwan had amended its inward FDI regulations to comply with WTO commitments. The revised regulations replaced the blanket China prohibition with allowance in principle for mainland investors to enter real estate and designated services industries, with case-by-case approval by Taiwan authorities.[42] However, these changes did not lead to a significant increase in FDI from China and only a handful of projects were recorded prior to 2008, mostly in retail and business services.[43] In addition to being involved with a low number of direct Chinese greenfield and M&A projects in Taiwan, Taiwanese regulators also were involved in several international M&A transactions in which a Chinese buyer acquired a globally operated firm with assets in Taiwan, such as Lenovo's acquisition of IBM's personal computer unit.

With Ma Ying-jeou's March 2008 election to the presidency in Taiwan the investment picture began to change. Making good on campaign

---

42. Item 69, *Act Governing Relations between Peoples of the Taiwan Area and China Area* (臺灣地區與大陸地區人民關係條例) (see footnote 32).

43. Summary of cross-border investment transactions between China and Taiwan in the period of 2003 to 2009, derived from subscription databases fDiMarkets (http://fdimarkets.com) and Thomson ONE (http://banker.thomsonib.com).

pledges to improve cross-strait economic relations, Taiwan reached agreement on expanding charter air services, triggering a wave of investment in Taiwan by China's airlines to set up required business infrastructure. In the summer of 2008, several policies supportive of Chinese investment in Taiwan were announced. In late June limited local currency convertibility for the new Taiwan dollar and the Chinese renminbi at Taiwan banks was announced, and in July cross-strait market access to the securities industry was widened. Additional normalization of transport links was agreed upon in the fall, paving the way for additional direct investment in support of sea transport and delivery services. The biggest development came in June 2009 with an agreement to ease the process for mainland firms to set up branches and offices in Taiwan, opening 192 sectors to Chinese investors—64 in manufacturing, 117 in services, and 11 in infrastructure. A regulatory cap on Chinese investors was raised from 20 percent to 30 percent of ownership.[44]

These changes in Taiwan complemented general outward investment liberalization taking place in China under the rubric of "go global," as commercial pressures on firms in China to invest abroad rose (Rosen and Hanemann 2009). In May 2009, the MOFCOM issued regulations specifically governing outward FDI to Taiwan, encouraging such investment as long as it did not harm national security interests, which principally meant special scrutiny by Beijing to ensure that investment overtures by Chinese firms did not provoke anxieties in Taiwan and a backlash against momentum for broader cross-strait economic liberalization.[45]

By the second half of 2009, actual investment flows from China to Taiwan confirmed that these changes were concrete and not just a rhetorical false start. Deal-tracking services reflect at least 15 greenfield investment overtures from China to Taiwan from May through December 2009 in the computer (Lenovo), automotive (SAIC), financial services (CMB), civil aviation, and other sectors, as well as a number of acquisition deals. The volume of inward mainland FDI approved by the MOEA spiked from virtually zero to over $30 million in both December 2009 and January 2010 (figure 1.20). Although these are small numbers (and not all of this "approved" investment will necessarily become "utilized"), this is a major change in the cross-strait context, and now that the "seal is broken" the annual value of China-to-Taiwan investment will likely rise significantly.

---

44. "Regulations on Investment Permission for Mainland Investors" (大陸地區人民來臺投資許可辦法), Ministry of Economic Affairs, Taiwan, June 30, 2009. Earlier drafts intended to raise the percentage to 50 percent. Available at: http://www.moeaic. gov.tw/system_external/ctlr?PRO= LawsLoad&id=64.

45. "Notice on Mainland Enterprise to Invest and Set Up Legal Entity in Taiwan" (关于大陆企业赴台湾地区投资或设立非企业法人有关事项的通知), Ministry of Commerce, People's Republic of China, May 17, 2009. Available at http://www.china.com.cn/policy/ txt/2009-05/17/content_17788032.htm.

**Figure 1.20  Approved foreign direct investment from China into Taiwan, monthly values, July 2009–January 2010**

millions of US dollars

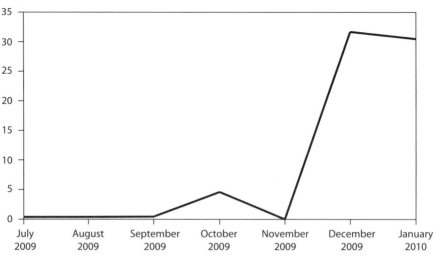

*Source:* Taiwan, Ministry of Economic Affairs Investment Commission.

Given that Taiwan's international investment position recorded total FDI stock of only $45.5 billion in 2008, with an average annual inflow of $5 billion over the past five years, China's marginal addition could soon be economically important.

## Portfolio Investment

Cross-border portfolio investment flows are an additional element of normal economic exchange. Portfolio investment is ownership of equity or debt securities in pursuit of a financial return, rather than as a manager or owner of a business for its own sake.[46] Direct cross-holdings of debt and equity securities by China and Taiwan are at an early stage, as both sides have restricted the other's portfolio investment activity until recently. This is changing as a result of the ad hoc steps taken in 2008–09 to liberalize cross-strait economic relations, and direct holdings are likely to increase significantly in the years ahead.

As of end-2008, Taiwan reported global portfolio assets of $189 billion and liabilities to foreigners of $111 billion in its international investment

---

46. According to the OECD's 2008 "Benchmark Definition of Foreign Direct Investment," the line between portfolio and direct investment equity stakes is generally drawn at 10 percent of total shares. Holdings below this threshold are classified as portfolio investment; a "controlling" stake of more than 10 percent is considered as direct investment.

position (IIP).[47] In 1990–2003, Taiwan used a qualified foreign institutional investor (QFII) system to introduce international capital into domestic financial markets in a conservative manner. After abolishing these QFII constraints in 2003, international capital flowed in more copiously—the stock of $40 billion doubled in the first year and then doubled again by the end of 2006, topping out at $208 billion in 2007 before falling by almost half again by the end of crisis year 2008 due to valuation effects and withdrawals. But investment from China was excluded from this flow, and uncertainties about Taiwan's relations with Beijing tempered investor enthusiasm, since the political risk associated with Taiwanese firms reliant on China-related income streams remained higher than in other economies.

With few exceptions, China still maintains a closed capital account and has taken a cautious approach to embracing portfolio capital flows. By end-2008, China held $252 billion in portfolio assets abroad and had sold $161 billion of portfolio liabilities to foreigners. Though these figures are slightly larger than those for Taiwan, the fact that China's population is 50 times larger and its economy 13 times bigger demonstrates how timid Beijing has been on this front. China studied Taiwan's use of the QFII system carefully in designing its own window on the otherwise closed capital account for portfolio investors, which it started to open in 2002. By 2006, Beijing permitted limited domestic portfolio investment firms to go out, in the other direction, under a corresponding qualified domestic institutional investor (QDII) program. To this were added licenses for state wealth managers, including the China Investment Corporation (China's sovereign wealth fund) and the National Social Security Fund, to invest pools of foreign exchange in diversified portfolios abroad, partly to help Beijing deal with its investment challenges regarding foreign exchange reserve management. But as with Taiwan's outbound flows, China's new forays in portfolio investment abroad could not flow across the Taiwan Strait until recently.

In June 2008, Taiwan relaxed quotas on Taiwanese fund investment in China's stock exchanges.[48] In August 2008, Taiwan started the liberalization of portfolio investment inflows from China, and in December 2008 passed a law that lifted the long-standing ban on investment from China in Taiwan's securities and futures.[49] In January 2010, a cross-strait bank-

47. International investment position data from Taiwan's Central Bank, www.cbc.gov.tw/public/Data/961517174971.pdf (accessed on September 15, 2010).

48. "Modification of Cross-Strait Securities Investment" (調整兩岸證券投資方案), Financial Supervisory Commission, Taiwan Executive Yuan, June 26, 2008. Available at http://www.mac.gov.tw/ct.asp?xItem=44258&ctNode=5613&mp=1

49. "Regulations Governing Securities Investment and Futures Trading in Taiwan by Mainland Area Investors" (大陸地區投資人來臺從事證券投資及期貨交易管理辦法), Financial Supervisory Commission, Taiwan Executive Yuan, December 4, 2008. Available at http://law.moj.gov.tw/LawClass/LawContent.aspx?Pcode=G0400147

ing, insurance, and securities MOU (signed in November 2009) took effect and Taiwan's Financial Supervisory Commission issued implementing regulations for China's QDIIs to enter Taiwan's financial markets.[50] In the initial stage the cap on Taiwanese securities market positions for these firms is $500 million. As of mid-2010, two funds—China AMC and China International Fund Management—have finished the registration processes and are preparing to start trading in Taiwan. While this ceiling is modest and several sectors are off limits, the quotas and coverage are likely to expand in the future. In the meantime, Taiwan is proceeding cautiously. China-controlled stakes are capped at 10 percent for important sectors, including public utilities and natural gas. The limit for shipping services is 8 percent. For the financial industry, the limit for each QDII is 5 percent, and 10 percent for all QDIIs.

## Flows of People

After trade and investment, the third factor that moves between economies in the normal course of exchange is people, and this too has been abnormal in the cross-strait context in the past. The movement of business travelers, expatriates, and tourists ordinarily follows bilateral trade and investment patterns closely. Whereas the number of Taiwanese business travelers and expatriates in China has grown steadily since the late 1980s, the number of visitors from China has been strictly limited by Taiwan. Taiwan's limits on visitation and residency paralleled trade and investment restrictions and reinforced them: for instance, the limited cases of investment opening to China that Taiwan had permitted (in real estate) were effectively nullified by travel prohibitions. The recent opening of Taiwan to investment from China described in the preceding section would be meaningless without relaxation of travel and residency restrictions, and likewise the regularization of transportation links is a prerequisite to meaningful investment flows. The total number of mainlanders traveling to Taiwan for business and tourism is expected to grow significantly and serve as a major source of economic growth for Taiwan.[51]

---

50. He Qian Xu, "MOU Took Effect and Mainland Investor Entered Taiwan" (MOU生效 陆资登台上路), Caing News, January 18, 2010. http://overseas.caing.com/2010-01-18/100109188. html (accessed on September 15, 2010).

51. The economic significance of Chinese tourists traveling to Taiwan is so great in fact that Beijing has used the threat of calling off tour groups to Taiwanese cities that lean toward the opposition Democratic Progressive Party as a tool of statecraft to punish perceived provocations. See Romberg (2009, 1–2). Such targeted commercial sanctions are precisely the kind of political pressure that skeptics of economic deepening in Taiwan are worried about.

**Figure 1.21  Number of annual cross-strait visitors, 1987–2009**

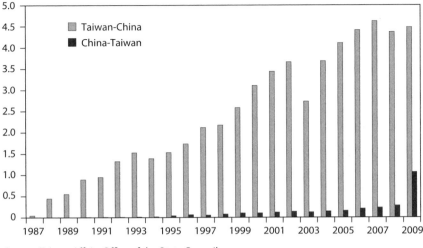

million individual entries

Source: Taiwan Affairs Office of the State Council.

## Business Travel and Tourism[52]

Figure 1.21 illustrates that the cross-strait flow of visitors has been asymmetric: visits by Taiwanese citizens to China grew from fewer than 1 million entries annually in 1990 to more than 4.5 million in 2007. This increase was largely driven by Taiwanese businessmen traveling temporarily to set up and manage production facilities, and mirrored the phases of economic engagement described above. The two-decade uptick correlates with flows of goods and investment from Taiwan to China. Temporary dips occurred in 2003 as a result of the SARS epidemic and in 2008 as a result of the global financial crisis, but otherwise the growth in the number of Taiwanese citizens traveling to China has been nearly constant.

Travel by Chinese citizens to Taiwan has remained limited to date, though it increased from trivial numbers in the late 1990s to about 250,000 in 2008, as both business and tourist travel were opened slightly. In 1995, Taiwan started allowing group business visits for attending exhibitions and trade shows. As of 2005 individual business visits were permitted, and Taiwanese firms can now issue invitations to Chinese businesses for stays of less than three months.[53] In 2002, Taiwan initiated group tourist

---

52. Tourism as an industry was reflected in the services trade discussion; here we are interested in openness to the movement of people for whatever reason.

53. "Regulations on Mainland Business Visitors in Taiwan" (大陸地區人民來臺從事商務活動許可辦法), Ministry of the Interior, Taiwan, February 1, 2005. Available at http://law.moj.gov.tw/LawClass/Law Content.aspx?pcode=D0080144

visas, and since 2008 individual tourist visas have been permitted.[54] This new visa policy along with relaxation of rules for passenger traffic across the strait has led to an explosion of visitors: in 2009, the number quadrupled compared to previous years and surpassed the 1 million mark for the first time (figure 1.21).

As with trade and investment, the cross-strait flow of people was distorted by Taiwan's prohibition on direct transportation links. After 1949, passenger travel between Taiwan and China was prohibited, necessitating transit through Hong Kong or other entrepôts, despite the reality of rising trade and investment over the past two decades. Indirect charter flights for holidays and other special events were permitted as of 2003, and in July 2008 direct flights between the mainland and Taiwan were allowed on weekends. In November 2008 and April 2009, the two sides signed new air transportation agreements to normalize flight traffic and allow direct daily flights.[55]

## Labor and Permanent Residency

While initially the cross-border flow of people from Taiwan to China was mostly short-term business visits, direct employment and residence of Taiwanese professionals in China became important by the late 1990s. With the increasing integration of China into Taiwan-driven production chains there was urgency to position skilled Taiwan professionals as expatriates in China, especially in the information and communication technology industry and other export-processing sectors. Key skills were in short supply in China at the time, and the mainland suffered from a brain drain of specialists. There are no official statistics available on how many Taiwanese citizens currently live and work in China, but unofficial estimates range from 400,000 to more than 1 million.[56]

While Taiwanese expatriates were mostly able to live and work in China, Taiwan's *Act Governing Relations between Peoples of the Taiwan Area*

---

54. "Regulations on Mainland Tourists in Taiwan" (大陸地區人民來臺從事觀光活動許可辦法), Ministry of the Interior, Taiwan, January 1, 2002; "Agreement on Mainland Tourists in Taiwan (海峽兩岸關于大陸居民赴臺灣旅游協議), Association for Relations across the Taiwan Strait, June 13, 2008. Available at http://law.moj.gov.tw/LawClass/LawContent.aspx?pcode=D0080141.

55. "Cross-Strait Air Transport Agreement" (海峽兩岸空運協議), Association for Relations across the Taiwan Strait, November 4, 2008. Available at http://law.moj.gov.tw/LawClass/LawContent.aspx?PCODE=Q0070009; "Supplement to Cross-Strait Air Transport Agreement" (海峽兩岸空運協議補充協議), Association for Relations across the Taiwan Strait, April 2009. Available at http://www.mac.gov.tw/public/Data/04269514771.pdf.

56. Media and even government officials from both sides often refer to an estimated 1 million Taiwanese citizens—or 5 percent of the total population—that currently live and work in China. But to our knowledge there is no statistical evidence that confirms this number.

*and China Area* in 1992 restricted employment of mainland Chinese in Taiwan, with partial exceptions for spouses and short-term workers in a limited range of industries. According to Taiwanese immigration data, around 300,000 mainland Chinese were granted residency by end-2009, which compares to around 400,000 nonmainland foreign residents.[57] Whereas more than 80 percent of those non-Chinese foreign residents are allowed to work—among them many blue-collar workers from Southeast Asian countries—those from China with permanent residency in Taiwan are not. The great majority of them—160,000 by end-2009 according to official statistics—are women married to Taiwanese men. Until recently, spouses from China were permitted to work only if they married into low-income families or in other cases of "special needs."[58]

In 1998, Taiwan introduced permits for professionals from China with special skills to apply for work visas, but the number issued under the program has remained minimal.[59] These rules were expanded in January 2002 to allow information technology professionals from China to apply for short- and long-term work visas in research and development and technical cooperation to overcome an acute shortage of talent in these fields. However, the number of workers under this program has remained very small as well: about 3,500 short-term visas had been issued by 2008, and the annual number of long-term visas has never exceeded 30. Since 2003, multinational corporations with large operations in Taiwan have been permitted to internally transfer employees from China to work in Taiwan for up to three years. In 2003–08, around 3,400 employees were transferred under this allowance.[60]

In his first year in office, President Ma submitted amendments to normalize work opportunities for mainland-born spouses and to permit greater latitude for Chinese students to live and study in Taiwan. Despite

---

57. Data from Taiwan National Immigration Agency. www.immigration.gov.tw/aspcode/info9811.asp (accessed on September 15, 2010); and www.immigration.gov.tw/immigration/FileSystem/Statistics/05%20Foreign%20990407.xls.

58. *Act Governing Relations between Peoples of the Taiwan Area and China Area* (臺灣地區與大陸地區人民關係條例) (see footnote 32), before the July 2009 revision.

59. "Rules Governing Permits for Professional Personnel from Mainland China Engaging in Professional Activities in Taiwan" (大陸地區專業人士來臺從事專業活動許可辦法), Ministry of the Interior, Taiwan, June 19, 1998 (first version for Chinese professionals with special skills). Available at http://law.moj.gov.tw/LawClass/LawContent.aspx?pcode=Q0020006

60. "Regulations on Inviting Mainland Employees to Work in Taiwan by Multinational Companies with Large-scale Business in Taiwan's Free Trade Zone" (在台湾自由贸易区内营业达一定规模之跨国企业邀请大陆地区雇员来台从事商务活动的许可办法), (Ministry of the Interior, Taiwan, May 16, 2003. Available at http://www.immigration.gov.tw/aspcode/searchmenu.asp?directoryid=910; "Regulations on Internal Transfer of Mainland Employees in Multinational Enterprises" (跨國企業內部調動之大陸地區人民申請來臺服務許可辦法), revised on August 20, 2007. Available at http://law.moj.gov. tw/Law Class/LawContent. aspx?pcode=Q0040007.

controversy, this revision to Article 17 of the act passed the legislature on June 9, 2009.[61] Yet the issue of labor pressure from China remains a political lightning rod in Taiwan, and most parties still compete with one another to be more populist in promising to shield Taiwan from labor pressures originating across the strait.

## Conclusions

This chapter has described the existing trade and economic relationship between China and Taiwan in order to set the stage for analyzing the implications of deepening that relationship. Before turning to that analysis in the following chapters, we can form a number of conclusions about the status quo in cross-strait economic relations that are useful in thinking about the future.

*First, there is no economic status quo in this relationship either for China-Taiwan economic relations narrowly or for the regional or global context surrounding them.* Whereas in the political context maintaining the status quo is the mainstay of agreement between Beijing, Taipei, and Washington, in the economic sphere everything is constantly changing and there is no status quo. It is common to hear people talk about economic change in cross-strait affairs as though it were an option to be embraced or rejected. That is an illusion. In terms of trade flows, direct investment and portfolio investment, and flows of people, cross-strait economic fundamentals are changing profoundly every day. In terms of Taiwan's export dependence on China, and final consumption in China as a share of those exports, the fundamentals are changing as well. The gap in technological capabilities between Taiwan and China is narrowing rapidly. Polls on public sentiment regarding economic interests and the importance of transcending past tensions also demonstrate significant changes.

The changes are just as stark in the multilateral context surrounding the cross-strait relationship. Economic agreements between China and most other economies in Asia are altering the relative costs of trade barriers between China and Taiwan. The ASEAN-China FTA has lowered China's tariffs to below MFN levels, and a host of other agreements are also altering tariff and nontariff barrier conditions. Value chains knit through Asia and across the Pacific are constantly reconfigured to reflect changing efficiencies and political risk realities, as long-standing political resistance to economic integration with China at the hub give way to the logic and durability of China's economic rise. The bottom line is that standing still is not an option, and much of what is being debated in cross-strait integration negotiations is already happening.

---

61. Article 17 states that "Any person who is permitted to have a spouse residency or long-term residency in the Taiwan Area in accordance with the provisions of Paragraphs 1, 3 or 4 of the preceding Article may work in the Taiwan Area during the residency period."

*Second, the trend of growing economic gains in Taiwan from its relationship with emerging China, while impressive, leaves mounting concerns about the risks to Taiwan's prosperity from incomplete normalization with China.* The existing and future disparities for Taiwan in economic relations with China are a serious concern in terms of economic outlook. Chapter 2 models and projects the implications of these disparities compared to scenarios in which they are resolved. But even before undertaking that formal exercise we can state that the existing relationship has given rise to doubts about Taiwan's economic development prospects and strategy. In trade, investment, and people flows, Taiwan is becoming more dependent on China, not less, and the absence of normalized economic interaction therefore presents a greater risk going forward. Taiwan's strategy to be a well-regulated gateway to continental China stalled due to ambiguities about its economic integration and tensions over political risk that could erode the value of operations in Taiwan in the future.

*Third, neither the quantity nor the quality of Taiwan's future economic relations with China can be assured through evolutionary and cyclical ad hoc processes, even though, per the first point above, much is changing in the cross-strait economic relationship in that very fashion.* These processes as we have known them are inherently cyclical because they start and stop with election cycles in Taiwan and leadership cycles in China, and are affected by election cycles in the United States as well. The ad hoc approach has been dribbling forth for almost two decades already, and yet cross-strait opening has been surpassed by shorter-lived plurilateral undertakings. Chapter 2 will define in more detail the forward agenda for more comprehensive normalization and liberalization of China-Taiwan economic relations, but based on just assessing the relationship to date one can surmise that the "occasionalism" that has characterized the approach to date is not sufficient to maintain a cross-strait relationship that is win-win over the long term.

*Fourth, most of the adjustments needed to deepen cross-strait economic relations will have to come from Taiwan's side, though the corollary is that Taiwan stands therefore to reap more of the economic benefits.* Our discussion of the structure of current relations has shown that China is largely in compliance with MFN-level WTO obligations to Taiwan, while Taiwan unilaterally imposes a broad range of barriers to trade in goods and services uniquely on China. These barriers need to be dismantled in order to normalize the relationship. Similarly, China is wide open to Taiwanese investment, which represents the largest single source of FDI in China, but Taiwan until recently has been almost entirely off limits to investment from China. This too will need to change in the course of deepening.

The chapters that follow will model the likely results of dismantling these barriers. But trade theory and experience make it clear why the work of liberalization and its subsequent benefits will fall disproportionately to Taiwan. Because Taiwan is largely WTO-compliant with practically every other member of the world trading community, its China-specific barriers have not so much protected Taiwanese business as marginally raised the costs to them, as well as to Taiwan's consumers. Our modeling in the following chapters confirms that Taiwan will gain from dismantling these barriers, not from increased net exports but from the domestic welfare benefits of increased imports and the structural adjustment and dynamic effects that follow.

*Fifth, while many of the residual distortions in China-Taiwan economic relations ultimately are economic in nature, they are maintained by Taiwan ostensibly for national security reasons.* Some of these—like limits on foreign control of public utilities—are typical in most other economies and are likely to remain. But many are not security oriented or have long since ceased to play a clear security role. The United States has debated for decades whether "national economic security" should stand along "national security" as a justification for blocking foreign investment and has consistently decided that the answer is no. The most important reason for that stance is that admitting national economic security as a basis for selectively excluding foreign investment and trade, especially in a democracy, is an open invitation to constant demands for protectionism by special interests that elected officials will find nearly impossible to repel. In the case at hand, China's behavior has already shown that for a small economy like Taiwan, national economic security can be a real concern, and a real source of vulnerability. Taiwan will need a filter to separate legitimate economic security concerns that could undermine the island's interests from special interests masquerading as security concerns.

Admitting that national economic security concerns are legitimate does not answer the question of whether defensive, protectionist measures are really a more effective response than proactive engagement and economic deepening. Not only can protectionist barriers masquerading as security fail to enhance national security, they can diminish it by threatening Taiwan's long-term competitiveness and economic success. However sympathetic one is to Taiwan's security imperative, one can just as easily argue that the island's security concerns are too important to be commingled in a stew of mixed, largely self-interested commercial motives.

*Sixth, cross-strait opening is not a recipe for Taiwan's competitiveness but just a step to prevent the erosion of existing strengths.* After all, by deepening economic relations, Taiwan is simply matching what its ASEAN and other regional competitors have done. Taiwan has done well despite cross-strait abnormalities for two reasons. First, China has tolerated the asymmetry. But second, Taiwan has produced comparative advantage in high-tech industries, which has paid the bills. The converse to this is that while optimizing cross-strait economic relations will support Taiwan's welfare, it is no more of sole importance on the upside than it was a detriment in the past. Improving cross-strait economic relations only provides a level playing field; what Taiwan does on that playing field to generate value is the hard question, and is largely separate from discussions between Taiwan and Beijing.

China's comparative advantage is relatively easy to ensure: low-cost labor, economies of scale and scope, and substantial room to improve the country's still-widespread relative impoverishment will propel China at high GDP growth for the next decade and beyond.[62] For Taiwan, comparative advantage can flow only from a highly sophisticated interaction of excellence in government policy and regulation, creativity and innovation by a highly educated population, and savvy risk taking in the corporate sector. While the unresolved risks to cross-strait trade and investment could diminish the likelihood that the highly mobile factors of high-skilled professionals and corporate capital will stay put and take their risks in Taiwan, resolving those risks (even perfectly, which is not in the cards) is just the first step to sufficiently reinvigorate the business environment and incentive structure in Taiwan to compete with the likes of Shanghai, Hong Kong, Tokyo, Osaka, and Singapore.

This conclusion draws only from our review of extant cross-strait conditions—it does not summarize the overall findings of this study. In particular, conclusions related to other parties, including the United States and the rest of Asia, as well as to regional trade dynamics, must await the forward-looking analysis in the following two chapters. We now turn to that analysis, defining and exploring the implications of cross-strait deepening for China and Taiwan in chapter 2, and extending that to an analysis of regional considerations in chapter 3.

---

62. We do not mean to be blithe: obviously, the disruption and adjustment that are a daily matter of course in China impose a grueling price on hundreds of millions of less well-off Chinese—the vast bulk of the population—whose fortunes are not secured. The challenges of policymaking in a transitional, unique economic context are epic, and the risks of social and political unrest are acute. Our point is that in growth accounting terms, the components needed to sustain growth are not in short supply.

# 2

# Bilateral Effects of Deepening the Economic Relationship

Chapter 1 laid out the current setting in China-Taiwan economic relations, which is the starting point for assessing the potential effects of liberalizing that relationship. Liberalization, rather than normalization, is the proper term for the prospect: normalization would just mean implementation of existing WTO obligations that Taiwan and China committed to extend to one another; liberalization entails going beyond that to keep pace with the WTO+ commitments proliferating in the region. On June 29, 2010, China and Taiwan took the initial steps toward economic deepening when Taiwan's Straits Exchange Foundation (SEF) and China's Association for Relations across the Taiwan Strait (ARATS) signed the Economic Cooperation Framework Agreement (ECFA) that provides the roadmap to a full set of economic agreements discussed below. Analyzing the implications of this undertaking is the concern of the remainder of this study.

Two overarching sets of questions are addressed in this chapter. First, what stands to be liberalized in the cross-strait economic relationship, what are the motivations for doing so, and what process is envisioned? Second, what are the estimated aggregate and sectoral effects Taiwan and China can anticipate from that liberalization, and conversely—in light of the changes taking place in the region around China and Taiwan—what are the consequences of maintaining the status quo instead? Since China and Taiwan have already signed an agreement to move beyond the status quo, some think that last question is irrelevant. However we take seriously the threat of some politicians not to ratify an agreement, and also the possibility of a change in party leading to withdrawal or abrogation.

Analyzing the impact of an economic policy change is always challenging. Policy impediments to commerce are not all easy to quantify and hence to model. Tariffs are straightforward, but in the case of Taiwan and China the ostensible applied tariff rates are not always in force in reality. Beyond tariffs, it is very difficult to put an accurate number on controls on services trade and investment flows. Still more difficult to quantify are premia arising from political risk or regulatory uncertainty, which have influenced the existing level of economic activity across the Taiwan Strait. Further, much of the two-way trade and investment flow has been obscured by the use of third-party intermediaries like Hong Kong, leaving analysts unsure whether the amount of Taiwanese investment in China, for instance, is less than $100 billion or closer to $200 billion. Finally, if this were not enough, the production chains linking Taiwan and China are closely linked to final demand in the OECD countries, which are undergoing a historic shock, leaving the analyst with more-than-usual trepidation about extrapolating even the most carefully derived baseline for past economic activity into the future. On the supply side of these production chains the setting around the Taiwan Strait is evolving with epic rapidity as well, with no fewer than 50 economic liberalization agreements phasing in or under negotiation with countries within a 10-hour flight of Taipei and Shanghai.[1]

While many of these considerations apply to trade policy analysis generally, the added challenges in the cross-strait case are extraordinary, and these all must be taken into consideration while making a best effort to explore the potential effects of liberalization with as much rigor as possible. We use a combination of qualitative analysis based on current data, information and interviews, and quantitative methods, including an economic modeling exercise, to explore the implications of liberalizing this bilateral economic relationship. Our approach reflects the view that we cannot gauge the implications of a given policy response in comparison to where we are now, but rather must consider where the two economies would otherwise be in the future given changes already taking place or foreseeable. The most pressing of these built-in changes to the status quo is the implementation of the ASEAN plus China agreement (also known as ASEAN+1, or AFTA), which came into effect in January 2010 for core ASEAN members (and comes into force in 2015 for other members).[2] But Taiwan's benefits from its proximity to rapidly growing China have been eroding relative to those of its neighbors since long before ASEAN FTAs

---

1. Any FTA after 2000 with China, Taiwan, Japan, Korea, India, Australia, or members of ASEAN as one of the partners is included in this list, from the WTO's regional trade agreement database.

2. The full title is "Framework Agreement on Comprehensive Economic Co-Operation between ASEAN and the People's Republic of China," agreed upon in Phnom Penh on November 5, 2002. www.aseansec.org/13196.htm (accessed on September 15, 2010).

became a topic of attention. This is discussed further below and details are available in appendix A.

## What, Why, and How?

### What Would Liberalization Include?

Chapter 1 described the abnormal conditions in China-Taiwan economic relations. After taking office in 2008, Taiwanese President Ma Ying-jeou undertook to resolve these abnormalities and push further to liberalization. Beijing engaged in this initiative enthusiastically. The United States, the foremost interested outside party, was cautiously supportive, and China and Taiwan signed the ECFA under which normalization and liberalization are to be negotiated.

Scenarios for cross-strait economic engagement can be grouped into three categories characterized by how far they go: normalization, liberalization, and integration.

*Normalization* entails compliance with the existing MFN-status obligations that WTO members commit to extend to one another. As summarized by the Chinese side, normalization means that indirect trade becomes direct trade, one-way trade becomes two-way trade, and unilateral prohibitions on imports from China maintained by Taiwan are rescinded. Neither China nor Taiwan notified a reservation toward the other in their WTO accession agreement, but subsequent to accession barriers have been maintained that are not imposed on other WTO members. This is especially true in the case of Taiwan, which prohibits more than 2,000 specific products from being imported from the mainland.[3] China has not formally challenged these departures from Taiwan's obligations because it is averse to underscoring Taiwan's independent standing in Geneva. Since 151 WTO members already have "normal" access to the Taiwan market, and many of those are less-developed economies with costs of production comparable to or lower than China's (for instance, Vietnam, Cambodia, Indonesia, and the Philippines), normalization does not entail special or preferential treatment. Nor is it likely to open Taiwan to competitive pressures that it has not already encountered in some measure. Mainland officials consider fidelity to these existing commitments a necessary starting point for further economic liberalization, although they stress that they are flexible in terms of the timing of compliance and exemptions for sensitive sectors.

Under WTO rules, MFN treatment is extended to all members, but there is the option to preferentially deepen openness by undertaking FTAs. Such

---

3. A list of these prohibited products is available on the website of Taiwan's Bureau of Foreign Trade. http://fbfh.trade.gov.tw/rich/test/indexfhE.asp (accessed on September 15, 2010).

preferential arrangements would be involved in the second scenario for cross-strait engagement: *liberalization*. For an FTA to be WTO-consistent, "duties and other restrictive regulations of commerce [should be] eliminated on substantially all the trade between the constituent territories in products originating in such territories."[4] What "substantially all" means has been variously interpreted: many FTAs neglect to cover a considerable share of trade, and no FTA has been challenged by the WTO for failure to be comprehensive. More recently, FTAs have gone beyond goods trade to "WTO+," dealing with services trade, investment flows, labor and the environment, regulatory transparency, competition policy, public procurement, mutual recognition of standards and professional qualifications, trade facilitation, and other business. Some agreements—such as the Closer Economic Partnership Arrangement between China and Hong Kong—incorporate pledges to forgo WTO rights that confer protectionist options, such as the ability to treat a member as a nonmarket economy or use antidumping policies on one another. Modern FTAs frequently include a specialized dispute settlement mechanism. Such liberalization beyond WTO-normal is the state of the game in Asia, as elsewhere, and it is this eventuality that China and Taiwan are discussing, and which is the focus of this study.

*Integration* is possible beyond the preferential arrangements of WTO+ FTAs, involving not just the elimination of barriers but active coordination and convergence of policy regimes. Such integration occurs in a customs union, which in addition to eliminating duties and other impediments between the parties goes further to establish a common external trade regime with third parties. Other vectors for economic integration include moving to a single currency under a monetary union, or forming a common labor market. The European Union provides an example of such integration and relinquishment of national authority over economic variables to a supranational undertaking. The North American Free Trade Agreement (NAFTA) between Canada, the United States, and Mexico certainly does *not* do so, and that is much more common. While there has been some academic discussion of such deeper economic integration between Taiwan and China (Cheung, Chinn, and Fujii 2007), this is not a subject of serious policy discussion between the two at this time, is not a necessary or even normal endpoint for an FTA, and is not a scenario explored further in this study.[5]

---

4. WTO, GATT Article XXIV, 8, b. www.wto.org/english/tratop_e/region_e/regatt_e.htm (accessed on September 15, 2010).

5. That said, Taiwan's President Ma has emphasized that he is not entertaining any discussion about deeper political relations across the strait "in his first term"—that is, in a second term such considerations are not beyond imagining. See "Taiwan President Ma Ying-jeou Prepared to Talk Politics with China after 2012," *Taiwan News*, May 10, 2010. www.etaiwan news.com/etn/news_content.php?id=944728&lang=eng_news&cate_img=logo_taiwan& cate_rss=TAIWAN_eng (accessed on September 15, 2010).

## Motivations: Why Does Each Side Want to Do This?

### *Taiwan's Perspective*

Taiwan's interest in economic liberalization with China arises from economic welfare concerns, while China's interests are largely political. One can describe Taiwan's interests either in terms of the economic upside from resolving economic tensions or the downside from failing to do so; both matter. Current circumstances are economically disadvantageous to Taiwan for numerous reasons.

First, Taiwan's import ban on goods from China means that in many cases only the second-most competitive products are available in Taiwan, imposing a welfare loss on Taiwanese households when they are the final consumers. In cases where Taiwan does import from the mainland but indirectly through transit trade via Hong Kong or elsewhere, Taiwanese consumers are disadvantaged by the added shipment cost. (It is important to recognize, however, that given Taiwanese manufacturers' affinity for south China and Hong Kong's proximity, much China-Taiwan trade would go through Hong Kong even without the direct shipping ban.)

Second, Taiwanese export competitiveness is undermined in industries where banned or indirectly imported intermediates push up production costs relative to economies without such bans. Such basic inputs as industrial fasteners (screws and bolts) naturally sourced from China are on Taiwan's banned list ostensibly for national security reasons, as are many other basic manufacturing inputs for light and heavier industry. While some observers work from the assumption that Taiwan's future lies in the higher-end services sector, the reality is that 37 percent of all employed persons in Taiwan work in industry, with 28 percent in manufacturing alone (2.9 million people in a workforce of 10.4 million).[6] Taiwan can no more afford to sacrifice manufacturing competitiveness to protect other domestic interests than the United States or Europe can. Of the more than 2,000 products Taiwan currently prohibits from the mainland—which include doughnuts, terrycloth towels, glass container lids, and solar panels—many are clearly nonstrategic in nature.

Third, Taiwan prohibits investment inflows from China, significantly reducing capital formation and complicating some outbound Taiwanese investment in the mainland (notably in financial services). These prohibitions have diminished both portfolio investment inflows and direct investment inflows. Progress on loosening Taiwan's investment ban is already being made separate from the more comprehensive FTA track (which is the subject of much of the remainder of the study). While Beijing has permitted Taiwanese investors to own and operate manufactur-

---

6. See Taiwan employment data at http://eng.stat.gov.tw/public/data/dgbas04/bc4/ english/table/tab05.xls (accessed on September 15, 2010).

ing facilities in China despite a lack of reciprocity, Taiwanese financial services providers have not been allowed to operate in China (with a few exceptions), depriving them of market opportunities and depriving Taiwanese firms in the mainland of support from their home bankers.

Fourth, and critically, the ambiguity about Taiwan's future economic relationship with the world's most important emerging economy undermines investment into Taiwan from the rest of the world.[7] Taiwan made several attempts to market itself as a regional services hub to support China-related business, but with the fundamental relationship across the strait fraught with political baggage, these campaigns have come up short. There have been inward investments in Taiwan in recent years, but few have been conceived as long-term investments in a Taiwanese business platform. In some cases, such as foreign stakes in Taiwanese financial firms, the goal included access to talent and assets that could be redeployed outside of Taiwan.

Fifth, there is capital flight by Taiwanese businesses and individuals themselves to avoid risks associated with trade and investment restrictions.[8] This is distinct from normal outbound direct investment to optimize operational efficiency. Rather, capital flight refers to investment that would otherwise be maintained in Taiwan based on comparative advantage but is shifted abroad (whether to China or elsewhere) due to potential shocks or weaknesses arising at home. This phenomenon is industry-specific when it involves plans for a particular production facility to side-step cross-strait tensions. Such capital flight can also be nonspecific, as when Taiwanese firms keep profits abroad instead of repatriating them in order to maintain freedom of action for future investment purposes. Individual investors have also shifted portfolio holdings to foreign securities in recent years, reflecting waning expectations for the ability of Taiwanese firms to maintain returns, and in reaction to China-Taiwan tensions. Normalization of relations or an FTA would not reduce the attraction of outbound Taiwanese investment to China, but it could surely mitigate the less commercially motivated capital flight that has taken place.

Sixth, over time this set of distortions adds up not just to static losses for Taiwan but to a negative dynamic effect as well: structural adjustment to changing relative comparative advantage between Taiwan and China has been retarded. Observers in Taiwan, China, and elsewhere in the region note that Taiwan's competitive edge has dulled over the past two decades as energy and money have been invested in sustaining limitations to economic liberalization with China rather than structural adjustment to new realities.

---

7. This finding is based on survey work (discussed further below) indicating that foreign firms would significantly increase their investments in Taiwan if China-related political risk concerns were removed.

8. Based on the survey work mentioned in the previous footnote.

Finally, the regional economic calculus is not in Taiwan's favor. Beijing and Taipei agree to "maintain the status quo" with one another politically, and the United States opposes unilateral action to alter that (though the parties have varying definitions of what the "status quo" actually means). But Beijing's ability to enter economic integration arrangements in the region while using its influence over neighbors to prevent Taiwan from doing the same is significantly changing the economic status quo. As trade and commerce deepen among nearly everyone *but* Taiwan, the island's competitiveness in the region declines. This integration has a long way to go and will become more important over time, and China's soft-power capacity to sway the policies of others will likely get stronger in the future. In fact, since the June 2010 signing of the ECFA, Taiwan has already begun bilateral trade consultations.

China has entered into at least 14 FTAs in the past decade, and is considering or negotiating another seven. China implemented the first stage of the ASEAN+1 agreement in January 2010. China's embrace of FTAs and the ASEAN+1 agreement constitute the new baseline against which Taiwan's action or inaction with the mainland must be analyzed.[9] The baseline would move further (that is, the costs of nonparticipation for Taiwan become higher) in the future with the conclusion of an ASEAN+3 agreement incorporating Japan and South Korea into the ASEAN-China accord, and even further should a broader East Asian FTA be concluded (incorporating Australia, New Zealand, and a handful of other economies; see modeling notes in appendix A for details).

In addition to angling for regional *lebensraum* in the wake of a cross-strait economic agreement, Taiwan is motivated to deepen trans-Pacific trade discussions with the United States as well. The prospect of a China-Taiwan FTA has heightened attention to US-Taiwan economic relations. Representatives from Taiwan and the United States have discussed undertaking an FTA and other options in the past. Some believe that in addition to possible economic benefits, such an agreement could help secure Taiwan's political confidence vis-à-vis China. The US perspective on these questions will be examined in chapter 4. It is fair to say that for bilateral commercial reasons and wider geoeconomic reasons the United States is likely to invest more in its relationship with Taiwan following cross-strait economic deepening.

Some of the welfare motivations described above could be achieved by Taiwan unilaterally. Simply by rescinding import prohibitions, for instance, Taiwan would generate producer and consumer welfare gains for

---

9. China's Ministry of Commerce maintains a special web resource for calculating the appropriate import duties on trade. We tested the resource on April 19, 2010, to confirm that China's import of chalk from Malaysia—an ASEAN+1 partner—would indeed be dutiable at zero, rather than at the 3 percent MFN rate China imposes on other WTO members. See http://ftatax.mofcom.gov.cn/fta/FTABrowser_en.html (by subscription; accessed on September 15, 2010).

its citizens and firms. However Taiwan's more acute concerns are perceptual and depend on expectations about whether the China-Taiwan economic relationship will be "normal" and stable in the future. To address these, a more formal framework for the cross-strait relationship is necessary. Some of the trade-related gains depend on mutual rather than unilateral action—for instance, mutual recognition of standards and certification. And while accepting China's imports is clearly a WTO "obligation" for Taiwan, in practice compliance with those obligations is a "concession" for which Taiwan can achieve WTO+ tradeoffs (from China). So it makes sense for Taiwan to undertake trade reform in the context of a joint undertaking rather than unilaterally.

### China's Perspective

China's principal interest in liberalizing cross-strait economic relations is a political move conducive to broader integration at an indefinite point in the future. Initially, Chinese officials underscored that they had no economic motive in considering a cross-strait economic agreement, and professed not to have conducted or studied a careful economic analysis of the economic implications of an FTA.[10] While China's FTA negotiations would normally be managed by the Ministry of Commerce, consultations with Taiwan on an economic deepening agreement were overseen by the China State Council's Taiwan Affairs Office—underscoring the inherently political nature of the matter for China. By late 2009, Beijing's tone on this point had evolved, and the mainland was emphasizing the economic interests on its side that needed consideration, economic analyses that had been undertaken, and economic objectives in potential negotiations. Chinese officials argue that a cross-strait agreement will confer significant economic benefits to Taiwan, and that by facilitating such benefits and fostering good will and an image of flexibility they will best promote the prospect of political unification down the road.

Of course, political considerations can arise from economic impact, for China as for others, and Beijing must consider geopolitical factors different from those of concern to Taiwan. The effects of an FTA for China may be minor relative to GDP, but even small impacts can generate political complexities. For instance, because they are not concerned primarily with trade analysis, China's Taiwan policy managers may have downplayed the fact that any FTA can have trade-diverting effects on third parties, which can give rise to political problems if not considered. Hong Kong will be affected, as it has served as a transshipment point for China-

---

10. China does not describe the intended economic agreement under the ECFA as an FTA, as it considers that FTAs are between sovereign states. However, as all the cross-strait terms and considerations are typical of an FTA, we use the term as though it were neutral with regard to the status of parties.

Taiwan commerce for decades. Beijing's view is that Hong Kong should "take one for the team" and endure any negative economic adjustment costs. No doubt China has the wherewithal to offset those negatives,[11] for Hong Kong or anywhere else, but the point is that even if China's motives are only political it must still concern itself with economic implications in order to maximize the chances of achieving those political goals. In addition, the volume of direct shipping across the strait has been growing in advance of an FTA, reducing the shock that will eventuate with an agreement and mitigating the weight of the FTA question for third parties.

While economic considerations are secondary for Beijing in the aggregate, for specific Chinese interests at the company, industry, and provincial levels the commercial implications are what matters. Fujian Province faces Taiwan and has designed much of its economic development policy planning around a new West Straits Economic Zone Initiative.[12] China's semiconductor industry has made great advances in recent years, but could move more quickly if it were to have unlimited interaction with Taiwan's still-leading firms in the industry. Taiwan's patent base and ability to nurture real innovation through such institutions as the Industrial Technology Research Institute still significantly exceed China's. When the West Straits concept was backed by China's State Council in 2009 in the context of rising prospects for a cross-strait pact, brokers immediately had lists available of firms likely to benefit from the initiative. These included Zhangzhou Development (water treatment), Yangguang Development (real estate), Fujian Expressway (transportation), China Wuyi Construction, SGMG Steel, Fujian Cement, Xiamen International Trade, Xiamen Ports, Xiamen Engineering (engineering and machinery), Jianfa (logistics and warehousing), GFJY Porcelain (light manufacturing), Xiamen Airport, and GCDT Property (real estate).

### The United States: A Motive in the Background

Both Beijing and Taipei have sought to ensure US support for their economic liberalization initiative for a variety of reasons. Most broadly, while moving ahead with the most profound adjustment in external policy in a generation or more, Taiwan hopes to maintain as much continuity as possible, where possible. Foremost, that means not alienating traditional sources of support in the United States in the course of moving closer to China, considering that relinquishing protectionist impediments to Chinese trade and investment does amount to a shift, even if nominally eco-

---

11. We find the negative effects on Hong Kong to be minor, largely factored in already, and of little concern to Hong Kong officials or business professionals.

12. "New Economic Zone West of Taiwan Strait to Broaden Cooperation," *China Daily*, May 18, 2010. http://www.chinadaily.com.cn/bw/2009-05/18/content_7785319.htm (accessed on September 15, 2010).

nomic only. Officials in Taipei are mindful that they are drawing nearer to Beijing at a time of regional adjustment: most polities in Asia are anxious to cultivate warm relations with Beijing while at the same time hedging against Chinese assertiveness (for instance, in the South China Sea).[13] This is a delicate balance.

Besides this geostrategic frame, many Taiwan advisors hope that talks under the US-Taiwan Trade and Investment Framework Agreement (TIFA) can be more quickly reactivated in light of the China undertaking, which they calculate will help balance rising dependence on cross-strait trade, or at least provide a *sense* of balance to help smooth the domestic political economy of cross-strait opening. Beyond the TIFA, some in Taipei eye the prospect of a US-Taiwan FTA, which they argue is significantly in Taiwan's interests economically, politically, or both. They expect a cross-strait agreement to motivate Washington to reorder its priorities to make this prospect more likely.

China's intimidation of other parties contemplating economic agreements with Taiwan may have disinclined others in Asia from doing so in the past, but they pose no similar obstacle to the United States. Domestic US trade politics have failed to line up behind a US-Taiwan FTA in the past, but with European businesses and trade officials contemplating an EU-Taiwan FTA, this could change.[14] As of the fall of 2010, US policymakers have set aside the notion of a US-Taiwan FTA for the time being, but will likely have restarted TIFA talks by the time this study is published. If Taiwan were blocked from pursuing reasonable economic integration through the normal course of discussions taking place in Asia, then a US-Taiwan FTA would need more urgent consideration, but it appears that Taiwan is starting to move forward on several other fronts (Lardy and Rosen 2004). Meanwhile, through TIFA talks the United States can clarify the case for a potential FTA of its own, resolve trade problems, discuss a possible bilateral investment agreement, and generally share views on the state of trade integration in Asia.

Finally, beyond the narrow trade policy machinations, China has larger reasons to be mindful of US reactions to cross-strait economic deepening. Beijing has calculated that this deepening promotes its grandest and highest-level strategic objective of reunification of greater China, and current leaders in particular are eager to secure a contribution to that end as part of their soon-to-be-closed legacy. We would argue that US reaction to this economic deepening is the weightiest variable in China's Taiwan diplomacy, more important even than the boisterous objections of Tai-

---

13. See Martin Fackler, "In Japan, U.S. Losing Diplomatic Ground to China," *New York Times*, January 24, 2010, A11. www.nytimes.com/2010/01/24/world/asia/24japan.html (accessed on September 15, 2010).

14. See the European Chamber of Commerce Taipei (ECCT 2008) report on release of a contracted study of economic benefits from such an undertaking.

wan's opposition Democratic Progressive Party (DPP), since the latter is predictable and not a variable.

## Process for Liberalization

### Cross-Strait Economic Cooperation Framework Agreement

From January 2009 until their signing of the ECFA in June 2010, China and Taiwan consulted on the form and scope of an initiative to deepen their two-way economic relationship. There was considerable uncertainty about the intended scope for most of this period, although officials on both sides briefed interested experts on the expected design. The framework agreement signed in Chongqing provides an early harvest agreement of near-term tariff elimination, with detailed product schedules for goods and services from each side, and a schedule for commencing talks on fuller trade in goods and liberalization of services trade within six months. China and Taiwan have stated that the agreement will be WTO-compliant, so we must assume that it will cover substantially all trade, at least to the degree typical. In addition to early harvest and FTA commitments, the ECFA committed the parties to a host of other elements found in FTAs today, including dispute resolution, investment promotion (which had already been addressed under a separate MOU), customs cooperation, and trade facilitation. The agreement also emphasizes joint industrial cooperation and sets up an Economic Cooperation Council that will be the steering committee for ongoing talks under the framework. At the same meeting, the two parties also signed a separate accord on intellectual property rights protection.

Mainland officials had no firm preference in terms of sequence or priorities for these negotiations, but rather insisted on two principles: that the undertaking lead to *normalization* of the economic relationship, meaning compliance with existing obligations under the WTO, and that an *institutionalized* mechanism be established for managing the economic relationship going forward rather than relying on ad hoc mechanisms. The scope of the framework for liberalizing the cross-strait economic relationship—first described as a comprehensive economic cooperation agreement and then reiterated as the ECFA—was thus defined largely by the Taiwan side. Taiwan also set out areas that it would not discuss: any question of sovereignty, labor market opening, or agricultural market access.

The ECFA package of commitments provides a set of asymmetric preferential tariff reductions for Taiwanese exports (greater than the opening afforded to Chinese exports) in the first instance of the early harvest agreement. However, provided the parties move in good faith to flesh out the FTA on schedule, the undertaking will indeed achieve China's goals of normalization and institutionalization within a reasonable time frame. We do not see those goals as entailing any concession from Taiwan, and indeed much of the economic benefits for Taiwan from the ECFA will arise from the domestic adjustment necessary for normalization. The benefits we compute for Taiwan from the ECFA will depend on timely and substantial implementation of a WTO-compliant FTA with China: if Taiwan does not do so, then our estimates are valuable for describing the likely shortfall versus potential gains. Deeper integration, such as formation of a common external tariff or monetary union, would not be necessitated by the requirements of an FTA, nor would they be likely.[15]

There is much more that could be said about the process of ratifying the ECFA in Taipei and the prospects for full negotiation and implementation of the FTA component starting at the end of 2010. Indeed, Taiwan has abrogated trade protocols in the recent past, so these questions are germane. However, the objective of this study is not to analyze Taiwan's trade politics but to assess the economic implications should Taiwan and China fulfill their aspirations for an economic framework. Therefore in our scenarios we assume that the ECFA is implemented in full and in a WTO-faithful manner, and our results answer the question of the economic effects in a reasonable timeframe. If one side drags its heels, and it takes 15 years to implement an FTA, so be it, the welfare gains from liberalization will take that much longer to achieve. Our goal is not to guess the timing but rather to estimate the potential gains.

### Opening Separate from the Economic Cooperation Framework Agreement

Cross-strait economic opening is not limited to the ECFA; significant liberalization has been accomplished through other mechanisms as well. From Ma Ying-jeou's election in March 2008 through January 2010, four rounds of talks were conducted between Taiwan's SEF and China's ARATS, restarting the semiofficial mechanism that had lapsed for a decade. The early 2008 round generated six agreements: on charter flights, tourist visas for mainland Chinese to visit Taiwan, air transport, sea transport, postal services, and food safety. In the December 2008 round, direct cross-strait shipping links were launched, as were weekday charter flights following more direct flight paths, and more direct postal services. The third round, held in Nanjing in late April 2009, produced additional agreements on moving from charter to regular transport links, financial services regulation (preliminary to market access), and a breakthrough on

---

15. Some observers have inferred from Ma administration comments that Taiwan does not intend to implement any opening for 10 years following the ECFA signing. We understand the comments that have led to this conjecture, but conclude that this is a misreading. We think that President Ma has retained the flexibility and the intention to implement Taiwan's commitments on a more expeditious schedule.

Taiwan's prohibitions on inbound investment from the mainland. Financial regulation memoranda were signed in November 2009 and went into effect in January 2010.[16] The fourth round of talks was held in Taichung, Taiwan in December 2009 and produced agreements on fisheries, agricultural product quality, and inspection and certification. Importantly, it also formally placed ECFA negotiations on the agenda for the fifth round of talks that successfully concluded the framework agreement in June 2010 in Chongqing, along with the intellectual property rights accord.

Thus a liberalization mechanism has already been institutionalized, albeit at the less than fully official level. And the achievements made through these Chiang-Chen talks (as they are called, after the respective chief representatives) entail *normalization* of economic relations; that is, implementation of MFN obligations promised to other WTO members. However this process is less suitable for comprehensive FTA liberalization, since SEF and ARATS are not trade policy agencies capable of managing a far-reaching economic negotiation. FTA-like undertakings are vastly more complex than the ad hoc MOUs agreed upon in 2008–09, though the latter are significant and complex as well, and neither semi-official representative entity is staffed to negotiate a broader agreement.

## Assessing the Economic Effects

### Modeling Methodology

To explore the economic implications of cross-strait economic deepening we use a global recursive dynamic computable general equilibrium (CGE) model. CGE models approximate economic activity with a set of equations and use real economic data to estimate how economies react to "shocks" like the change in trade tariffs and other barriers intended under the ECFA. Our model is an extension of the CGE models used in China WTO accession studies by Wang (1997, 1999, 2003a, 2003b), with import-embodied technology transfer and trade-policy-induced total factor productivity (TFP) growth. It is part of a family of models widely used to analyze the impact of global trade liberalization and structural adjustment programs. The model focuses on the real side of the world economy and incorporates considerable detail on sectoral output and real trade flows, both bilateral and global. It is not designed to generate short-term macroeconomic forecasts. Rather, under exogenous assumptions on future world economic growth it generates the pattern of production and trade resulting from world economic adjustment to the shocks specified in the alternative policy scenarios using a recursive dynamic framework.

16. "FSC Inked Three MOUs with Chinese Authorities," Financial Supervisory Authority press release, Taiwan Executive Yuan. www.fscey.gov.tw/Layout/main_en/News_NewsContent. aspx?NewsID=38541&LanguageType=2&path=1878 (accessed on September 15, 2010)

Detail on this model is provided in the appendices to this study, but all readers should understand some characteristics of this modeling, which will be well known to modeling aficionados. First, the model does not *forecast* growth but rather provides a projection of how much growth would *differ* under different policy scenarios. Baseline growth itself is simply fed into our model from a reputed source, not calculated by us, and we then test how much growth would change from that baseline given different policy choices. Second, the model does not fully capture trade in services, FDI, or portfolio investment flows, and it holds many other variables constant in order to derive the direction and order of magnitude of change in social welfare, terms of trade, volume of trade, output, consumption, real wages, and changes in prices and resource allocation. These estimates must also be regarded as *conditional projections* rather than as forecasts. In reality, actual trade and output patterns are affected by much more than just trade liberalization. The results from our modeling explored below are outcomes in 2020 in terms of GDP, trade effects, and welfare.

The model has 20 fully endogenized regions and 32 production sectors in each region to represent the world economy. Three types of gains from trade liberalization are captured by the model:

- the gains from more efficient utilization of resources leading to a one-time permanent increase in GDP and social welfare;

- more rapid physical capital accumulation from a "medium-run growth bonus" that compounds the efficiency gain from trade liberalization and leads to higher saving and investment; and

- import-embodied (through capital and intermediate goods) technology transfer among regions, which links sector-specific TFP growth with each region's imports of capital- and technology-intensive products.[17] Technology transfer is assumed to flow in one direction—from more-developed regions to less-developed regions.

As will be pointed out repeatedly, our model underestimates nongoods trade effects of economic liberalization, including services trade and investment flows, and it does not address some realities like higher transaction costs created by mushrooming sets of "rules of origin." Some studies suggest these are quite high in the Asian agreements to date.

---

17. Empirical evidence suggests that there is strong positive feedback between trade expansion and productivity growth. Trade liberalization increases the prevalence of technology transfer as trade barriers are reduced. Firms in the liberalized regions will import more capital- and technology-intensive goods as both investment and intermediate inputs from abroad at cheaper prices. Those goods are usually embodied with advanced technology from other countries, thus stimulating productivity growth for all production factors.

## Baseline and Scenarios

The economies of Taiwan, China, and their neighbors are changing quickly, and a constellation of bilateral and plurilateral agreements are at various stages of completion (figure 2.1). These factors make analyzing the economic implications of cross-strait liberalization challenging; to clarify them, one must define likely scenarios.

There are two axes to the dynamic situation across the strait. First, what, if any, changes would take place in China-Taiwan economic relations? And second, what, if any, changes would take place in economic relations between the two and other economies in the region? Table 2.1 summarizes the matrix of possibilities.

The three column headings (ASEAN+1/ASEAN+3/East Asian FTA) describe a range of actions that China has taken or may take that would change the economic significance of whether there is liberalization across the Taiwan Strait: completing ASEAN+1 commitments in January 2010 (done); inclusion of Japan and South Korea in the ASEAN+1 framework to make a +3 agreement;[18] and a complete East Asian FTA, including Australia, New Zealand, Macau, Mongolia, and other smaller East Asian countries.

The numbered rows in table 2.1 present possible Taiwan policy responses, including (1) nothing, that is, stopping with the implementation of links that have been achieved so far, as Taiwan's DPP had essentially counseled; the ECFA gets bogged down in implementation; and (2) the WTO+ outcome reflected in the ECFA. Though most observers believe Taiwan will proceed toward implementing the terms of the ECFA now that it is signed, even under a return of DPP to power, we retain the "status quo" scenario because Taiwan has failed to implement trade agreements in the past and the cost of that outcome is worth quantifying. Row (3) offers the scenario of full Taiwan-China economic integration, but we disregard this possibility as unlikely for the time being. While the first three scenarios explore the significance of bilateral liberalization for Taiwan and China in the dynamic context of ongoing integration in Asia, scenarios (4)–(6) envision Taiwan building on the bilateral foundation to join plurilateral regional agreements, which are addressed in chapter 3.

---

18. While ASEAN+1 is phasing in with a real timeline, ASEAN+3—known as "APT" in ASEAN parlance—does not yet have such tangibility. There are separate framework agreements between ASEAN and Japan and South Korea individually that are already in our baseline, but there is no framework that would extend the arrangements to cover trade among the three parties in the APT. There are other variants worth exploring: China and Korea are now preparing to consult on an FTA in 2011, and Korean preferences in China would be profound for Taiwan. However, the ASEAN+3 scenario captures that, and we cannot hope to model every conceivable array.

## Figure 2.1 Selected current and proposed regional agreements in the Asia-Pacific region

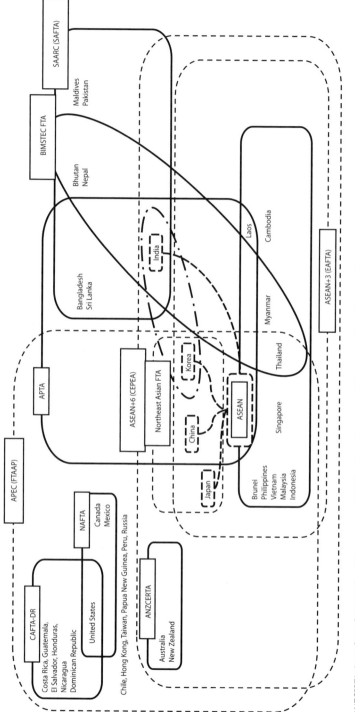

ANZCERTA: Australia and New Zealand Closer Economic Relations Trade Agreement; AFTA: Association of East Asian Nations Free Trade Area; APEC (FTAAP) = Asia-Pacific Economic Cooperation (Free Trade Area of the Asia-Pacific); APTA = Asia-Pacific Trade Agreement; ASEAN = Association of Southeast Asian Nations; BIMSTEC FTA = Bay of Bengal Initiative for MultiSectoral Technical and Economic Cooperation Free Trade Agreement; CAFTA-DR = Central America–United States–Dominican Republic Free Trade Area; CEPEA = Comprehensive Economic Partnership in East Asia; EAFTA = East Asia Free Trade Agreement; NAFTA = North American Free Trade Agreement; SAARC (SAFTA) = South Asian Association for Regional Cooperation (South Asian Free Trade Area).

*Source:* Updated using the World Trade Organization regional trade agreement database.

**Table 2.1  Scenarios: Taiwan's economic participation limited to ECFA**

| Scenario | ASEAN+1 | ASEAN+3 | East Asian FTA |
|---|---|---|---|
| 1    Taiwan status quo | | | |
| 2    Taiwan-China ECFA (WTO+ liberalization) | | | |
| 3    Taiwan-China integration | | | |
| 4    ECFA, Taiwan joins ASEAN+1 | | | |
| 5    ECFA, Taiwan joins ASEAN+1, ASEAN+3 | | | |
| 6    ECFA, Taiwan joins ASEAN+3 | | | |

ECFA = Economic Cooperation Framework Agreement; ASEAN = Association of Southeast Asian Nations; FTA = free trade agreement; WTO = World Trade Organization.

Our baseline for examining the effects of these various "policy shocks" is the set of agreements in place as of 2009: Taiwan has implemented limited links with the mainland but is not in WTO compliance, while China extends MFN-level trade treatment to Taiwan and has entered into a number of WTO+ FTAs in the region as well as an ASEAN-China FTA (ASEAN+1). Bilaterally, we think the most likely outcomes through 2020 are those shown in the shaded boxes in table 2.1: that China fully implements the ASEAN+1 or takes part in an ASEAN+3 agreement, while Taiwan either does or does not implement the ECFA.

The matrix of scenarios makes several things readily apparent. First, as figure 2.1 illustrates, East Asia is beset by a spaghetti bowl of interwoven trade initiatives that make analysis more difficult. Second, there is no "preserving the status quo" in cross-strait economic relations, given the raft of ongoing integration projects. And third, normalizing cross-strait trade is not the endpoint for Taiwan in terms of keeping the playing field level—it is only the first step.

## Time Frame

The significance of liberalizing cross-strait economic relations depends on which scenario plays out, and the picture is different depending on the time frame one considers. The immediate, static impact of most scenarios is modest compared to the longer-term implications. The most profound economic effects of the liberalization scenarios we examined occur four to six years after an agreement commences, and over time the welfare gains cumulate and compound to present a much more impressive difference from the baseline outlook. We think it is appropriate to look at the consequences of the choices Taiwan and China make today 10 years out in order to fully assess the significance. As will be apparent, our estimates of potential gains from cross-strait economic deepening are greater than those arrived at by others, and we attribute this to our decision to apply a time frame that fully captures longer-term dynamic effects and structural adjustment.

## Aggregate Effects

As discussed above, Beijing expresses little concern about the economic effects of an FTA, while in Taipei the arguments offered in support of the ECFA have been decidedly sectoral, with a particular emphasis on petrochemicals, agriculture, machinery, and auto parts. We will turn to sectoral considerations in due course, but the correct point of departure for assessing cross-strait economic liberalization is the aggregate effects over time.

Given the importance of quantitative assessment to policymaking, it is significant that an economic assessment of the ECFA was not undertaken until the spring of 2009 and thus available only in the late summer of 2009. We may take Beijing's position that it is unconcerned with the economic effects at face value, but what about Taiwan, given its insistence that the objective of the ECFA is Taiwan's economic welfare, not a political rapprochement? Preparation of a comprehensive analysis of the ECFA was not requested by Taiwanese leaders until the spring of 2009. It may be that the aggregate benefits were simply taken as a given by President Ma and his administration, or it may be that leaders were anxious that publicizing the aggregate gains to be achieved in an FTA would also involve identifying who among the locals would be on the losing end of such an agreement. It may be that the pace of preliminary discussions simply got ahead of expectations. Or it may be that the generally high margins of error associated with modeling FTAs in a dynamic environment, combined with the particular difficulties of modeling the economic relationship between China and Taiwan, dissuaded politicians and their economic advisors from attempting to do so. In any case, at least three aggregate studies were ultimately begun, including the present volume.

### GDP

Table 2.2 summarizes our projections of change in GDP in 2020 attributable to bilateral liberalization for China and Taiwan under three scenarios.

The ASEAN-China FTA (ASEAN+1) is built into our baseline scenario, therefore we cannot project the negative consequences of that for Taiwan. However, the effects would very likely be negative, since ASEAN+1 lowers barriers to ASEAN trade in China while Taiwan continues to face China's standard, MFN-applied tariffs. In an Asian Development Bank (ADB) analysis of East Asian trade agreements, Kawai and Wignaraja (2008) estimate the income loss for Taiwan in 2017 from ASEAN+1 at $2.5 billion, or about half a percentage point of GDP (in constant 2001 dollars). In an analysis produced by Taiwan's MOEA in early 2009, ASEAN+1

**Table 2.2  Change in 2020 GDP** (billions of 2004 US dollars and percent)

|         | ECFA (China-Taiwan) | No ECFA, ASEAN+3 | ECFA, ASEAN+3 |
|---------|---------------------|------------------|---------------|
| Taiwan  | 20.6 (4.40)         | −3.5 (−0.75)     | 16.4 (3.50)   |
| China   | 4.2 (0.08)          | 18.3 (0.34)      | 24.4 (0.45)   |

ECFA = Economic Cooperation Framework Agreement; ASEAN = Association of Southeast Asian Nations.

Note: Numbers in parentheses represent percent change.

*Source:* Model estimates.

is forecast to adversely affect export-dependent Taiwanese industries, including petrochemicals (43 percent of Taiwan's industrial production goes to China) and machinery (32 percent to China), by creating a tariff differential for Taiwanese exports to China as high as 14 percent.[19]

Against this backdrop of negative aggregate and sectoral consequences of an ASEAN+1 for Taiwan, our simulation of the results of the ECFA presents a stark contrast. In 2020, when the effects of trade liberalization will have had time to sink in, Taiwan's GDP would be on the order of 4.4 percent higher than otherwise, assuming only ASEAN+1. This would amount to $21 billion (in 2004 dollars). Consistent with Beijing's modest attitude about its own economic benefits, the ECFA's impact on China is smaller given its much larger size, but positive nonetheless.

At first glance, the balance of GDP growth in Taiwan's favor might seem counterintuitive to some. After all, China gets more market access in Taiwan out of the deal than Taiwan gets in China, where MFN-level tariffs are already maintained. But recall that the baseline portends a significant downside for Taiwan from preferential ASEAN market access in China in the years ahead, which does not affect China, and these GDP effects are from that baseline.

The other two bilateral scenarios for Taiwan presented in table 2.2 further illustrate the importance of whether Taiwan pursues something like the ECFA in light of deepening trade integration in the region. If China and ASEAN extend their FTA to Japan and South Korea in an ASEAN+3 arrangement, which is under discussion,[20] and Taiwan remains aloof from China, then the negative consequence for Taiwan is increased by

---

19. MOEA Minister Chii-Ming Yiin, "Possible Content for Advancing the Cross-Strait Economic Cooperation Framework," March 29, 2009. Available at http://www.roc-taiwan.org/ct.asp?xItem=90233&ctNode=4761&mp=1&nowPage=13&pagesize=30

20. In fact, hub-and-spoke frameworks between ASEAN (hub) and, individually, Japan and South Korea are already signed. What is missing is the critical "plurilateralization" of these openings, among those northeast Asian parties and China.

**Figure 2.2  Change in Taiwanese GDP over baseline, 2010–20**

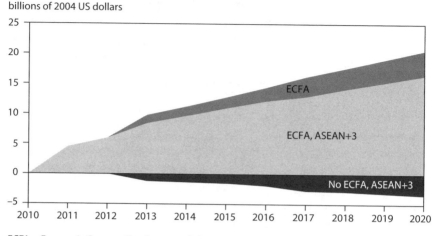

billions of 2004 US dollars

ECFA = Economic Cooperation Framework Agreement; ASEAN = Association of Southeast Asian Nations.

*Source:* Model estimates.

0.75 percent of GDP by 2020. If the ECFA *does* play out concurrent with ASEAN+3, then the outcome for Taiwan in 2020 swings to positive 3.5 percent for GDP from the baseline—a total benefit of 4.3 percent of GDP between the negative outcome of an unfulfilled ECFA and the positive outcome of getting it done. Thus all the negative effects of an ASEAN+3 scenario that excludes Taiwan can be offset by the bilateral ECFA. These outcomes are presented graphically in figure 2.2.[21]

There is a large discrepancy between our headline GDP result of 4.48 percent and results reported in the Taiwanese government-sponsored CGE estimates of about 1.72 percent GDP increase.[22] We are reporting cumulated gains in 2020, after the dynamic gains of structural adjustment have time to eventuate. It appears that other studies are confined to more near-term effects. In fact we assert that our estimate is just a floor, and that the total implications are considerably greater, due to the variety of gains having to do with services trade and investment that models such as ours are likely to undercount.

---

21. In our modeling, ECFA starts phasing in as of 2011, while ASEAN+3 starts to phase in as of 2013. Keep in mind that we are projecting the stakes for Taiwan under scenarios, not forecasting what we think is inevitable. Our ECFA assumptions are state of the art, whereas the ASEAN+3 assumptions might be considered optimistic.

22. The study, titled "Impact of the Economic Cooperation Framework Agreement across the Taiwan Strait," was published by the Chung Hua Institute of Economic Research (Taipei) in July 2009.

**Table 2.3  Change in 2020 global trade and welfare indicators**
(billions of 2004 US dollars and percent)

| | ECFA | | No ECFA, ASEAN+3 | | ECFA, ASEAN+3 | |
|---|---|---|---|---|---|---|
| | Taiwan | China | Taiwan | China | Taiwan | China |
| Trade balance | −9.5 | 6.4 | 0 | 20.8 | −9.30 | 26.50 |
| Exports | 26.3 (6.3) | 38.8 (1.7) | −4.5 (−1.1) | 71.5 (3.1) | 21.00 (5.1) | 109.10 (4.7) |
| Imports | 35.8 (11.0) | 32.4 (1.9) | −4.5 (−1.4) | 50.7 (3.0) | 30.30 (9.3) | 82.60 (4.8) |
| Terms of trade (percent) | 3.83 | 0.16 | −0.42 | 0.15 | 3.33 | 0.34 |
| Absorption | 15.30 (3.9) | 4.20 (0.1) | −2.70 (−0.7) | 17.90 (0.3) | 12.10 (3.1) | 23.90 (0.5) |

ECFA = Economic Cooperation Framework Agreement; ASEAN = Association of Southeast Asian Nations.

Note: Numbers may not tally due to rounding. Numbers in parentheses represent percent change.

*Source:* Model estimates.

## Trade

Table 2.3 summarizes the results of our modeling of cross-strait trade policy effects in 2020. As with other results, these illuminate the direction and magnitude of the impact from liberalizing China-Taiwan trade from a baseline; they are not forecasts of absolute gains or losses. We can reasonably assume that they represent a low boundary of likely outcomes, since there are four limitations to the upside inherent in the modeling tools: services trade liberalization is undercounted; Taiwan's initial trade bans, which bias gains downward, cannot be properly modeled; investment-driven trade is undercounted;[23] and the dynamic gains from the liberalization of FDI driving structural adjustment are undercounted.

We should expect the ECFA to increase trade from the baseline, and this is the result of our modeling (figure 2.3). Global trade effects by 2020 are significant for Taiwan: 6.3 percent higher exports than otherwise and 11 percent higher imports (Taiwan having done the lion's share of trade barrier reduction). In the baseline projection Taiwan continues to run a large but shrinking global trade surplus through 2020, and the net narrowing of its trade balance by $9.5 billion in 2020 does not materially change its position as a trade surplus economy (and of course by fostering structural adjustment contributes to the overall welfare gains for Taiwan—see below). Though smaller in percentage terms given a much larger base, im-

---

23. Trade tends to follow outward investment. It is known that many Taiwanese firms have managed to circumvent existing restrictions on Taiwanese investment to the mainland; however there are additional sectoral opportunities for Taiwanese firms that are not open yet, and we assume normalization will lead to some additional investment-related trade flows.

**Figure 2.3   Change in exports and imports of China and Taiwan**

billions of 2004 US dollars

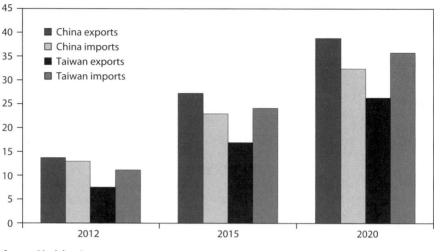

*Source:* Model estimates.

port and export growth for China as a result of the ECFA is comparable to or larger than for Taiwan in value—$32 billion and $39 billion, respectively, by 2020, for a net increase of $6.4 billion in global trade balance.

In the ECFA-only scenario, Taiwan's exports to China as a share of all Taiwanese exports go from 41.5 percent in 2008 to 62 percent in 2020, while China grows as a source of Taiwan's imports from 14.2 to 23 percent (table 2.4).[24] This outcome in terms of trade dependence is a concern to some in Taiwan, since the degree of trade dependence is not mutual and this leads to concerns about Beijing's leverage to pressure Taiwan using economic sanctions.[25] As noted in chapter 1, however, a significant share of these exports are and will continue to be for China's processing and re-export trade, not for final consumption in China, and this mitigates some of the sense of imbalance and vulnerability for Taiwan.

If ASEAN+3 transpires, then the growth in China-Taiwan trade interdependence is slightly muted. Compared to our baseline projection of Taiwan's trade in 2020, ASEAN+3 reduces Taiwan's global exports and imports by about $4.5 billion each—declines of 1.1 and 1.4 percent, respectively. This reflects trade diversion away from Taiwan as other economies in the region deepen their economic links. While this means no net change in trade balance for Taiwan, it contributes to the negative change in GDP as efficiencies are lost. By contrast, if the ECFA is con-

---

24. The trade shares are calculated based on nominal rather than real exports and imports.

25. The utility of economic sanctions to compel political outcomes has a dubious track record. See Hufbauer et al. (2008).

**Table 2.4    Trade dependence between China and Taiwan** (percent of total trade flows)

| | Baseline | | ECFA | No ECFA, ASEAN+3 | ECFA, ASEAN+3 |
|---|---|---|---|---|---|
| | 2008 | 2020 | 2020 | 2020 | 2020 |
| Taiwan's exports to China | 41.5[a] | 52.0 | 62.0 | 51.3 | 61.3 |
| China's exports to Taiwan | 2.7 | 3.3 | 4.2 | 3.2 | 4.2 |
| Taiwan's imports from China | 14.2 | 19.5 | 23.0 | 20.1 | 23.5 |
| China's imports from Taiwan | 11.4 | 12.0 | 15.2 | 11.3 | 14.3 |

ECFA = Economic Cooperation Framework Agreement; ASEAN = Association of Southeast Asian Nations.

a. The baseline numbers calculated endogenously in the model arise from the 2004 dataset used to populate data in our model from Version 7 of the Global Trade Analysis Project (GTAP) database, leading to 2008 baseline figures that are somehow different from those computed from official trade statistics in recent years. This is not only caused by the prediction error from an economic model, but largely due to Hong Kong reexports for China-Taiwan shipment back to their direct trade routine in the GTAP database, so the number largely reflects Taiwan's dependence on both China and Hong Kong, given that domestic exports to and imports from Taiwan by Hong Kong are of a much smaller scale.

*Source:* Model results.

cluded concurrent with ASEAN+3, then the effects on Taiwan's exports and imports are both significantly positive, as they rise 5.3 and 9.6 percent, respectively, from the baseline in value terms, generating outcomes for trade dependence comparable to those under the ECFA-only scenario. As with other metrics, it is important to look not just at the change from the baseline under the ECFA scenario but also at the difference between the ECFA (or ECFA plus ASEAN+3) scenario and the negative without-ECFA scenario to get a full sense of the effects of policy choices.[26]

## Welfare: Terms of Trade and Real Absorption

The change in an economy's terms of trade is a change in the ratio of its export price index to its import price index. That is, if bananas are all the rage this year and so you can trade one ton of them for 100 cases of beer, whereas last year they would only fetch you 50 cases of beer, then your terms of trade have improved (considerably, in this example: bottoms

26. See comments on modeling methodology in the appendices for details on macro closure and other considerations that condition these results.

up!). Tariff changes following enactment of an FTA can have the effect of improving terms of trade, while being excluded from an FTA among neighbors can have the opposite, negative effect. Terms of trade gains are typically attributable to a shift of production away from areas of low comparative advantage toward products of higher comparative advantage. Terms of trade improvements are an important element of welfare gains for an economy (in addition to efficiency gains and absorption—the domestic component of GDP growth). Our modeling shows a 3.84 percent terms of trade gain from the ECFA for Taiwan in 2020 from the baseline projection, as it shifts its production structure after dismantling unilateral barriers to trade with the mainland (table 2.3). China's bigger export gains occur in sectors it already focuses on, so China sees very little change in terms of trade (as would be expected).

In the event of ASEAN+3 transpiring without the ECFA in place, Taiwan sees minor negative terms of trade effects due to trade diversion, while if the ECFA is completed then the positive terms of trade effects for Taiwan are 95 percent as high as they would be without the ASEAN+3. With or without the ECFA, Beijing sees modest terms of trade gains after an ASEAN+3 from the baseline (which, recall, reflects ASEAN+1). Though the terms of trade gains for China are fairly modest in either case, they are higher for China if the ECFA is undertaken in addition to the ASEAN+3.

While terms of trade describe changes in the amount of domestic product needed to acquire a given amount of foreign product, *real absorption* describes another kind of welfare metric, total domestic purchasing power, which is composed of household consumption, firm investment, and government consumption. This measure of gross domestic *consumption* differs from gross domestic *product* in that it counts imports for domestic use, not the balance of exports minus imports. Inasmuch as growth in the level of consumption is an indication of welfare gains, real absorption provides an additional, if qualified, metric (given the specific nature of our model; see the appendices).[27]

Our modeling suggests that for Taiwan, carrying out the ECFA with China would mean real absorption in 2020 that is 3.9 percent higher than in the baseline. If ASEAN+3 takes place, then Taiwan experiences a seven-tenths of a percent reduction in real absorption from failure to liberalize cross-strait trade, and a 3.3 percent gain from the baseline from concluding the ECFA. For China, the percentage changes in real absorption arising from the ECFA are trivial though positive, and slightly more significant from ASEAN+3, again with a positive premium from doing both. As with other aggregate measures, the bottom line is that the ECFA is moderately positive for Taiwan, offsets negative consequences for Taiwan

---

27. Qualified, of course, because this domestic consumption may reflect an unsustainable trade deficit financed through foreign purchases of long-term national debt, as in the case of the United States.

from remaining outside regional undertakings, and is less significant for Beijing in welfare terms.

The effects discussed above must be considered as the lower boundary of possible effects due to a number of limitations inherent in our modeling of Taiwan-China liberalization. First, the starting point in Taiwan's imports from China of prohibiting more than 2,000 goods is zero in the Global Trade Analysis Project (GTAP) modeling database we work with (because while there is some import from China, it comes through Hong Kong), and models such as ours cannot show growth in trade from a zero base, though in reality these product lines will be an important part of prospective gains. (See box 2.1 on inferring prospective Taiwan import values from actual Korean imports.) Second, models such as ours cannot take full account of the benefits from increased investment flows either within the two economies or from third parties. Third, the models omit gains from services trade, except for the reduced transportation costs arising from more direct cargo shipment. Finally, such models provide a limited estimate of dynamic effects—that is, the gains from more efficient investment decisions over time, once distortions are dismantled.

Investment flows require elaboration. As noted in chapter 1, Taiwan's direct investment in China is massive, while reciprocal investment is blocked unilaterally by Taiwan. One could assume from this that a normalization agreement or even a WTO+ liberalization agreement would do little to further augment the trend in Taiwanese investment to China, but rather only open Taiwan to investment flows from China. Certainly the relative growth in investment would be greatest coming into Taiwan. However, Taiwan's outbound investment restrictions *have* constrained some amount of investment, and moreover, restrictions enforced by Beijing have held Taiwan back from some important sectors, notably financial services. While Taiwanese financial services firms might not be considered to have comparative advantage to operate in most markets away from home, they do have a special potential to operate profitably in China. Finally, survey work on the investment intentions of Taiwanese firms does suggest that a successful ECFA would indeed stimulate significant additional investment in Taiwan and into Taiwan by foreign firms as well.

The changes from FTA policies are long-run outcomes, so we focus on 2020, by which time adjustments will have set in. The ramp-up of these effects in the intervening years is shaped by the sequencing of competing agreements: if Taiwan enjoys the ECFA without ASEAN+3 extending similar benefits to Japan and Korea, then the economic gains accrued by Taiwan are greatest. When we explore the impact of ASEAN+3 on Taiwan's gains, we set it to begin in 2013 in order to highlight its ultimate effects. Figure 2.4 shows that the impact on Taiwan's terms of trade ensues fairly quickly (within three years) and then plateaus. Figure 2.5 shows the change in Taiwan's real absorption occurring over the period,

## Box 2.1 Impact of removing Taiwan's trade bans on imports from China

Taiwan has banned more than 2,000 product categories (at the harmonized system [HS] eight-digit or 10-digit level) to be imported from China. Global computable general equilibrium models usually cannot capture the impact of elimination of such bans, as it is hard to translate these nontariff barriers into tariff equivalents. To evaluate the impact of Taiwan lifting these bans, we compare the structure of Taiwan's imports from China with the structure of South Korea's imports from China. We choose South Korea as the benchmark because the economic structures of Taiwan and Korea have many similarities, and Korea does not have bans on imports from China. China's share of Korea's imports of these banned products provides a rough indication of a potential increase in Taiwan's imports of these goods from China when the product ban is eliminated. This exercise estimates the static impact of removing the ban without considering broader implications. It further illustrates why we emphasize that our modeling results provide only a lower bound for Taiwan's gain from economic integration with China.

The analysis is conducted in three steps. First, we aggregate the imports of Korea and Taiwan into HS six-digit categories. Second, we compute China's share in each economy's import of the banned products. Finally, we compute the difference between the shares and use that to extrapolate Taiwan's total imports from China once the bans are eliminated (see table B2.1.1). Increased Taiwanese imports from China would reduce prices for consumers and producers, and increase varieties of products Taiwan could choose from, thus increasing Taiwan's welfare. Such calculations implicitly assume that without the product ban, the share of imports in categories with banned products as total imports would be the same for Taiwan and South Korea, which is surely an imperfect assumption.

### Table B2.1.1 Impact of eliminating trade bans by Taiwan

| Year | Total imports from China[a] (billions of US dollars) | | Share of imports in categories with banned products (percent) | | Estimated increase in Taiwan's imports in categories with banned products (millions of US dollars) |
|---|---|---|---|---|---|
| | South Korea | Taiwan | South Korea | Taiwan | |
| 1997 | 9.1 | 3.4 | 22.50 | 8.70 | 468.90 |
| 1998 | 6.3 | 3.9 | 20.47 | 6.83 | 527.10 |
| 1999 | 7.8 | 4.0 | 19.13 | 6.98 | 479.90 |
| 2000 | 11.3 | 5.0 | 20.58 | 6.62 | 704.00 |
| 2001 | 12.5 | 5.0 | 17.67 | 6.15 | 576.10 |
| 2002 | 15.5 | 6.6 | 18.94 | 6.11 | 845.30 |
| 2003 | 20.1 | 9.0 | 17.80 | 5.09 | 1,145.20 |
| 2004 | 27.8 | 13.5 | 14.26 | 4.98 | 1,256.00 |
| 2005 | 35.1 | 16.5 | 16.88 | 5.67 | 1,855.90 |
| 2006 | 44.5 | 20.7 | 17.50 | 6.80 | 2,217.90 |
| 2007 | 56.1 | 23.5 | 22.51 | 11.40 | 2,605.90 |
| 2008 | 73.9 | 25.9 | 25.72 | 13.81 | 3,082.40 |

a. Includes reexports.

*Source:* Authors' calculations based on data provided by China Customs and Bureau of Foreign Trade, Taiwan.

**Figure 2.4    Percent change in Taiwanese terms of trade, 2010–20**

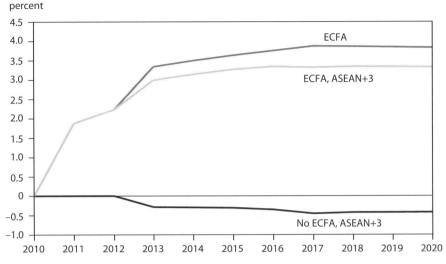

ECFA = Economic Cooperation Framework Agreement; ASEAN = Association of Southeast Asian Nations.

*Source:* Model estimates.

**Figure 2.5    Change in Taiwanese absorption, 2010–20**

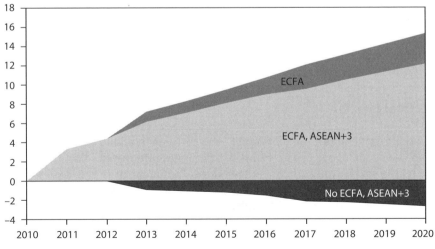

ECFA = Economic Cooperation Framework Agreement; ASEAN = Association of Southeast Asian Nations.

*Source:* Model estimates.

**Figure 2.6 Change in Chinese absorption, 2010–20**

billions of 2004 US dollars

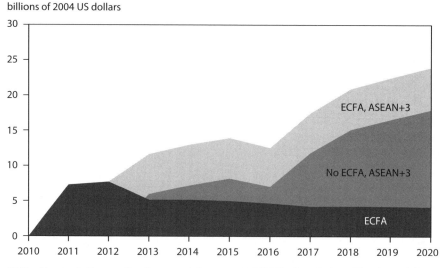

ECFA = Economic Cooperation Framework Agreement; ASEAN = Association of Southeast Asian Nations.

*Source:* Model estimates.

and illustrates the binary nature of the ECFA question for Taiwan: there is no economic status quo for the island. Since the rest of the region is moving forward, standing still for Taiwan means a loss, whereas the bilateral option across the strait claws back those losses and then some.

Meanwhile, to conclude with the time series picture from Beijing's perspective, figure 2.6 shows the change in China's real absorption over the period to 2020. The implication is that, in the aggregate, the economic gains to China from the ECFA are minor and eventuate rapidly, while the benefits from ASEAN+3 are more significant and accumulate over time.

## Sectoral Effects

There is a joke about an economist who drowns in a lake that is only one inch deep—*on average.* The point is that aggregate metrics can fail to describe the significance of concentrated local impacts, or in this case the extent of gains and losses sector by sector or locality by locality. Concentrated losses anticipated by industries or even specific firms, and by localities within a larger polity, can be decisive in whether an economic policy change is undertaken.

In the case of economic liberalization across the Taiwan Strait, the shortcomings of CGE modeling are amplified the more disaggregated one chooses to go. We therefore apply the patterns and implications of the aggregate analysis to the sectoral situation with a hefty dose of qualitative assessment. We consider the winners and losers from Taiwan's perspective and then from China's perspective.

### Taiwan: Winners and Losers

In Taiwan, President Ma's administration used the sectoral consequences of our baseline scenario—that ASEAN+1 transpires and Taiwan takes no steps toward parity—as the central argument for the ECFA.[28] Here we take a similar approach to ascertain which Taiwanese sectors are most at risk should Taiwan remain on the FTA sidelines by failing to implement or by abrogating the now-signed ECFA agreement.

To identify which sectors in Taiwan will be impacted by trade policy changes, we apply a number of criteria filters on existing cross-strait trade. First we select sectors with Taiwanese world exports in 2008 greater than $1 billion; 28 of 97 sectors at the HS two-digit level meet this criterion. Next we cull these for dependence on China as the destination for at least 25 percent of those exports in 2008 (or over a 40-month average); 10 of these 28 sectors meet that criterion. The result is the 10 sectors listed in table 2.5.

These 10 sectors alone generated $33.7 billion of exports to China in 2008, which is over half of Taiwan's world exports in these sectors. The share of Taiwan's exports going to China in these sectors ranges as high as 76 percent for HS-90 (optical devices, predominantly liquid crystal diode-related manufactures), which happens to be by far Taiwan's single largest export to China by value, with nearly $16 billion a year (2008) just for LCDs (liquid crystal displays) used in digital electronics.

Table 2.6 looks closer within these 10 sectors at the 20 disaggregated categories of product (at the six-digit level) with the greatest value of 2008 exports to China, led by LCD sales. Approximately $1.6 billion a year each of ABS polymers (a type of plastic that such products as Lego toys are made of) and terephthalic acid (for production of synthetic fibers and plastic packaging) go to China. Another $1.5 billion in optical device parts and ethylene glycol (used as an antifreeze and in China more commonly as a synthetic fiber and plastics production input) round out the top five billion-dollar-plus list. The rest of the top 20 are other petrochemical products, processed metal products, and optical and semiconductor-related products.

Given Taiwan's significance in the information technology industry, one might think that the zero-tariff provisions of the Information Technology Agreement (ITA), to which both China and Taiwan are party,

---

28. See commentary on the official Taiwan ECFA website, www.ecfa.org.tw (accessed on September 15, 2010).

**Table 2.5  Taiwanese exports of significant value that go predominantly to China**

| HS code | Product name | Taiwan's exports to China (millions of US dollars) | | Taiwan's exports to the world (millions of US dollars) | | Trade dependence (percent) | | Weighted average tariff for Taiwan | Bound: simple average |
|---|---|---|---|---|---|---|---|---|---|
| | | 40-month | 2008 | 40-month | 2008 | 40-month total | 2008 | | |
| 90 | Optical, photographic, cinematographic, measuring, checking, precision, medical or surgical instruments and apparatus; parts and accessories thereof | 42,049.40 | 16,384.73 | 62,324.14 | 21,464.42 | 67.47 | 76.33 | 7.87 | 7.46 |
| 29 | Organic chemicals | 17,362.93 | 6,495.81 | 27,437.52 | 10,583.82 | 63.28 | 61.37 | 4.89 | 5.66 |
| 74 | Copper and articles thereof | 6,215.39 | 1,918.05 | 13,281.96 | 4,016.46 | 46.80 | 47.75 | 4.80 | 6.58 |
| 39 | Plastics and articles thereof | 18,466.98 | 5,932.52 | 51,910.67 | 17,189.31 | 35.57 | 34.51 | 6.75 | 8.11 |
| 32 | Tanning or dyeing extracts; dyes, pigments, paints, varnishes, putty and mastics | 1,310.68 | 388.39 | 3,962.05 | 1,275.79 | 33.08 | 30.44 | 7.67 | 7.55 |
| 28 | Inorganic chemicals; compounds of precious metal, radioactive elements | 1,070.07 | 421.67 | 3,547.40 | 1,404.75 | 30.16 | 30.02 | 5.01 | 5.59 |
| 38 | Miscellaneous chemical products | 2,012.16 | 634.92 | 7,078.72 | 2,330.44 | 28.43 | 27.24 | 4.30 | 7.55 |
| 48 | Paper and paperboard; articles of paper pulp, of paper or of paperboard | 1,158.60 | 348.10 | 4,378.98 | 1,406.73 | 26.46 | 24.75 | 6.03 | 6.86 |
| 76 | Aluminum and articles thereof | 1,192.46 | 340.48 | 4,689.83 | 1,517.06 | 25.43 | 22.44 | 6.62 | 9.11 |
| 54 | Man-made filaments | 2,803.79 | 846.01 | 11,295.44 | 3,322.75 | 24.82 | 25.46 | 7.62 | 7.46 |

Note: Data are sorted by 40-month trade dependence.

Source: UNCTAD, Trade Analysis and Information (TRAINS) database, accessed through the World Bank's World Integrated Trade Solution (WITS) software.

**Table 2.6  Disaggregation of Taiwan's most China-dependent exports**

| HS code | Product name | Duty type | Simple average | Weighted average | China's imports from Taiwan in 2007 (billions of US dollars) |
|---|---|---|---|---|---|
| 901380 | Liquid crystal devices (LCDs) not constituting articles provided for more specifically in other headings; other optical appliances and instruments, nes in chapter 90 | MFN | 8.0 | 8.0 | 15.9 |
| 390330 | Acrylonitrilebutadienestyrene (ABS) copolymers | MFN | 6.5 | 6.5 | 1.6 |
| 291736 | Terephthalic acid and its salts | MFN | 6.5 | 6.5 | 1.6 |
| 901390 | Parts and accessories for LCDs and other related devices | MFN | 7.0 | 7.0 | 1.5 |
| 290531 | Ethylene glycol (ethanediol) | MFN | 5.5 | 5.5 | 1.0 |
| 390210 | Polypropylene | MFN | 6.5 | 6.5 | 0.8 |
| 390810 | Polyamide-6, -11, -12, -6,6, -6,9, -6,10 or -6,12 | MFN | 6.5 | 6.5 | 0.7 |
| 741021 | Copper foil without backing | MFN | 4.0 | 4.0 | 0.6 |
| 741011 | Copper foil with backing | MFN | 4.0 | 4.0 | 0.5 |
| 900120 | Sheets and plates of polarizing material | MFN | 8.0 | 8.0 | 0.5 |
| 900190 | Lenses, prisms, mirrors, and other optical elements | MFN | 8.0 | 8.0 | 0.5 |
| 390319 | Polystyrene (other than expansible) | MFN | 6.5 | 6.5 | 0.5 |
| 290250 | Styrene | MFN | 2.0 | 2.0 | 0.4 |
| 740811 | Copper wire | MFN | 4.0 | 4.0 | 0.4 |
| 381800 | Chemical elements doped for use in electronics, in the form of discs, wafers or similar forms; chemical compounds doped for use in electronics | MFN | 0 | 0 | 0.4 |
| 290723 | 4,4'-Isopropylidenediphenol (bisphenol A, diphenylolpropane) and its salts | MFN | 5.5 | 5.5 | 0.3 |
| 390410 | Poly vinyl chloride, not mixed with any other substances | MFN | 6.5 | 6.5 | 0.3 |
| 390730 | Epoxide resins | MFN | 6.5 | 6.5 | 0.3 |
| 390740 | Polycarbonates | MFN | 6.5 | 6.5 | 0.3 |
| 382490 | Chemical products and preparations of the chemical/allied industries | MFN | 7.0 | 7.0 | 0.3 |

MFN = most favored nation.

*Source:* UNCTAD, Trade Analysis and Information (TRAINS) database, accessed through the World Bank's World Integrated Trade Solution (WITS) software.

would exempt most Taiwanese exports from duties. However, on our list of high-value, highly China-dependent Taiwanese exports, only one item (the 15th—chemical elements doped for use in electronics) is listed in the ITA schedule and enjoys zero duties.[29] In fact, only one other item in the *top 100* Taiwanese exports to China by value (six-digit level) is ITA-scheduled. The remainder face applied duties ranging from 2 to 8 percent, with bound rates sometimes a little higher, such as 9.7 percent for LCDs. While these duties may seem low, Taiwan's MOEA argues that in the high-volume production businesses at issue here—both petrochemical, and microelectronics—tariff wedges of 5 to 7 percent that ASEAN-based producers will enjoy after 2010 would make Taiwanese producers uncompetitive.[30]

It is worth noting that on the list of highest-export-value Taiwanese products regardless of China dependence ratio, there are plenty of zero-tariff ITA scheduled items, most obviously semiconductors and integrated circuits (table 2.7, shown in bold). These important Taiwanese industries are therefore not at risk from differential tariff reduction agreements. However, other nontariff elements of ASEAN+1 and ECFA, including dispute resolution, investment, mutual standards recognition, and skilled labor mobility, may be important factors of competition for Taiwanese firms vis-à-vis their ASEAN and northeast Asian competitors.

Finally, there are eight industries with significant global exports for Taiwan (greater than $600 million in 2008) and very low reliance on China as an export market (6.8 percent or lower). These range from $7.4 billion of autos and auto parts to steel, pearls, toys, bedding, seafood, watercraft, and knitwear (table 2.8). In some of these cases, such as vehicle parts and toys, past Taiwanese comparative advantages and the firms that possess them have migrated to China, so it is not surprising that Taiwan's export market share in China is not pronounced (while Taiwan's exports *plus* the export share held by Taiwanese firms in China might be very high). However, it is also notable that the weighted average tariffs applied by China to these goods are higher than typical—10 percent or more in five of eight cases. While the minor market share to start means that ASEAN+1 will not heavily impact these Taiwanese products, the tariff structure implies that the ECFA could bring significant export growth in these areas for Taiwan.

---

29. See "WTO: Information Technology Agreement," December 13, 1996. http://tcc.export. gov/Trade_Agreements/All_Trade_Agreements/WTO_IT_TA.asp#ANNEX (accessed on September 15, 2010).

30. Flat-screen television producers, major users of thin film transistors (TFT) and LCDs, report operating profit margins in the range of 4 to 5 percent. See http://seekingalpha. com/article/137774-sony-corporation-f4q08-qtr-end-3-31-09-earnings-call-transcript? page=-1 (accessed on September 15, 2010). In its 2005 cover story "Why Taiwan Matters," *Business Week* noted: "Net margins at Asustek have fallen to 6.4 percent, from 19 percent in 2001." www.businessweek.com/magazine/content/05_20/b3933011.htm (accessed on September 15, 2010).

**Table 2.7  Highest-value Taiwanese exports to China**

| HS code | Product name | Duty type | Simple average (2008) | Weighted average (2008) | Chinese imports from Taiwan in 2007 (billions of US dollars) |
|---|---|---|---|---|---|
| 901380 | Liquid crystal devices (LCDs) not constituting articles provided for more specifically in other headings; other optical appliances, and instruments, nes in chapter 90 | MFN | 8.0 | 8.0 | 15.9 |
| 854231 | **Electronic integrated circuits, processors & controllers, whether/not combined with memories, converters, logic circuits, amplifiers, clock & timing circuits/ other circuits** | **MFN** | **0** | **0** | **15.6** |
| 854232 | **Electronic integrated circuits, memories** | **MFN** | **0** | **0** | **7.0** |
| 854239 | **Other electronic integrated circuits, other than amplifiers/memories/processors & controllers** | **MFN** | **0** | **0** | **5.8** |
| 853400 | **Printed circuits** | **MFN** | **0** | **0** | **3.0** |
| 847330 | **Parts & accessories of the machines of heading 84.71** | **MFN** | **0** | **0** | **1.6** |
| 390330 | Acrylonitrilebutadienestyrene (ABS) copolymers | MFN | 6.5 | 6.5 | 1.6 |
| 291736 | Terephthalic acid and its salts | MFN | 6.5 | 6.5 | 1.6 |
| 901390 | Parts and accessories for LCDs and other related devices | MFN | 7.0 | 7.0 | 1.5 |
| 290531 | Ethylene glycol (ethanediol) | MFN | 5.5 | 5.5 | 1.0 |
| 854140 | **Photosensitive semiconductor devices, including photovoltaic cells whether/not assembled in modules/ made up into panels; light emitting diodes** | **MFN** | **0** | **0** | **0.9** |
| 852990 | Various parts for electrical machinery and equipment | MFN | 4.2 | 4.2 | 0.8 |
| 271019 | Petroleum oils and oils obtained from bituminous minerals (other than crude) | MFN | 5.1 | 5.1 | 0.8 |
| 390210 | Polypropylene | MFN | 6.5 | 6.5 | 0.8 |
| 390810 | Polyamide-6, -11, -12, -6,6, -6,9, -6,10 or -6,12 | MFN | 6.5 | 6.5 | 0.7 |
| 741021 | Copper foil without backing | MFN | 4.0 | 4.0 | 0.6 |

*(continued on next page)*

83

**Table 2.7  Highest-value Taiwanese exports to China** *(continued)*

| HS code | Product name | Duty type | Simple average (2008) | Weighted average (2008) | Chinese imports from Taiwan in 2007 (billions of US dollars) |
|---|---|---|---|---|---|
| **853224** | **Ceramic dielectric, multilayer** | **MFN** | **0** | **0** | **0.6** |
| **854190** | **Parts for diodes, transistors and similar semiconductor devices and other devices** | **MFN** | **0** | **0** | **0.6** |
| 741011 | Copper foil with backing | MFN | 4.0 | 4.0 | 0.5 |
| **854233** | **Electronic integrated circuits, amplifiers** | **MFN** | **0** | **0** | **0.5** |
| 851770 | Parts of telephone sets, including telephones for cellular networks | MFN | 1.4 | 1.4 | 0.5 |
| 900120 | Sheets and plates of polarizing material | MFN | 8.0 | 8.0 | 0.5 |
| **847989** | **Other machines and mechanical appliances not for treating metal** | **MFN** | **0** | **0** | **0.5** |
| 900190 | Lenses, prisms, mirrors and other optical elements | MFN | 8.0 | 8.0 | 0.5 |
| **852351** | **Semiconductor media, solid-state nonvolatile storage devices, for the recording of sound/of other phenomena, but excluding products of Chapter 37** | **MFN** | **0** | **0** | **0.5** |
| 390319 | Polystyrene (other than expansible) | MFN | 6.5 | 6.5 | 0.5 |
| 290250 | Styrene | MFN | 2.0 | 2.0 | 0.4 |
| 721049 | Flat-rolled products of iron/nonalloy steel | MFN | 4.0 | 4.0 | 0.4 |
| **854121** | **Transistors (including photosensitive transistors), with a dissipation rate of less than 1 W** | **MFN** | **0** | **0** | **0.4** |
| 740811 | Copper wire, of refined copper of which the maximum cross-sectional dimension exceeds 6mm | MFN | 4.0 | 4.0 | 0.4 |
| **854110** | **Diodes (excluding photosensitive/light emitting diodes)** | **MFN** | **0** | **0** | **0.4** |
| **381800** | **Chemical elements doped for use in electronics, in the form of discs/wafers/similar forms; chemical compounds doped for use in electronics** | **MFN** | **0** | **0** | **0.4** |

MFN = most favored nation.

Note: Products exempt from the Information Technology Agreement are in bold.

*Source:* UNCTAD, Trade Analysis and Information (TRAINS) database, accessed through the World Bank's World Integrated Trade Solution (WITS) software.

**Table 2.8　High-value Taiwanese exports to the world, but not to China**

| HS code | Product name | Taiwan's exports to China (millions of US dollars) | | Taiwan's exports to the world (millions of US dollars) | | Trade dependence | | Weighted average tariff for Taiwan |
|---|---|---|---|---|---|---|---|---|
| | | 40-month | 2008 | 40-month | 2008 | 40-month total | 2008 | |
| 87 | Vehicles other than railway or tramway rolling stock, and parts and accessories thereof | 966.35 | 242.92 | 22,544.88 | 7,418.72 | 4.29 | 3.27 | 11.27 |
| 73 | Articles of iron or steel | 1,550.73 | 459.33 | 19,946.65 | 6,746.21 | 7.77 | 6.81 | 8.20 |
| 71 | Natural or cultured pearls, precious or semiprecious stones, precious metals, metals clad with precious metal and articles thereof; imitation jewelry; coins | 96.83 | 31.48 | 5,738.57 | 2,506.68 | 1.69 | 1.26 | 5.61 |
| 95 | Toys, games and sports requisites; parts and accessories thereof | 225.48 | 63.34 | 5,870.32 | 1,804.68 | 3.84 | 3.51 | 12.13 |
| 94 | Furniture; bedding, mattresses, mattress supports, cushions and similar stuffed furnishings; lamps and lighting fittings, not elsewhere specified or included; illuminated signs, illuminated nameplates and the like; prefabricated buildings | 213.69 | 72.31 | 5,192.17 | 1,625.16 | 4.12 | 4.45 | 5.53 |
| 3 | Fish and crustaceans, mollusks, and other aquatic invertebrates | 106.45 | 41.01 | 4,051.22 | 1,398.97 | 2.63 | 2.93 | 11.16 |
| 89 | Ships, boats, and floating structures | 33.44 | 10.92 | 3,553.66 | 1,347.79 | 0.94 | 0.81 | 10.00 |
| 61 | Articles of apparel and clothing access, knitted or crocheted | 68.17 | 25.42 | 2,329.83 | 658.94 | 2.93 | 3.86 | 14.76 |

*Source:* UNCTAD, Trade Analysis and Information (TRAINS) database, accessed through the World Bank's World Integrated Trade Solution (WITS) software.

## Sectoral Preferences and Exclusions

The anticipated sectoral effects fail to occur for industries excluded from agreements. This is common in FTAs. In the case of ASEAN expansion agreements, there are long lists of exclusions notified individually by each member party, some temporary and some permanent.[31] In preliminary ECFA discussions, Taiwan started with a blanket exclusion of the agriculture sector and requirements to retain protection for "traditional industries," including toys and textiles.[32] Taiwanese officials talked about the need for "asymmetric reciprocity" in some sectors. For example, they argued that one state-owned Chinese bank is financially larger than all the banks in Taiwan put together, and so one-for-one market access opening is not appropriate. Officials from China, meanwhile, did not emphasize particular sectors for exclusion as a starting point for ECFA. That said, given the extent of beyond-the-border regulation and nontariff barriers available to constrain foreign investors in many sectors, they didn't have to.

Inverse to exclusions from liberalization are areas for accelerated opening, or early harvest. In this area as well it was Taiwan that did most of the asking, promoting the opportunity to achieve parity with the FTA to be afforded ASEAN members under ASEAN+1 through the ECFA early harvest agreement. Taiwan's MOEA highlighted those sectors that, as in our analysis above, both depend on Chinese demand and stand to suffer a major disadvantage after phase-in of ASEAN+1. Sectors benefiting from the early harvest include machinery, petrochemicals, steel, textiles, and auto parts. Financial services, including banking and insurance, are already moving faster to liberalization through MOUs on a separate track, but were codified along with other services under the ECFA.

The habit of announcing lists of "no's" is common in Taiwan and China alike but is somewhat unfortunate for several reasons. First, it is misleading. Taiwanese officials trumpet a refusal to include agriculture in talks, but as many as 830 Chinese agricultural products are already imported legally into Taiwan. Second, such blunt treatment obscures the fact that Taiwan should enjoy competitive strength in many higher-value niches of food and horticulture that are not fought and won based on labor costs or economies of scale, that is, niches that depend on quality and reputation. And finally, no trade agreement can produce only winners: in the long

---

31. See Frost (2008, 134). See www.aseansec.org/13196.htm for the extension agreement with China; note in particular the annexes at the end (accessed on September 15, 2010).

32. This is typical in FTAs, not least in Asia. Under the 2008 China-Singapore FTA, for instance, 5 percent of Singapore's exports to China are not covered. According to Singapore's Ministry of Trade and Industry, products not covered include animal products, vegetables and fruits, cereals, tobacco, fertilizers, explosives, wood pulp, printed material, silk, nickel, lead, zinc, tin, and aircraft.

run, the dynamic shift of resources within an economy is an important wellspring of gains.

### Quantitative Results on Sectors

As discussed in the aggregate quantitative analysis, economic models cannot project gains well for the 2,000-plus products that start with zero export from China to Taiwan in modeling databases, normalization of which will induce some of the most important sectoral effects for both sides (but especially Taiwan). Nonetheless, the sectoral model results do provide broadly indicative results for an important subset of winners and losers. Table 2.9 presents changes in Taiwan from the baseline (no ECFA, ASEAN+1) in output (industrial production) for the 32 sectors in our model in three bilateral scenarios.

A number of observations can be made. First, the result of an ECFA is to induce structural adjustment. Half as many sectors see some shrinkage of output from the policy shock of cross-strait deepening as see expansion (11 versus 21), and by a roughly comparable range of magnitudes. In this dynamism lies the greatest potential for economic growth. This is particularly noticeable in comparison to the scenario of ASEAN+3 transpiring without the ECFA taking place, which is characterized by nothing so much as stasis, with sectoral output moving mostly within a band of +/–2 percent around zero. Second, as in the aggregate, once the ECFA is in place its benefits are not nullified by the conclusion of an ASEAN+3 arrangement to which Taiwan is not a party. In many cases Taiwan is the same or better off with an ASEAN+3 among its neighbors and the ECFA for itself than with just the ECFA. Finally, the industries that Taiwan hopes to front load with an early harvest of liberalization do show up in our modeling as the biggest potential gainers—petrochemicals and plastics, auto parts, and machinery. The greatest reduction compared to the baseline arises for electronic equipment, which, given Taiwan's traditional strength in electronics, may strike some as odd. The section that follows briefly discusses this and other specific sectors.

### Sectors of Particular Significance

*Electronic equipment.* Electronics is a core industry for Taiwan's economy and virtually synonymous with the island's strength and relevance to the global economy. A 2005 *Business Week* cover story that asked "why Taiwan matters" found the answer in electronics.[33] In our modeling (and any aggregation), this category ranges widely from very mature, commoditized products such as typewriters, calculators, fax machines, and the like to

---

33. See footnote 29.

**Table 2.9    Change in Taiwan's industrial output, 2020** (percent)

| Product name | ECFA | No ECFA, ASEAN+3 | ECFA, ASEAN+3 |
|---|---|---|---|
| Chemical rubber and plastic products | 29.415 | −1.423 | 27.496 |
| Textile | 27.913 | −3.576 | 23.510 |
| Petroleum, coal, and other mineral products | 13.855 | −1.095 | 12.503 |
| Motor vehicles and parts | 10.881 | −2.848 | 4.745 |
| Machinery and equipment | 6.520 | −2.054 | 4.333 |
| Leather and sporting goods | 5.037 | 0.666 | 6.068 |
| Forest and fishery products | 4.435 | 0.158 | 4.701 |
| Nongrain crops | 3.913 | −1.199 | 3.265 |
| Coal and other minerals | 3.279 | 0.033 | 3.353 |
| Construction | 3.268 | −0.601 | 2.563 |
| Metal and metal products | 2.978 | 0.056 | 3.123 |
| Utility and other nontraded services | 2.934 | −0.445 | 2.404 |
| Tobacco and beverages | 1.520 | −0.203 | 1.265 |
| Recreational and other services | 1.490 | −0.090 | 1.359 |
| Trade and transportation | 1.367 | −0.249 | 1.038 |
| Rice | 1.240 | −0.161 | 1.044 |
| Finance and insurance | 1.017 | −0.253 | 0.704 |
| Wood and paper products | 0.646 | 1.262 | 2.213 |
| Communication | 0.464 | −0.118 | 0.288 |
| Livestock | 0.441 | 0.221 | 0.719 |
| Wearing apparel | 0.337 | −0.766 | −0.121 |
| Meat and milk products | −0.375 | 0.090 | −0.217 |
| Sugar | −0.430 | 0.130 | −0.202 |
| Fruits and vegetables | −0.779 | 0.274 | −0.483 |
| Oil and gas | −0.894 | 0.340 | −0.510 |
| Mineral products | −0.920 | 0.116 | −0.868 |
| Other processed food products | −1.191 | −0.093 | −1.130 |
| Business services | −1.480 | 0.265 | −1.255 |
| Other light manufactures | −6.278 | 1.879 | −4.579 |
| Transport equipment | −7.419 | 1.838 | −5.563 |
| Other grains | −8.569 | 0.436 | −7.961 |
| Electronic equipment | −11.086 | −0.394 | −11.216 |

ECFA = Economic Cooperation Framework Agreement; ASEAN = Association of Southeast Asian Nations.

Notes: Data are sorted by ECFA-only column. Positive or negative numbers represent changes in projected industrial output relative to the baseline; they do not mean the industry is expanding or contracting during the simulation period. For example, gross output in Taiwan's electronic equipment sector (last row in table) doubles from 2010 to 2020 in the baseline projection but expands only 1.8 times in the ECFA policy simulation. Therefore, our 2020 projection is minus 11.086 percent from the baseline projection, but this is still a 180 percent expansion of gross output in 2010. In other words, ECFA means relative slowing of growth for this sector, not negative growth in absolute terms.

*Source:* Model results.

high-volume but uniquely sophisticated devices including semiconductors and integrated circuits, TFTs, and LCDs.

While the baseline outlook for the sector in Taiwan is continued growth in absolute terms, under the ECFA scenarios output is 11 percent lower in 2020 than otherwise. There are several factors that could explain this outcome. First, freer cross-strait trade would hasten the ongoing migration of the lower end of many electronics products to China due to lower production costs. These more mature products generally incorporate greater labor inputs in production, and hence the wage differential matters. While the shipping costs to bring production back to Taiwan are slightly higher, most Taiwanese output is for final consumption elsewhere, and since final assembly is typically in China total shipping costs might actually be lower thanks to sourcing in China. Second, at the higher end, China's low-labor-cost advantage amounts to little, given the capital intensity of production. However, production on both sides of the strait involves the same Taiwanese producers, and with freedom to service Taiwan both for final demand and with intermediates that are reexported elsewhere from new, high-scale economy facilities in China, production would be shifted intrafirm to mainland facilities in many cases.

Leading Taiwanese executives in the semiconductor segment seem neither to care much about the prospective output effects of the ECFA nor to have much to ask for from negotiations over it. Their firms are already global, or at least regional. From interviews with senior business leaders we conclude that in terms of Taiwan's continued dominance in this industry, the value of the ECFA is indirect. The determinant of success in this industry is the pool of extremely talented, hard-working, experienced engineering and other technical talent, which is completely mobile. China's semiconductor and other high-end electronics prowess is largely already managed by Taiwanese staff. Having said that, the ambiguity in cross-strait economic relations is a cloud that has undermined Taiwan's position as the fertile breeding ground of new ideas and generator of professional opportunities in this industry. By clarifying expectations and refocusing Taiwan's domestic competitiveness debate back on fundamentals rather than quixotic hopes of limiting Chinese impact on the sector, the ECFA can enhance Taiwan's prospects.

*Services.* Services sector industries in China and Taiwan will be affected in many ways by liberalization of cross-strait economic relations. Bilateral MOUs (for shipping, tourism, financial services, media) directly expand market access for two-way trade and investment in services. More general services sector opening is intended for inclusion under the comprehensive ECFA as well. Services sector activity would also be indirectly driven up by the industrial and manufacturing sector opening under the ECFA, as noted in the review of firm-level expectations for investment growth below.

Services activity is not easily captured in CGE models such as the one employed in this study. This is because services trade is not limited by tariff barriers, which are relatively straightforward to quantify, but rather by nontariff barriers. In a 2004 assessment of US-Taiwan FTA prospects by one of the authors of this study it was noted that attempts to include services sector effects raised the aggregate gains projected by models for goods-only liberalization by as much as 40 percent (Lardy and Rosen 2004, 32). As with sectoral implications for goods trade, the impact on Taiwan's services sector is likely to be more significant than on China's, and hence is of more interest as a potential source of support for liberalization. More than 70 percent of Taiwanese GDP is composed of services sector activity. Finance and insurance (10 percent), transportation/storage/communications (6 percent), and real estate (8 percent) are all large industries for Taiwan that should see considerable impact from cross-strait opening.

Taiwan's financial services sector (banking, insurance, and securities) will see direct benefits from market opening via an MOU currently slated for implementation. Taiwanese banks in China are awaiting permission to convert seven representative offices to branches (with the exception of Fubon, which bought into mainland-based Xiamen Bank indirectly via a transaction in Hong Kong, and several legacy banks—Concord in Ningbo and First Sino in Shanghai—that were established in the 1980s before prohibitions were formalized). Taiwan's Mainland Affairs Council has prohibited Taiwanese banks from investing in branches in China, while Beijing requires that an MOU on mutual recognition of government regulators be in place (a commitment to mutual recognition of financial authorities was achieved at the third round of Chiang-Chen talks, though it remains to be implemented).[34] Chinese banks are precluded from operating in Taiwan by the blanket prohibition on mainland investment, which is being relaxed (see below), paving the way for discussion of banking licenses in Taiwan for Chinese players. Taiwanese bankers are hopeful that the agreement might secure them preferential treatment in China exceeding the standard terms of access other foreign invested banks are permitted, such as permission to start taking local currency deposits earlier than the standard three-year waiting period (two with profitability despite not being able to take deposits), permission to exceed a 20 percent cap on foreign bank ownership, and relaxation of requirements to hold $20 billion in capital assets. The case can be made that waiving the three-year waiting period is not really preferential, since these banks have been waiting for approvals for many years.

Opening market access for banking (and similarly for insurance and the securities industry) will create growth opportunities for both sides. For

---

34. "Taiwan Looking At China's Financial Market," Cathay United Bank, March 23, 2007, www.banking.nccu.edu.tw/data/course/20070323_2.ppt (accessed on September 15, 2010). "The Third Round of Chiang-Chen Talks: Economics and Trade Matters (MAC)." Available at http://www.mac.gov.tw/public/Data/972210564271.pdf.

Taiwanese banks, the total available market would expand massively even if limited to Taiwanese businesses on the mainland.[35] An estimate prepared for this study by a senior Fubon Bank analyst for strategic planning purposes quantifies the annual pretax profit potential for Taiwan's banks for expanded market access to Taiwanese firms alone for lending and wealth management services at a midpoint of $800 million, with potential up to $1.3 billion. These are very large numbers for Taiwan's banks in light of recent total annual profits for the domestic banking industry of $1.1 billion.[36] Taiwanese businesses on the mainland (referred to as *Taishang*) would benefit from access to their home bankers and greater access to capital services at better cost. China would benefit as well, since the small and medium-sized enterprises that Taiwan's banks excel at servicing are severely underserved in China, and would benefit from Taiwanese banks' appetite for risk-taking in this area.

Direct cross-strait transportation services links are one of the "three links" that defined the extent of economic liberalization negotiations until recently (the others being postal links and direct trade). A 2003 CGE analysis sponsored by Taiwan's Executive Yuan identified cost savings of $24 million to $36 million a year for seaborne transportation services, $400 million for passenger air transport, and $24 million for air cargo.[37] These figures do not reflect the value of lost time incurred by shippers and passengers as well, which are huge—for instance, 8.6 million man-hours a year as of 2003, compelling many executives to simply move to the mainland, taking the positive externality of their skills with them.[38] Shipping cost reduction estimates amount to 15 to 30 percent. Taiwanese reports after these links were agreed upon in December 2008 put the total value from direct maritime and aviation links at just shy of $1 billion per year—apparently using the same estimates employed in the 2003 analysis.[39] Taiwanese analysts point out that the net benefit of this services sector liberalization depends on Taiwan's ability to respond more broadly to the integration of the Asian marketplace. Some of these cost savings are achieved by displacing

---

35. This limitation is likely to be seen in practice for a period of time.

36. Average of 2007 and 2008 pretax profits. See the "Consolidated Income Statement of Domestic Banks," Taiwan's Central Bank. Available at http://www.cbc.gov.tw/ct.asp?xItem=36479&ctNode=903&mp=2.

37. "Assessment of the Impact of Direct Cross-Strait Transportation," by agencies related to the Taiwan Executive Yuan, August 2003. Available at http://www.mac.gov.tw/public/MMO/mac/dlink01.pdf. See also Shen and Wang (2004).

38. There were an estimated 1 million Taiwanese, predominantly business professionals, living on the mainland in 2007. See "Analysis: Absentee Voting Needs Careful Study," *Taipei Times,* March 30, 2007. www.taipeitimes.com/News/taiwan/archives/2007/03/30/2003354483 (accessed on September 15, 2010).

39. See "Direct Cross-Strait Links in Place," *China Post,* December 15, 2008.

more expensive Taiwanese services with cheaper offerings from the mainland, and therefore the impact on the transport industries in Taiwan may be negative even if the island benefits in the aggregate.

Another services sector where speculation has run high that cross-strait liberalization may bring significant benefits in Taiwan is real estate. Notwithstanding some limited opening to Chinese investment in real estate starting in 2002, Taiwan essentially remained closed until 2009. Changes to the laws on inward mainland investment passed in May 2009 removed many of these restrictions (although implementing regulations remain to be promulgated in a number of areas). Comprehensive liberalization would mean (1) more Taiwanese business professionals working in China but spending more time (and hence investing) in properties at home; (2) an increase in China's residential and commercial investment in Taiwan; and (3) growth in third-party investment to use Taiwan as a regional service center, or for its own sake.

### Investment Growth

Investment growth is not well captured by CGE models, and yet investment flow changes—inward from abroad, indigenous, and investments kept at home instead of sent abroad—can be a significant consequence of FTAs. While this is true in most FTAs, it is especially important in the case of Taiwan and China. On investment, the biggest distortion arising from the status quo in cross-strait relations is not the constraint of Taiwanese investment in the mainland (upwards of $150 billion), but a triple hit on investment in Taiwan: first, mainland investment has been largely impossible; second, FDI in Taiwan has been scared away by the mounting political risk associated with the irregular relations with China; and third, even Taiwanese businesses have deferred investments at home.

Chen-yuan Tung (2010) of Taiwan's National Chengchi University has concluded through large-scale surveys that Taiwanese firms will reduce domestic investment if Taiwan eschews liberalization with the mainland, and increase it if an agreement is undertaken. He found the same outlook for foreign-invested enterprises in Taiwan. The reasons for reducing investment if Taiwan continues abnormal relations include competition for regional markets from firms domiciled in economies with more normal economic relations with China; lost opportunities to increase economies of scale; and disadvantage in participating in the growth created by regional integration (Tung 2010, table 8). Investment growth should Taiwan join in the integration process results from integrating production capacity and using Taiwan as a base for high-value-added niches, research and development, services, and marketing (Tung 2010, table 9). This survey work is premised on Taiwan's participation in East Asian integration, not just cross-strait; but as the quantitative results above foreshadow, the commercial benefits accruing to Taiwan from the ECFA dominate the expected gains (Tung 2010). And in any case, the ECFA is expected to be a necessary initial step toward the inclusion of Taiwan in regional integration, and so in terms of investment-flow implications it is the initial driver.

The third round of Chen-Chiang talks resulted in Taiwan agreeing to open significantly to investment from China. Taiwan scheduled 117 services sector classifications, 11 infrastructure areas, and 64 manufacturing industries for opening, and began accepting applications immediately. While this is an important step, the bulk of the investment benefits that are now possible will be trade-related. That is, the now-signed ECFA undertaking is the catalyst that will generate the incentive to invest into Taiwan for Chinese and other firms, and for Taiwanese companies to step up their fixed investment at home rather than abroad. And the prospect of inward investment from the mainland not only matters in terms of cross-border capital flows; it also brings an immediate change in mindset as the cloistering walls that have shielded Taiwanese producers from acquisition from across the strait are dismantled.

### From China's Perspective

In 2008–09, Beijing generally played down concerns with sectoral outcomes as a result of an ECFA, assuming that, because it is so large relative to Taiwan and most of the trade opening is on Taiwan's side, China has little negative adjustment to worry about. That seems correct to us. Quantitatively, our model, which showed sector output changes for Taiwan under the ECFA ranging from +29 percent to –11 percent, shows only trivial output changes for China (table 2.10). Nonetheless, for a mix of reasons China expressed a greater interest in economic benefits for its side in the final ECFA negotiations, and has conspicuously drawn attention to its emphasis on the economic nature of the talks. This may have been in earnest or, just as easily, can be understood as an effort to downplay its inherently political objectives.

While sectoral effects for China on a national level are minimal, positive opportunities will be more notable in specific geographies—Fujian Province, for example. In May 2009, China's State Council approved a regional economic development plan for the West Straits area that had been discussed for some years. The program plans call for infrastructure investment, a Taiwan-led petrochemical industrial park, and other support to accelerate economic integration in the region. Fujian's prospects are deeply related to China's economic relationship with Taiwan and stand to be disproportionately boosted by the liberalization of cross-strait economic relations in terms both of trade and investment flows. A cross-strait financial sector memorandum finalized in the Chiang-Chen talks but separate from the ECFA discussion will benefit mainland asset managers by giving them the ability to invest in Taiwan's stock market, and will likely provide accelerated market opening starting in Fujian Province for Taiwanese

**Table 2.10    Change in China's output in final year, 2020** (percent)

| Product name | ECFA | No ECFA, ASEAN+3 | ECFA, ASEAN+3 |
|---|---|---|---|
| Wearing apparel | 1.131 | 2.711 | 3.784 |
| Transport equipment | 1.127 | 0.040 | 1.156 |
| Machinery and equipment | 0.793 | 0.848 | 1.648 |
| Other light manufactures | 0.632 | 0.115 | 0.717 |
| Metal and metal products | 0.557 | 0.433 | 0.980 |
| Electronic equipment | 0.476 | 3.061 | 3.539 |
| Mineral products | 0.363 | 0.470 | 0.846 |
| Wood and paper products | 0.360 | 0.267 | 0.605 |
| Motor vehicles and parts | 0.347 | −1.750 | −1.342 |
| Coal and other minerals | 0.285 | 0.372 | 0.664 |
| Business services | 0.238 | 0.549 | 0.806 |
| Recreational and other services | 0.237 | 0.289 | 0.546 |
| Communication | 0.226 | 0.450 | 0.697 |
| Finance and Insurance | 0.220 | 0.445 | 0.683 |
| Oil and gas | 0.177 | 0.152 | 0.325 |
| Trade and transportation | 0.158 | 0.509 | 0.681 |
| Utility and other nontraded services | 0.137 | 0.248 | 0.413 |
| Leather and sporting goods | 0.125 | 2.188 | 2.243 |
| Construction | 0.059 | 0.335 | 0.426 |
| Tobacco and beverages | 0.021 | −0.092 | −0.050 |
| Petroleum, coal, and other mineral products | 0.017 | 0.014 | 0.045 |
| Sugar | −0.053 | −4.325 | −4.418 |
| Forest and fishery products | −0.078 | 0.313 | 0.245 |
| Fruits and vegetables | −0.139 | 0.212 | 0.084 |
| Other grains | −0.144 | 0.267 | 0.125 |
| Rice | −0.166 | 0.121 | −0.030 |
| Other processed food products | −0.181 | 0.932 | 0.731 |
| Textiles | −0.277 | 0.571 | 0.272 |
| Livestock | −0.310 | 0.151 | −0.157 |
| Meat and milk products | −0.353 | 1.163 | 0.756 |
| Chemical rubber and plastic products | −0.805 | 0.276 | −0.495 |
| Nongrain crops | −0.889 | 3.056 | 2.087 |

ECFA = Economic Cooperation Framework Agreement; ASEAN = Association of Southeast Asian Nations.

Note: Data are sorted by ECFA-only column. Positive or negative numbers represent changes in projected industrial output relative to the baseline; they do not mean the industry is expanding or contracting during the simulation period.

*Source:* Model results.

financial services firms, bringing additional sources of capital that are particularly useful for the myriad small and medium-sized private enterprises operating in China's central coast region. Those have traditionally been underserved by China's domestic financial firms.

Beyond goods and services trade flows, China already benefits from the presence of up to 1 million skilled Taiwanese professionals who live and work on the mainland, and from upwards of $150 billion of inward investment from Taiwan. This extraordinary capital and labor mobility has occurred without the benefit of a more formal liberalization agreement, and therefore one should not expect an agreement to shock the current trend but rather to help sustain it. One area where a cross-strait agreement *is* capable of making a policy breakthrough that could benefit China is technology transfer. Relaxation of Taiwan's most stringent China-specific technology restrictions—for instance, on the transfer of 12-inch semiconductor wafer fabrication technology—is likely independent of a larger economic agreement, as it has been in the works for some time. While particular industries and areas of China would no doubt see additional benefits from this migration, the fact is that Taiwan's technological lead over China has diminished over the past 10 years, and Taiwan's leverage in terms of dangling technology transfer is not what it used to be. Finally, whatever technology transfer is newly permitted to China, the island's technology controls will not likely exceed the permissiveness of the United States, thus reducing the maximum appeal of Taiwan as a source of new technology for China.

## Conclusions

The forces driving a cross-strait economic liberalization agreement are strong, compelling, and mounting. China's economic gravity in the region that includes Taiwan is undeniable and growing. The global financial crisis has increased the relative weight of the Chinese economy worldwide, and crisis-specific policy measures have underscored the relevance of China to Taiwan in particular, not just as a place for final assembly before reexport to OECD countries but as a final demand market. Regional integration arrangements long discounted as futuristic from the Western perspective are on the verge of implementation and are the impetus for policy formation in Taiwan. China is approaching Taiwan under the Ma administration with maximum flexibility in terms of economic policy in order to facilitate an agreement. The conditions are fundamentally supportive for a breakthrough from the economic perspective.

Cross-strait liberalization is taking shape on two tracks. Ad hoc meetings are generating MOUs to make immediate progress on economic relations piece by piece, while the template for a broader framework to go beyond WTO normalization to achieve parity with the region's FTAs is coming into focus. An implemented ECFA would emphasize an early harvest in those sectors where the greatest spreads between losses from inaction and gains from action would be possible, followed by comprehensive work on the remainder of typical FTA business over the medium term.

This work would portend a more institutionalized and normalized process of "government to government" interaction across the strait.

The projected benefits of the ECFA compared to business as usual—which assumes ASEAN+1 but no cross-strait liberalization—are large for Taiwan and modest for China. Taiwan would see gains greater than 4 percent on whatever GDP turns out to be after 10 years as a result of the ECFA, while China's gains would be modest. On a sectoral level, Taiwan would experience considerable structural adjustment under the ECFA, versus very little otherwise. In addition to the gains for the winning sectors in Taiwan, the agreement would generate dynamic gains for the economy as it more rapidly reallocated resources including money and people away from sunset industries toward areas of promise for the future. Most of the economic regime adjustment would be on Taiwan's side; therefore that is where most of the benefits would occur.

The downside effects on Taiwan from exclusion from regional FTAs would be mostly mitigated by cross-strait liberalization. In the next chapter we will ask what the upside additional benefits from Taiwan's inclusion in those FTAs might be. The anticipated structural adjustment in Taiwan portends a challenging political-economy environment on the way to making the ECFA a reality. And the political security implications of cross-strait economic liberalization remain to be considered in the chapters ahead as well. However, there are consequences from the status quo as well, as Taiwan's competitiveness erodes as private parties seek a more advantageous environment for taking advantage of China's exceptional development. Finally, we stress that the ECFA is not the complete strategy for Taiwan's success, but rather a step toward a level playing field, with the rest of the region moving rapidly to plan around China's marketplace. It is what Taiwan does once it has secured such parity that will determine its future prosperity.

# 3

# Regional Implications

In the previous chapter we confined ourselves to assessing the bilateral effects of China-Taiwan economic liberalization in the context of both agreed-upon and prospective regional economic deepening. We pointedly set aside two closely related questions. First, what are the additional gains for Taiwan and China if, building on cross-strait opening, Taiwan joins in regional trade liberalization arrangements? And second, what are the economic implications of China-Taiwan economic liberalization for others in the region?

We have separated these questions from those addressed in the previous chapter because much of the debate in Taiwan about economic welfare has centered on whether cross-strait trade is the key to Taiwan's welfare, or rather just the key to unlocking economic agreements with other economies. This question is frequently asked in Washington as well, where the possibility of a US-Taiwan FTA has been debated in the past and is being reconsidered in light of the ECFA.[1]

To address these questions we add three scenarios, as highlighted in table 3.1, for comparison against the baseline (ASEAN plus China, no ECFA) and ECFA-only eventualities introduced in chapter 2. First, we gauge the results if, following the ECFA, Taiwan were to join ASEAN+1. Second, we explore that event should the region meanwhile complete an ASEAN+3. And finally, we examine what happens if Taiwan joins in ASEAN+3. We present our quantitative aggregate results for these scenarios, as well as qualitative observations. We do not significantly address the question of how much more assertively China might behave in the re-

---

1. As of this writing, the US Department of State has indicated that the FTA option is not under active consideration. However, the topic is more a part of policy discussion than it has been in some time, as will be discussed in this chapter.

**Table 3.1    Scenarios: Taiwan's participation beyond ECFA**

| Scenario | ASEAN+1 | ASEAN+3 | East Asian FTA |
|---|---|---|---|
| 1  Taiwan status quo | | | |
| 2  Taiwan-China ECFA (WTO+ liberalization) | | | |
| 3  Taiwan-China integration | | | |
| 4  ECFA, Taiwan joins ASEAN+1 | ▓ | ▓ | |
| 5  ECFA, Taiwan joins ASEAN+1, ASEAN+3 | ▓ | ▓ | |
| 6  ECFA, Taiwan joins ASEAN+3 | ▓ | ▓ | |

ECFA = Economic Cooperation Framework Agreement; ASEAN = Association of Southeast Asian Nations; FTA = free trade agreement; WTO = World Trade Organization.

gion were cross-strait relations to be normalized, nor do we deeply assess the behavior of other pairs in the region under that scenario. These are important questions, but we leave them for political scientists to ponder.[2]

## Taiwan's Liberalization beyond China

Taiwan is a member of the WTO and enjoys the MFN-level economic treatment that members extend to one another. However with the increasing complexity of the WTO agenda, and with the mounting difficulties of lowering residual barriers and the cropping up of new ones after eight rounds of multilateral talks since 1947, most economies have embraced, either strategically or tactically or both, plurilateral and bilateral economic negotiations in recent years. Taiwan is a member of the Asia Pacific Economic Cooperation (APEC) forum, and has FTAs with Panama (2003), Guatemala (2005), Nicaragua (2006), El Salvador (2007), and Honduras (2007), all of which are marginal economies in terms of size and significance. APEC has played a valuable role over the years as a forum for agreeing upon liberalization commitments supplemental to the WTO. However, it has not succeeded as a vehicle for meaningful FTA-like liberalization.

The list of economic integration initiatives in Asia is lengthy. In *Asia's New Regionalism*, Ellen Frost (2008) explains that the tangle of undertakings includes a mix of top-down ambitions redolent of regional*ism*—a political agenda for Asia as opposed to elsewhere—and a bottom-up force of regional*ization* driven by the myriad men and women of commerce in lit-

---

2. Eric Ramstetter (authors' communication) points out that with Taiwanese matters on a more predictable footing, Beijing could variously be expected to be more assertive or—conversely—more self-assured and thus willing to work on resolution of other problems, like Korea.

toral Asia, who knit a tapestry of production chains through the region with minimal attention to nation building and maximum attention to balance sheets. Figure 2.1 mapped the Asia Pacific-centered preferential trade agreement scene. Our baseline for modeling in this study reflects this reality: ASEAN+1 is implemented, along with a number of other recently concluded agreements (see table A.1 in appendix A).

Among the many characteristics that can be attributed to the ascendant web of regional liberalization initiatives in Asia prior to the ECFA negotiations, one must be stated in the negative: none involved Taiwan. Pressure from Beijing, direct or feared, constrained Taiwan's ability to enter into bilateral or plurilateral economic agreements in the region. While this study is not an analysis of the geopolitics of Taiwan's international room to conduct such economic relations, it is an exploration of the economic significance of doing so (Tanner 2007). In the short period since Beijing and Taipei signed the ECFA agreement, Taiwan and Singapore have already announced talks on economic deepening, demonstrating the relevance of this element of the calculation for Taiwan. To test the significance of Taiwan moving beyond China-only preferential arrangements in the region, we model Taiwan acceding to the larger groupings of ASEAN+1 (in force) and ASEAN+3 (prospective), rather than knitting together lots of smaller bilateral effects, in order to get a general picture of the significance.

## Aggregate Effects for Taiwan and China

### GDP

The previous chapter summarized the impact on GDP of Taiwan and China undertaking the ECFA under a variety of regional scenarios ranging from the pre-ECFA status quo to the completion of an ASEAN+3 (table 2.2 in chapter 2). Table 2.3 extended the analysis to three additional scenarios, all post-ECFA: Taiwan goes on to join ASEAN+1; Taiwan joins ASEAN+1 while the rest of the region goes to ASEAN+3; and Taiwan joins a successful ASEAN+3.

The results suggest that the *additional* GDP effect on Taiwan from extending economic deepening arrangements beyond China to the rest of Asia after the ECFA are positive but modest, especially in comparison with the initial ECFA benefits. If Taiwan went on to join ASEAN+1, it could then anticipate in 2020 roughly an additional half percent of GDP gain on top of the 4.4 percent boost achieved through the ECFA. If ASEAN+3 were to transpire and Taiwan were on board, then we project eight-tenths of a percent greater GDP (the outcome for Taiwan in the third column of table 2.3 against the baseline in the third column of table 2.2). Were Taiwan to implement the ECFA, then it would, narrowly speaking, be better off *not* seeing competitors South Korea and Japan in an FTA with China (although the difference is slight). The implication is that the ECFA is where the main benefits are for Taiwan, rather than whether it is able to complete other FTAs. Once Taiwan secures the ECFA and joins ASEAN+1, then whether Taiwan is in or out of an ASEAN+3 that follows makes only a modest difference in GDP terms. This is not to say that progress by South Korea—Taiwan's most closely matched peer competitor—in negotiating FTAs with the United States (completed, ratification expected in 2010), European Union (negotiations completed in 2009, agreed upon but not finalized), and China (consultations planned for 2011) is not a competitive threat to Taiwan. Rather, our insight is that the benefits Taiwan achieves by keeping pace in regional integration are modest in comparison to the initial benefit of cross-strait opening.

For China, Taiwan's inclusion in ASEAN+1 subtracts trivially (as a percent of GDP, given China's larger GDP) from 2020 GDP without Taiwan in that agreement. And likewise, if after the ECFA Taiwan were to accede to ASEAN+3, then the 2020 effect for China would be insignificantly lower.

### Trade

Our modeling tells a similar story for the trade effects. The main event for Taiwan is completing a cross-strait FTA; the additional shocks from participation in regional undertakings are modest. This can be seen by comparing table 2.3 in chapter 2 with table 3.2. For instance, if Taiwan were able to go all the way to ASEAN+3 accession, its exports in 2020 would be $7 billion higher than the $26 billion increase from ECFA alone, and imports would be $6 billion greater than the $36 billion ECFA-induced growth. The effect on Taiwan's trade balance would be roughly identical—a modest reduction of Taiwan's trade surplus, on net, as the economy takes advantage of the comparative advantage of foreign production in some areas.

For China, the trade story is not changed significantly by Taiwan's presence or absence from regionwide undertakings. China sees a trade boost from the ECFA and a separate boost from ASEAN+3; adding Taiwan to the ASEAN+ accords changes these outcomes only minimally for China. ASEAN+3 is more valuable for China economically than the ECFA is.

As discussed in other chapters, there are qualitative factors not captured in these quantitative projections. An Asia where China has free trade with the southeastern tier and with the northeastern powerhouses of Japan and South Korea, and has included Taiwan on an equal economic basis in all this deepening, would portend an extraordinary outcome with vastly diminished political risks. The scenario in which China-Taiwan tensions are resolved to the extent that Taiwan could join in ASEAN+3

**Table 3.2  Change in 2020 trade and welfare indicators in scenarios where Taiwan extends regional integration beyond ECFA** (billions of 2004 US dollars and percent)

| | Taiwan joins ASEAN+1 | | Taiwan joins ASEAN+1, ASEAN+3 | | Taiwan joins ASEAN+3 | |
|---|---|---|---|---|---|---|
| | Taiwan | China | Taiwan | China | Taiwan | China |
| Trade balance | −10.50 | 8.70 | −10.40 | 27.80 | −8.50 | 27.20 |
| Exports | 31.20 (7.5) | 36.10 (1.5) | 25.90 (6.2) | 107.50 (4.6) | 33.10 (7.9) | 106.00 (4.5) |
| Imports | 41.70 (12.8) | 27.40 (1.6) | 36.30 (11.1) | 79.70 (4.6) | 41.60 (12.7) | 78.80 (4.6) |
| Terms of trade (percent) | 3.82 | 0.03 | 3.35 | 0.29 | 3.57 | 0.26 |
| Absorption | 17.00 (4.4) | 2.70 (0.05) | 13.90 (3.6) | 23.40 (0.4) | 14.90 (3.8) | 21.30 (0.4) |

ECFA = Economic Cooperation Framework Agreement; ASEAN = Association of Southeast Asian Nations.

Notes: Numbers in parentheses represent percent change. Numbers may not tally due to rounding.

*Source:* Model estimates.

portends major political progress in the region. And we surmise that such reduced political tensions would confer significant economic benefits on China and the other members of the Asia-Pacific in the form of trade deepening beyond what is captured in this model.

### *Welfare: Terms of Trade and Real Absorption*

The indicators of welfare presented in table 2.3 in chapter 2 also can be used for our regional scenarios. Taiwan and China both see modest additional terms of trade gains when Taiwan's trade liberalization is extended regionally, but these are minor compared to the initial gains from the ECFA itself. China sees more notable gains in welfare as indicated by terms of trade and also by real absorption when ASEAN+3 scenarios are introduced, whereas Taiwan's narrow interests are better served by stopping at ASEAN+1 and leaving peer competitors in Japan and South Korea outside China's innermost circle of barrier reduction.

As in the case of trade, welfare gains for Taiwan (and China) would be enhanced in an Asia where political and security threats were diminishing. We assume this would be the case in the event of Taiwan's accession to ASEAN+ agreements, while we are mindful that such considerations are not captured in our models of welfare effects. So the upside could be greater. On the other hand, as we have stressed, Taiwan's relative prosperity is in no way guaranteed by even the best outcome for inclusion in free trade covenants, cross-strait or regional: these regimes are just playing-field levelers; what Taiwan builds on that field once it is leveled will determine its relative success.

## Sectoral and Qualitative Observations

The model permits us to explore the sectoral winners and losers under various policy scenarios as well. To do so, we look at the different changes in production in 2020 under the various scenarios, and rank the most positively and negatively affected sectors in table 3.3. In general, the Taiwanese industries with the most to gain should Taiwan go beyond the ECFA to join ASEAN+1 and ASEAN+3 are leather and sporting goods, textiles, and parts of the food and agriculture industries. Taiwanese sugar sees major shrinkage and fruit and vegetables see minor production shrinkage; but these are areas expected to be excluded from full liberalization.[3] So long as the ECFA happens, no other sector stands to shrink by more than an additional 2.3 percent from Taiwan's inclusion in or exclusion from ASEAN+ agreements.[4]

For China, the sectoral implications of Taiwan going beyond the ECFA to join regional integration are more muted still. No sectors in China see an additional production gain greater than 0.4 percent by 2020 from Taiwan joining ASEAN+1 or ASEAN+3. A handful of sectors see modest downsides in China if after the ECFA Taiwan proceeds to join the ASEAN arrangements, specifically sugar and leather/sporting goods. It should be noted that the absolute values of percentage gains or losses in China are much larger than similar percentage moves in Taiwan, given the relative size of their economies, although these economic implications for China are not large enough to drive policy decisions.

Several observations can be drawn from this discussion of Taiwan's economic liberalization beyond the strait. First, Taiwan accomplishes the most by addressing the cross-strait agenda and matching preferential FTA terms of commerce with China, ideally without Japan and South Korea doing so (although that is unlikely *not* to happen, as China and Korea are already preparing for consultations). China maximizes its economic interests under the full regional integration of ASEAN+3. For China, whether Taiwan is along for the ASEAN+3 ride is less important. Some readers will be concerned at this point about whether Taiwan's pursuit of an FTA with the United States post-ECFA might hold more benefits than the regional integration explored in this chapter. The short answer is no, but we

---

3. Agriculture is commonly excluded from FTAs. In the case of Taiwan, leaders assert that the sector is one of the "three no's." However, there is not a complete prohibition on two-way food trade. For instance, Taiwan already imports sorghum, some vegetables, and tea from China. And under the ECFA China opens to significant fish and produce from Taiwan. These factors are reflected in our modeling.

4. This refers to the 32 aggregated sectors in our CGE model. Specific subsectors at a greater level of disaggregation could see more pronounced effects—on both the upside and the downside.

## Table 3.3 Percent change in production in 2020

| Sector | ECFA (1) | Taiwan joins ASEAN+1 (2) | Percent change in (2) with respect to (1) |
|---|---|---|---|
| **Taiwan** | | | |
| Winners | | | |
| Leather and sporting goods | 5.037 | 74.329 | 69.292 |
| Other processed food products | −1.191 | 9.478 | 10.669 |
| Textiles | 27.913 | 38.293 | 10.380 |
| Other grains | −8.569 | −0.658 | 7.911 |
| Livestock | 0.441 | 8.261 | 7.820 |
| Nongrain crops | 3.913 | 7.784 | 3.871 |
| Losers | | | |
| Sugar | −0.430 | −62.313 | −61.883 |
| Fruits and vegetables | −0.779 | −5.750 | −4.971 |
| Meat and milk products | −0.375 | −2.107 | −1.732 |
| Electronic equipment | −11.086 | −12.445 | −1.359 |
| Machinery and equipment | 6.520 | 5.777 | −0.743 |
| Mineral products | −0.920 | −1.581 | −0.661 |
| **China** | | | |
| Winners | | | |
| Electronic equipment | 0.476 | 0.840 | 0.364 |
| Other light manufactures | 0.632 | 0.702 | 0.070 |
| Machinery and equipment | 0.793 | 0.853 | 0.060 |
| Metal and metal products | 0.557 | 0.600 | 0.043 |
| Oil and gas | 0.177 | 0.212 | 0.035 |
| Chemicals, rubber, and plastic products | −0.805 | −0.782 | 0.023 |
| Losers | | | |
| Sugar | −0.053 | −2.940 | −2.887 |
| Leather and sporting goods | 0.125 | −1.120 | −1.245 |
| Transport equipment | 1.127 | 0.486 | −0.641 |
| Textiles | −0.277 | −0.691 | −0.414 |
| Tobacco and beverages | 0.021 | −0.362 | −0.383 |
| Nongrain crops | −0.889 | −1.258 | −0.369 |

ECFA = Economic Cooperation Framework Agreement; ASEAN = Association of Southeast Asian Nations.

*(continued on next page)*

will address that question in chapter 4, which looks at considerations concerning the United States in particular.

Second, the sectoral effects are limited in the aggregate, and even more so if the two sides continue to limit agriculture opening. The greatest sectoral gainers in Taiwan under these scenarios are not the high-tech busi-

**Table 3.3    Percent change in production in 2020** *(continued)*

| Sectors | No ECFA ASEAN +3 (3) | Taiwan + ASEAN+1, ASEAN+3 (4) | Percent change in (4) with respect to (3) |
|---|---|---|---|
| **Taiwan** | | | |
| Winners | | | |
| Leather and sporting goods | 0.666 | 76.761 | 76.095 |
| Textiles | −3.576 | 33.951 | 37.527 |
| Chemical rubber and plastic products | −1.423 | 28.798 | 30.221 |
| Petroleum, coal, and other mineral products | −1.095 | 14.188 | 15.283 |
| Motor vehicles and parts | −2.848 | 7.973 | 10.821 |
| Other processed food products | −0.093 | 9.991 | 10.084 |
| Losers | | | |
| Sugar | 0.13 | −62.179 | −62.309 |
| Electronic equipment | −0.394 | −12.865 | −12.471 |
| Fruits and vegetables | 0.274 | −5.684 | −5.958 |
| Other light manufactures | 1.879 | −2.967 | −4.846 |
| Transport equipment | 1.838 | −2.112 | −3.950 |
| Meat and milk products | 0.090 | −1.925 | −2.015 |
| **China** | | | |
| Winners | | | |
| Transport equipment | 0.040 | 1.142 | 1.102 |
| Wearing apparel | 2.711 | 3.635 | 0.924 |
| Machinery and equipment | 0.848 | 1.708 | 0.860 |
| Electronic equipment | 3.061 | 3.735 | 0.674 |
| Other light manufactures | 0.115 | 0.744 | 0.629 |
| Metal and metal products | 0.433 | 1.024 | 0.591 |
| Losers | | | |
| Leather and sporting goods | 2.188 | 0.964 | −1.224 |
| Nongrain crops | 3.056 | 2.021 | −1.035 |
| Chemicals, rubber, and plastic products | 0.276 | −0.445 | −0.721 |
| Textiles | 0.571 | −0.127 | −0.698 |
| Meat and milk products | 1.163 | 0.570 | −0.593 |
| Livestock | 0.151 | −0.232 | −0.383 |

ECFA = Economic Cooperation Framework Agreement; ASEAN = Association of Southeast Asian Nations.

nesses Taiwan is most respected for, which already enjoy fairly open trade conditions, but more traditional industries like leather and sporting goods. We are reminded that textiles are different from apparel and that Taiwan has comparative advantage in this industry (including capital-intensive nonwoven synthetic fabrics, for instance).

**Table 3.3   Percent change in production in 2020** *(continued)*

| Sectors | ECFA ASEAN +3 (5) | Taiwan joins ASEAN+3 (6) | Percent change in (6) with respect to (5) |
|---|---|---|---|
| **Taiwan** | | | |
| Winners | | | |
| Leather and sporting goods | 6.068 | 77.392 | 71.324 |
| Other processed food products | −1.130 | 13.079 | 14.209 |
| Textiles | 23.510 | 34.336 | 10.826 |
| Other grains | −7.961 | 2.411 | 10.372 |
| Livestock | 0.719 | 11.044 | 10.325 |
| Nongrain crops | 3.265 | 9.341 | 6.076 |
| Losers | | | |
| Sugar | −0.202 | −62.349 | −62.147 |
| Fruits and vegetables | −0.483 | −7.245 | −6.762 |
| Mineral products | −0.868 | −3.186 | −2.318 |
| Oil and gas | −0.510 | −0.927 | −0.417 |
| Wearing apparel | −0.121 | −0.220 | −0.099 |
| Business services | −1.255 | −1.353 | −0.098 |
| **China** | | | |
| Winners | | | |
| Electronic equipment | 3.539 | 3.636 | 0.097 |
| Sugar | −4.418 | −4.329 | 0.089 |
| Other light manufactures | 0.717 | 0.784 | 0.067 |
| Wood and paper products | 0.605 | 0.651 | 0.046 |
| Oil and gas | 0.325 | 0.348 | 0.023 |
| Metal and metal products | 0.980 | 0.988 | 0.008 |
| Losers | | | |
| Leather and sporting goods | 2.243 | 1.028 | −1.215 |
| Textiles | 0.272 | −0.108 | −0.380 |
| Meat and milk products | 0.756 | 0.574 | −0.182 |
| Motor vehicles and parts | −1.342 | −1.475 | −0.133 |
| Wearing apparel | 3.784 | 3.672 | −0.112 |
| Livestock | −0.157 | −0.236 | −0.079 |

ECFA = Economic Cooperation Framework Agreement; ASEAN = Association of Southeast Asian Nations.

Note: Positive or negative numbers represent changes in projected industrial output relative to the baseline; they do not mean the industry is expanding or contracting during the simulation period.

*Source:* Model estimates and authors' calculations.

Third, agriculture is not only a sensitive sector with adjustment challenges for Taiwan, it is potentially a source of real comparative advantage. This applies bilaterally as well as in regional scenarios. This shows up in our modeling but is likely to be even more interesting in the future given

Taiwan's position as the only member of the Greater China club with both the regulatory institutions and the farming space to develop a major high-value organic food cluster.

Finally, from Beijing's perspective there is little economic incentive to either include or exclude Taiwan from regionwide arrangements: it does not change the outcome much for either China or Taiwan. The dynamic effects are a different story, but less so in terms of the long-term structural adjustment that our model underestimates than from the reduction in political risk concerns, which act as perennial taxes on firms that must hedge against the unlikely but nontrivial chance of conflict in the region. And of course Beijing asserts that whatever the economic effects, static or dynamic, they are not material: the political value of a step toward potential reunification is more important to China.

## Impact on Others in Asia

So far we have considered the cost-benefit analysis facing China and Taiwan. The next question is whether China-Taiwan economic liberalization matters for other economies in Asia. During the decades when cross-strait economic relations were constrained by policy interventions, the economies around this tension zone evolved to make up the difference. The normalization of China-Taiwan commerce will result in some rediversion of trade and investment from the economies that had filled the gap, eliminating transshipment and other trade facilitation services that had emerged to intermediate, and affecting financial markets as well. Some of this has already occurred. Taiwan is a global player in electronics and semiconductors, for one thing, and major policy shocks could affect production chains in the industry. Regional trade arrangements have reflected Beijing's pressure on other Asian governments not to undertake agreements with Taiwan. Therefore with cross-strait economic normalization comes the possibility of a sudden snap-back to a more natural state of affairs, including a rapid move to secure a "second mover" (China being first) advantage in FTA arrangements with Taiwan and its competitive production chains.

Tables 3.4 and 3.5 lay out our modeling results for winners and losers among other economies in the region from the ECFA-only and ECFA-then-regional-integration scenarios for Taiwan explored in this study. Starting with ECFA-only, we are not surprised to see Hong Kong and Singapore experience modest reductions in GDP, as the transshipment role they have played and the special regional headquarters advantages they have enjoyed vis-à-vis Taiwan are diminished. Hong Kong sees negative impacts under all scenarios, but these are modest. If Taiwan joins ASEAN+1 then it achieves a temporary advantage vis-à-vis rival South Korea, which sees a $1.9 billion shrinkage in GDP, though with ASEAN+3 that swings to a much larger positive effect regardless of whether Taiwan

**Table 3.4  Change in 2020 GDP of economies other than China and Taiwan when Taiwan is limited to ECFA**

| | ECFA (China–Taiwan) | | | No ECFA, ASEAN+3 | | | ECFA, ASEAN+3 | |
| --- | --- | --- | --- | --- | --- | --- | --- | --- |
| | Billions of 2004 US dollars | Percent | | Billions of 2004 US dollars | Percent | | Billions of 2004 US dollars | Percent |
| **Winners** | | | | | | | | |
| Rest of Southeast Asia | 0.940 | 0.461 | Korea | 10.785 | 0.993 | Korea | 8.997 | 0.828 |
| Vietnam | 0.297 | 0.315 | Japan | 16.768 | 0.333 | Rest of Southeast Asia | 0.780 | 0.382 |
| Indonesia | 0.708 | 0.138 | Singapore | 0.547 | 0.289 | Japan | 14.529 | 0.289 |
| Rest of the world | 4.330 | 0.080 | Rest of the world | 2.862 | 0.053 | Rest of the world | 7.127 | 0.131 |
| **Losers** | | | | | | | | |
| Hong Kong | −0.863 | −0.337 | Philippines | −0.721 | −0.393 | Hong Kong | −1.310 | −0.512 |
| Singapore | −0.499 | −0.264 | Vietnam | −0.313 | −0.333 | Philippines | −0.631 | −0.344 |

ECFA = Economic Cooperation Framework Agreement; ASEAN = Association of Southeast Asian Nations.

*Source:* Model estimates and authors' calculations.

**Table 3.5 Change in 2020 GDP of economies other than China and Taiwan when Taiwan participates in other regional agreements**

| Taiwan joins ASEAN+1 | Billions of 2004 US dollars | Percent | Taiwan joins ASEAN+1, ASEAN+3 | Billions of 2004 US dollars | Percent | Taiwan joins ASEAN+3 | Billions of 2004 US dollars | Percent |
|---|---|---|---|---|---|---|---|---|
| Winners | | | | | | | | |
| Vietnam | 0.920 | 0.978 | Korea | 8.827 | 0.813 | Korea | 8.901 | 0.819 |
| Rest of Southeast Asia | 0.997 | 0.488 | Vietnam | 0.512 | 0.545 | Vietnam | 0.497 | 0.528 |
| Singapore | 0.725 | 0.384 | Rest of Southeast Asia | 0.770 | 0.377 | Rest of Southeast Asia | 0.749 | 0.367 |
| Thailand | 1.005 | 0.352 | Japan | 14.221 | 0.283 | Japan | 16.347 | 0.325 |
| Losers | | | | | | | | |
| Hong Kong | −0.508 | −0.198 | Hong Kong | −1.207 | −0.472 | Hong Kong | −1.273 | −0.498 |
| Korea | −1.897 | −0.175 | Philippines | −0.475 | −0.258 | Philippines | −0.677 | −0.369 |

ECFA = Economic Cooperation Framework Agreement; ASEAN = Association of Southeast Asian Nations.

*Source:* Model estimates and authors' calculations.

is party. And in reality South Korea is preparing for FTA consultations with China bilaterally that would likely offset some of the effect of Taiwan's momentary ECFA advantage.

The ECFA alone brings some modest benefits for Vietnam and other less-developed members of ASEAN. We interpret these gains for newly globalized but still less-developed economies in Asia from Taiwan's inclusion as a result of the complementarity of higher- and lower-income economies in trade agreements. For instance, while gains in trade between comparable-income economies like the United States and the nations of Europe are somewhat limited, the potential between the United States and Mexico under NAFTA was greater as a result of dissimilar development levels and associated differences in factor costs. After the 4.8 million citizens of Singapore (with per capita income averaging $39,000), Taiwan's 25 million at $16,500 would be the wealthiest population in ASEAN+1 in per capita terms, and thus a desirable market within a grouping clustered around the lower end, including Vietnam. Conversely, the modest but negative performance of the Philippines under ASEAN+3 results from sharing a similar production structure with China in sectors of comparative advantage—once Japan and Korea open to China, the Philippines' exports tend to be displaced.

Generally, the economic side effects of China-Taiwan economic liberalization for neighbors do not appear to present major complications. Even for the economy most notably affected, Hong Kong, the outlook is not particularly threatening (see below). Taiwan's inclusion in regional arrangements would benefit Vietnam and a few other neighbors to a significant degree, as they are in the right position to deal with Taiwan's well-off, middle-class population. And of course taking into account the longer-term, dynamic reality that an Asia in which Taiwan joined ASEAN+3 would be an Asia that had moved well beyond the principal political risk plaguing it today, we assume that other nations would add a major geo-economic premium that is not reflected in the modeled effects.

## Hong Kong

Hong Kong is the standout in terms of negative effects from cross-strait liberalization in the first analysis, which results directly from its having previously benefited from cross-strait frictions. Practically speaking, Hong Kong's situation is not a concern as regards the cross-strait outlook. The reintroduction of direct links across the strait has already siphoned off much of the Hong Kong transshipment work that is at risk. Hong Kong's external affairs are Beijing's responsibility, and Beijing officials are certain beyond any doubt that Hong Kong will not muddy any step toward consolidation of a greater Chinese marketplace with narrow, self-interested concerns. More importantly, the industries in which Taiwan and Hong Kong have overlapping competitiveness are limited, and Hong Kong's competitive abilities are well honed. Hong Kong is focused on business services; Taiwan's prowess lies in manufacturing, especially in the high-tech segment. Hong Kong's comparative advantages are clear and systematic, and it will be difficult for Taiwan to produce a value proposition that rivals these capabilities.

Qualitatively, Hong Kong's exposure appears concentrated in finance, shipping and transportation, tourism, and business services (such as the domiciling of regional headquarters). Quantitatively, our model shows noticeable negative output growth for Hong Kong only in textiles and in chemicals/rubber/plastics, neither of which is an important manufacturing sector for the city (that is, the "output" reported for Hong Kong is probably a reflection of factors moving through the city produced elsewhere, and is an artifact that appears in the model).

By March 2008, 54 Taiwanese companies had listed on the Hong Kong stock exchange, and from January 2007 to March 2008 Taiwanese listings accounted for 40 percent of all funds raised by non-Chinese initial public offerings. This trend was driven by a desire to escape Taiwanese restrictions on total investment in the mainland by Taiwan-listed firms (40 percent maximum) (Securities and Futures Commission 2008). As of mid-2008 Taiwan relaxed these restrictions, and the motivation for its firms to raise capital through Hong Kong was reduced. Taiwan occasionally expresses aspirations to be a regional financial sector hub, but no senior business or policy professionals we spoke to in Taiwan or Hong Kong expect Taiwan to challenge Hong Kong's position in this regard based on the effects of the ECFA per se.

Prior to being referred to as the ECFA, the cross-strait initiative was labeled a Closer Economic Cooperation Agreement, a term obviously similar to Hong Kong's Closer Economic Partnership Agreement (CEPA). Despite the politically expedient midcourse change in nomenclature, there remains the question of whether Hong Kong's experience in deepening its economic engagement with the mainland under the CEPA provides any lessons for Taiwan. In fact, the relevance is limited, because the preexisting policy conditions are so dissimilar. Hong Kong is a free port and exports few home-origin goods, so the goods trade elements of the CEPA were not that important, whereas in the case of Taiwan its unilateral tariff and nontariff goods trade barriers are key. In Taiwan, "traditional manufacturing industries" (such as toys) garner political attention, as does agriculture, whereas in Hong Kong such protection-seeking sectors are largely absent. A number of nongoods elements of the CEPA *are* envisioned by Taiwan's leadership as part of the ECFA process, but for later staging, including mutual recognition of professional qualifications and cooperative inspection and quarantine procedures. In the case of Hong Kong's waiver under the CEPA of WTO rights to employ nonmarket economy methodology for China, challenge imports based on antidumping and subsidies concerns, or use tariff rate quotas, there has been no similar intention expressed by Taiwan.[5]

Senior officials and executives in Hong Kong make a persuasive case that not only is the negative impact of cross-strait rapprochement manageable, the upside is larger. Hong Kong will continue to be the transshipment point for Taiwanese manufacturing in southern China, not for reasons of policy but just due to geography and established infrastructure. Hong Kong is promoting itself as a venue to handle higher-end business services for Chinese and Taiwanese firms that require a neutral setting, such as commercial arbitration.

## Conclusions

Extending Taiwan's trade liberalization beyond China to regional plurilateral undertakings brings only limited additional benefits to Taiwan beyond those generated by the ECFA. A handful of Taiwanese industries do see notable gains in output as a result of broader trade liberalization. However, these effects are concentrated in more mature, old-line industries such as leather and sporting goods rather than in sectors of future importance for Taiwan like information technology, which already has a free trade regime under the WTO Information Technology Agreement. Otherwise, an important conclusion is that adding post-ECFA opening to Taiwan brings potentially very important gains for the economy's agricultural sector, but there is the likelihood that such sectors would be excluded to some extent from liberalization, more due to Taiwan's insistence than China's. The differences for China arising from these variations in Taiwan liberalization are, meanwhile, minor.

The static effects our model projects for China-Taiwan economic liberalization on neighboring economies in Asia are modest, both on the upside and downside. Where the downside shows up most, for Hong Kong, it is manageable and politically important to play down. There are some winners in the region from Taiwanese inclusion in ASEAN+, notably Vietnam. These quantitative projections are compatible with our qualitative assessment and with interviews with officials and business professionals.

The dynamic effects of liberalization are likely to be valuable to other economies in the region. These include both dynamic effects in the economic sense—changes in output, demand, and employment over time as economies redirect resources to better reflect underlying comparative advantages undistorted by policy interventions—and also in political terms: less political risk hanging over the region will bolster the share of GDP that can be directed to productive use instead of applied to national defense or simply forgone as a hedge against overdependence.

---

5. For the text of the CEPA see www.tid.gov.hk/english/cepa/files/main_e.pdf (accessed on September 15, 2010).

# Cross-Strait Economic Relations and the United States

Economic normalization between China and Taiwan and its convergence with regional liberalization trends would affect the United States in a variety of ways, including commercially, in terms of economic leadership in the region, and in security terms as well. Peaceful conditions across the Taiwan Strait depend on the careful handling of the process of economic deepening, so the United States has a profound, perhaps even core interest in the progress of that deepening.[1] This chapter explores the implications of China-Taiwan economic deepening from the US perspective. We first summarize the present trade and investment connections among the three, and then review the quantitative results of our modeling of the ECFA for the United States. We consider US policy options related to this arena. Having worked through the economic dimensions, we consider some of the security implications of cross-strait economic deepening.

## The US-China-Taiwan Economic Relationship

The United States has serious economic relationships with both China and Taiwan.[2] In 2009, US-China two-way trade was $366 billion—$296 billion

---

1. See "China-Taiwan: Recent Economic, Political and Military Developments Across the Strait and Implications for the United States," testimony by David B. Shear, Deputy Assistant Secretary, Bureau of East Asian and Pacific Affairs, US-China Economic and Security Review Commission, March 18, 2010.

2. Data in this and the following paragraph are from US International Transactions Accounts Data, Bureau of Economic Analysis (balance of payments basis).

to imports and $70 billion to exports. The two-way totals over 2006–08 were $343 billion, $387 billion, and $409 billion, respectively. Thus, China represented 14 percent of total US goods trade through December 2009, having passed Mexico to become the second largest trading partner of the United States, behind only Canada, in 2006. US exports of services to China reached $15 billion in 2009, almost double services imports of around $8.6 billion in the same year.

Taiwan and the United States share a deep trade relationship as well. In 2009, US-Taiwan trade amounted to $47 billion, with the United States exporting $18 billion to and importing $28 billion from Taiwan. While this represents a smaller 1.8 percent of US global goods trade through 2009, making Taiwan the United States' 10th largest trading partner, on a per capita basis few economies ship more to the United States. The export of US services to Taiwan totaled $7 billion in 2009, while services imports were around $6 billion.

Growth in US-Taiwan trade has been moderated by the regionalization of Asian production chains. This is to say that many Taiwanese manufacturers have migrated final assembly operations (and much of their value added as well) to China over the past two decades; so Taiwan-branded or -owned products largely ship to the United States from China. And of course Taiwanese firms are not the only ones to situate assembly operations in China. In light of the fragmentation of production chains across borders, it would be a mistake to see the trade effects of the ECFA purely in terms of Chinese manufacturers displacing American goods in Taiwan (for instance) as Taiwan's prohibitions on importation from China are dismantled. In many cases, US firms have production facilities in China designed to service Asian markets, and would simply be shifting production within their global networks.

US business interests consulted with Taiwanese officials about product coverage of the ECFA during the agreement's preparatory stage to request that certain items be included for liberalization, including food products that by default would be excluded under Taiwan's "three no's," some medical-related products that could be excluded under sanitary/phytosanitary exemptions, and specific products like "other distilled cereal beverages"—that is, Chinese *baijiu*, or white liquor, which might be excluded because it competes with traditional craft products such as Taiwan's *gaoliang* sorghum liquor from Kinmen and Matsu. The European Chamber of Commerce Taipei proposed its own list of priorities for inclusion in the ECFA (ECCT 2009–10). Of course, products manufactured for export in China by US and European firms are *Chinese* exports, but they do generate revenues that contribute to repatriated profit.

Knitting these production chains together are flows of cross-border direct investment, as discussed in chapter 1. The US international investment position for year-end 2008 records $46 billion of FDI in China, and nearly $17 billion in Taiwan (on a historical-cost basis).[3] US investment in Taiwan is concentrated in manufacturing (particularly the computer and electronics segment), finance, and wholesale trading. US investment in China is even more focused on manufacturing (computer/electronics, chemicals, and transportation), along with wholesale trade and a growing flow into financial services. China accounted for almost half of the growth of US FDI to Asia in 2008, although over four-fifths of that went to non-manufacturing. These numbers almost certainly understate the extent of US investment in these markets due to use of "switchyard" domiciles to hold investments abroad for tax and other purposes, including Hong Kong, Singapore, and Caribbean offshore financial centers such as Bermuda and the British Virgin Islands. The ratio of income to investment position for the United States in China was 13.4 percent in 2008; for Taiwan it was 9 percent.

Structural adjustment on each side of the strait, and cross-border investment flows that are both a product and cause of that adjustment, suggest more extensive growth in services sector export opportunities for the United States than our model can project. Adjustment will bolster the demand for financial services, transportation, and other business services, sectors in which the United States maintains comparative advantage despite the disruptions of the global financial crisis. Through 2008 services exports represented 30 percent of total US exports, and unlike the $840 billion goods trade deficit, the United States ran a $144 billion services trade surplus.

Taiwan and China have also increased their direct investment in the United States in recent years. US statistics report a very modest $1.2 billion of Chinese investment in the United States through 2008 (almost entirely in wholesale trading), up about $300 million year-on-year.[4] (China's figures are about double that.[5]) Preliminary numbers for greenfield investment and M&A deals indicate that Chinese investment volume has fundamentally increased in 2009 compared to previous years.[6] However, these are still very small numbers by US or Chinese standards—through 2008, China had a total outward FDI stock of about $184 billion and the United States a total inward stock of about $2.3 trillion, by comparison.

---

3. Investment-related figures are available at US Bureau of Economic Analysis, "International Economic Accounts." www.bea.gov/international/ai1.htm#usdia (accessed on September 15, 2010).

4. Data from the US Bureau of Economic Analysis (op. cit.); direct investment position on a historical-cost basis.

5. The Chinese Ministry of Commerce's "2008 Statistical Bulletin of China's Outward FDI" reports an FDI stock in the United States of $2.39 billion.

6. Based on 2009 data on greenfield and M&A equity investment from Thomson ONE and FDIntelligence and quarterly estimates from US and Chinese government sources.

For Taiwan, the 2008 investment position in the United States was $3.9 billion, concentrated in manufacturing, wholesale trade, and banking. US data also track FDI by country of "ultimate beneficial ownership," which tries to trace origins behind switchyard domiciles and shell companies. These 2008 figures are $1.9 billion and $5.5 billion for China and Taiwan, respectively, marginally higher but still small compared to other bilateral investment relationships.

These two-way investment flows have the potential to rise significantly in the years ahead, especially between the United States and China. China is entering an era of expanded outbound investment. Its firms are underrepresented abroad and have mounting incentives to get closer to their global customers (Rosen and Hanemann 2009). From Beijing's governmental perspective, adding more direct investment relative to low-risk but low-return holdings of US Treasury securities has been identified as a goal. For their part, US investors see China as a singular investment opportunity for the decades ahead and are actively looking to expand their exposure. As discussed in chapter 2 and validated by US business representatives in Taiwan, US investors see potential in Taiwan in light of cross-strait normalization. US firms will have particular interests in the effects of the ECFA for the computer and semiconductor value chain, and for the utility of Taiwan as a "greater China" financial and business services hub, given the superior legal system. But while the ECFA makes Taiwan's outperformance in these and other sectors possible, in no way does it alone achieve such success, which depends on the agility Taiwan displays above and beyond the ECFA.

In general, the United States is a huge net importer of portfolio investment from both Taiwan and China.[7] As of 2008, Taiwanese investors held $150 billion in long- and short-term US securities, including more than $66 billion of treasury securities and more than $11 billion in corporate debt and equity—about 1.5 percent of total foreign portfolio investment in the United States in all. US investors held around $41 billion of Taiwanese securities in 2008, overwhelmingly corporate equities.

China is one of the most important foreign portfolio investors in the United States. US Treasury survey data suggest that through June 2009 Chinese entities held $1.23 trillion in long-term US debt, $160 billion in shorter-term debt, and $76 billion in portfolio equities, for a total portfolio of $1.46 trillion. Such figures, which amount to more than 12 percent of total foreign holdings for the United States, likely understate reality due to secondary market purchases. In other words, treasury bills bought by a broker in London are recorded as UK purchases, but might well be an order placed by Chinese entities (Setser and Pandey 2009). The majority of those holdings are US government treasury securities and agencies

---

7. Data from US Treasury's Treasury International Capital system. www.ustreas.gov/tic/shlptab1.html (accessed on September 15, 2010).

held by China's State Administration of Foreign Exchange and other government vehicles, and corporate debt and equity owned by sovereign vehicles such as the China Investment Corporation. Private investors through China's QDII program are a much smaller story. Through 2008, US investors were holding around $55 billion of portfolio investment in China, most of it equities ($53 billion) and the rest corporate debt.

In sum, the United States relies on capital inflows from China and Taiwan to help it finance its external deficits that arise in significant part from a systemic trade deficit run with these two Chinese economies. At the same time, many of the goods-exporting firms behind those trade deficits in China and Taiwan are not Chinese but multinationals, including many US firms that build up assets in their host countries as a result. Given such complex interdependence, the United States would be concerned if China and Taiwan were to increase their cumulative trade surpluses with the United States as a result of the ECFA, and/or divert a large portion of the capital flows they send to the United States as a result of the agreement. Our modeling of the effect of China-Taiwan deepening and related scenarios helps us address those concerns.

## Modeling Results for the Economic Cooperation Framework Agreement and the United States

### GDP

Our modeling indicates that the aggregate economic impact on US GDP (as other variables) from the ECFA will be small in relation to the US economy. Given the imprecision inherent in the model, these results must be used with care. However, they do provide the starting point for discussing the effects of cross-strait economic rapprochement on the United States.

Our modeling projects a modest $690 million reduction in headline US GDP in 2020 resulting from implementation of the ECFA (table 4.1). The first thing to be said about this result is that it is very small and statistically insignificant in the context of the $14.5 trillion US economy. However it is useful to explore the interactions that generate this result. As discussed further below, US global imports and exports both fall very modestly, with an even more modest resulting fall in trade balance. But given input-output effects, industrial output and GDP in the United States decline somewhat more than the net trade balance change.

With China and Taiwan delivering more of their aggregate production to one another, the US import prices for some goods from these two rise slightly, leading to a modest fall in US imports (and hence slightly higher average prices for these products in the United States). Similarly, there is slight trade diversion impacting the United States, with Taiwan and China replacing US exports in their trade with one another. Hence there

**Table 4.1    Change in US macroeconomic variables**
(billions of 2004 US dollars and percent)

|  | ECFA | Taiwan joins ASEAN+3 |
|---|---|---|
| GDP | −0.69 (−0.004) | −6.81 (−0.043) |

Note: Numbers may not tally due to rounding. Numbers in parentheses represent percent changes.

Source: Model results.

is a slight fall in US global exports too. While the slight declines in imports and exports largely offset one another, resulting in a more modest change in the US trade balance (a mere $83 million), each of these channels—imports and exports—has a greater than one-to-one negative effect on US industrial production and hence GDP ($690 million). This is the reverse of the beneficial effect of opening an economy to trade, in which both exports *and imports* can contribute greater than one-to-one to GDP growth. The sections below consider the winners and losers more closely in terms of industrial production and trade.

In the event that Taiwan follows the ECFA with entry into an ASEAN+3, our model projects a much greater negative outcome for US GDP in 2020. It is the eventuality of ASEAN+3 coming to fruition, not so much the question of Taiwan's inclusion in it, that generates this outcome. Under ASEAN+3 scenarios, the reduction in US GDP is an order of magnitude greater: $6.8 billion annually. This is still a small number for the United States, but not as easy to ignore. The United States could match ASEAN+ integration with its own trade liberalization over the coming decade and offset some of these effects.[8] This is a key insight from our analysis: if the US concern is Taiwan's prosperity, then the ECFA and subsequent regional inclusion for Taiwan are great, but this is not necessarily positive for the United States economically. The ECFA portion is not problematic from the latter perspective, but the broader regional integration is. Whether this is a major negative for the United States depends on participation in ongoing Asian economic integration.

## Industrial Output

The 2020 impact on US industrial output by sector is reported in table 4.2. No US industry in the 32-industry model sees positive or negative change in output greater than 0.8 percent as a result of ECFA implementation. In

---

8. In a paper submitted to the US Trade Representative in support of a Trans-Pacific Partnership Agreement on behalf of the Peterson Institute for International Economics, Bergsten and Schott (2010) note that such an agreement could catalyze a new center of gravity for open regionalism in Asian trade politics, but that this initiative currently does not involve the fastest-growth economies in the region.

**Table 4.2  Change in US output by industry under ECFA and Taiwan and ASEAN+3 scenarios, 2020**

| Industry | ECFA only Millions of 2004 US dollars | ECFA only Percent of industry output | Taiwan joins ASEAN+3 Millions of 2004 US dollars | Taiwan joins ASEAN+3 Percent of industry output |
|---|---|---|---|---|
| Electronic equipment | 2,123.7 | 0.42 | −279.3 | −0.06 |
| Business services | 250.7 | 0.01 | 640.7 | 0.03 |
| Metal and metal products | 223.5 | 0.03 | 288.2 | 0.04 |
| Finance and Insurance | 158.8 | 0.01 | −56.4 | 0 |
| Oil and gas | 129.7 | 0.09 | 269.5 | 0.19 |
| Nongrain crops | 108.8 | 0.13 | −889.6 | −1.09 |
| Utility and other nontraded services | 107.6 | 0 | −1,660.0 | −0.02 |
| Meat and milk products | 81.4 | 0.04 | 53.2 | 0.03 |
| Other processed food products | 78.6 | 0.02 | −943.0 | −0.18 |
| Livestock | 72.0 | 0.05 | 121.5 | 0.09 |
| Coal and other minerals | 36.1 | 0.03 | 80.4 | 0.07 |
| Construction | 33.5 | 0.00 | −523.8 | −0.03 |
| Rice | 23.2 | 0.24 | 29.1 | 0.30 |
| Forest and fishery products | 23.1 | 0.07 | 6.5 | 0.02 |
| Other grains | 21.6 | 0.04 | 417.3 | 0.82 |
| Fruits and vegetables | 21.3 | 0.03 | 57.1 | 0.08 |
| Communication | 20.9 | 0 | −3.7 | 0 |
| Recreational and other services | 8.6 | 0 | −19.7 | 0 |
| Sugar | 0.4 | 0 | −3.7 | −0.02 |
| Tobacco and beverages | −5.7 | 0 | −61.3 | −0.04 |
| Leather and sporting goods | −36.3 | −0.21 | −296.1 | −1.68 |
| Mineral products | −59.8 | −0.04 | −163.5 | −0.10 |
| Wood and paper products | −130.6 | −0.02 | 93.9 | 0.01 |
| Petroleum, coal, and other mineral products | −131.2 | −0.04 | −390.4 | −0.11 |
| Other light manufactures | −145.7 | −0.15 | 28.2 | 0.03 |
| Motor vehicles and parts | −199.7 | −0.03 | 652.1 | 0.11 |
| Transport equipment | −222.7 | −0.08 | 651.7 | 0.22 |
| Trade and transportation | −254.0 | −0.01 | −387.7 | −0.01 |
| Wearing apparel | −328.3 | −0.79 | −620.3 | −1.50 |
| Textiles | −495.5 | −0.35 | −1,180.0 | −0.82 |
| Chemicals, rubber, and plastic products | −939.4 | −0.09 | −2,890.0 | −0.28 |
| Machinery and equipment | −1,160.0 | −0.10 | −3,630.0 | −0.31 |
| Total | −585.5 | | −10,609.2 | |

ECFA = Economic Cooperation Framework Agreement; ASEAN = Association of Southeast Asian Nations.

Note: Data are sorted by dollar amount under the ECFA-only scenario. Positive or negative numbers represent changes in projected industrial output relative to the baseline; they do not mean the industry is expanding or contracting during the simulation period.

dollar amounts and as a percent of industry output, most of the winners in the US economy are in food production and natural resources. This results from general equilibrium effects; that is, China and Taiwan are growing faster than the baseline scenario, and hence global demand for resources increases more quickly. These sectors are negatively affected by the price and trade diversion impact on US output discussed above under GDP.

The US manufacturing sector that sees the single most significant output growth (in dollar terms and as a percent of output) is electronic equipment, which is interesting in light of the significant shrinkage observed for this sector in Taiwan in chapter 2. While Taiwan's import prohibitions may have helped sustain some lower-value-added manufacturing in the sector despite the extensive migration of the industry from Taiwan to China, in the United States the electronic equipment industry has already been fully exposed to foreign competition. Thus, if further industry rationalization between Taiwan and China drives costs down further and hence increases demand, US production stands to benefit.

Apparel and textiles sees the largest shrinkage (though still very modest) of output for the United States as a result of the ECFA. Taiwan currently maintains prohibitions on imports from China on about 500 textile and apparel product categories, and removal of those barriers would naturally result in some trade diversion from third parties, including the United States. Though smaller than the garment sector in percentage terms, industrial and manufactured products see larger output declines in dollar terms: machinery and equipment, and chemicals and plastics, each fall by about a billion dollars. All the other nonextractive manufacturing industries (except metal and metal products) see modest output declines as a result of the ECFA.

Beyond $585 million in net output reduction under ECFA-only, our model projects $10.6 billion in output shrinkage under ASEAN+3 scenarios. Recall this is true with or without Taiwan's inclusion. Leather goods and apparel and nongrain crops see output reductions greater than 1 percent, while the biggest dollar contractions occur—as under the ECFA—in machinery and chemicals. The US gains in electronic equipment and food and hard commodities are eroded by overlapping comparative advantages in these industries in the ASEAN+3 grouping. In a few sectors, particularly vehicles and transport equipment, it appears that the general equilibrium growth of Asia under ASEAN+3 contributes to output gains for the United States.

## Trade

The results from our model regarding the aggregate impact of the ECFA on US trade are reported in table 4.3. As a result of the ECFA, US global

**Table 4.3  Aggregate trade effects for the United States, 2020**
(billions of 2004 dollars and percent)

| | ECFA | Taiwan joins ASEAN+3 |
|---|---|---|
| Exports | −0.298 (−0.017) | −3.592 (−0.207) |
| Imports | −0.215 (−0.009) | −3.483 (−0.152) |
| Balance | −0.083 | −0.109 |

ECFA = Economic Cooperation Framework Agreement; ASEAN = Association of Southeast Asian Nations.

Notes: Numbers may not tally due to rounding. Numbers in parentheses represent percent changes.

*Source:* Model results.

exports in 2020 are $298 million lower than they would otherwise be, and imports are $215 million lower, representing a tiny $83 million deterioration in the trade deficit. If Taiwan joins ASEAN+3, the effects for the United States are an order of magnitude greater for both exports and imports, which is offsetting, leaving the trade balance little changed from the ECFA-only case. Again it is the ASEAN+3 transpiring, not the question of Taiwan's involvement, that matters for US trade results. US exports shrink because preferential trade integration among major Asian players displaces them. US imports decline as well, as a faster-growing and more-specialized Asia absorbs more of its productive capacity at home instead of producing for trans-Pacific export. Local demand for Taiwanese and Chinese production effectively pushes up US prices marginally, producing the follow-on input-output effect on GDP described above. The United States would offset some of these effects, of course, if it were party to the same Asian integration.

Table 4.4 shows the trade effects of the ECFA for the United States by industry in percentage terms. The impact on US exports and imports is consistent with the industrial output story. Food and agricultural products would spur the most pronounced growth in US exports due to more rapidly growing demand in Asia. Electronic equipment would see the largest percent growth in exports versus the baseline, and services trade growth would be positive, while most other manufacturing would see modest displacement from the ECFA. China's textiles and apparel would displace other producers' market share in Taiwan, including the United States. In the auto sector, Taiwan is still phasing out quota restrictions under the terms of WTO accession (Lardy and Rosen 2004, 30), but will retain a high MFN tariff thereafter, so an FTA-like agreement that liberalizes China-Taiwan auto trade would confer a tremendous advantage on producers in the mainland, both foreign and indigenous. This helps explain the modest motor vehicle and parts export shrinkage our model pro-

**Table 4.4  US change in exports and imports under ECFA-only scenario, 2020** (percent)

| Industry | Exports | Imports |
|---|---|---|
| Electronic equipment | 0.75 | −0.20 |
| Livestock | 0.73 | −0.18 |
| Meat and milk products | 0.55 | −0.03 |
| Forest and fishery products | 0.49 | −0.07 |
| Construction | 0.44 | −0.28 |
| Oil and gas | 0.44 | −0.12 |
| Nongrain crops | 0.40 | 0.02 |
| Rice | 0.31 | −0.69 |
| Coal and other minerals | 0.28 | −0.06 |
| Finance and insurance | 0.25 | −0.12 |
| Communication | 0.25 | −0.11 |
| Utility and other nontraded services | 0.23 | −0.08 |
| Trade and transportation | 0.20 | −0.07 |
| Business services | 0.19 | −0.13 |
| Fruits and vegetables | 0.16 | −0.01 |
| Recreational and other services | 0.16 | −0.17 |
| Other processed food products | 0.12 | −0.09 |
| Sugar | 0.05 | −0.13 |
| Tobacco and beverages | 0.05 | −0.02 |
| Other grains | 0.04 | 0.11 |
| Petroleum, coal, and other mineral products | −0.01 | −0.06 |
| Metal and metal products | −0.05 | −0.26 |
| Motor vehicles and parts | −0.07 | 0.02 |
| Wood and paper products | −0.16 | −0.03 |
| Transport equipment | −0.19 | −0.05 |
| Chemicals, rubber, and plastic products | −0.25 | 0.00 |
| Other light manufactures | −0.30 | 0.19 |
| Machinery and equipments | −0.36 | 0.00 |
| Mineral products | −0.37 | 0.01 |
| Leather and sporting goods | −0.58 | 0.01 |
| Wearing apparel | −0.64 | 0.46 |
| Textiles | −0.81 | 0.27 |

ECFA = Economic Cooperation Framework Agreement.

Note: Data are sorted by exports column.

*Source:* Model estimates.

duced. (There would be a similar effect on Japanese and Korean automakers, which have built share in Taiwan in recent years.)

Table 4.5 shows the change by 2020 for US trade by partner country. Under the ECFA, US exports to Taiwan go up because the Taiwanese economy grows faster, and US imports from Taiwan go down because more of what Taiwan manufactures for the United States either migrates to China or gets consumed locally as the cross-strait relationship deepens.

**Table 4.5    Change in US trade by selected country or region, 2020** (percent)

| Country/region | ECFA | | Taiwan joins ASEAN+3 | |
|---|---|---|---|---|
| | **Exports** | **Imports** | **Exports** | **Imports** |
| Taiwan | 5.0 | −13.4 | 2.1 | −13.2 |
| Philippines | 0.9 | 0.4 | 0.4 | −1.9 |
| Rest of East Asia | 0.5 | 0.5 | 0.3 | 0.6 |
| Malaysia | 0.5 | 0.9 | −2.4 | −2.1 |
| Thailand | 0.3 | 0.9 | −2.7 | 0.7 |
| Indonesia | 0.1 | 0.9 | −0.5 | 0.2 |
| Australia | 0.0 | 0.1 | 0.3 | 0.3 |
| Vietnam | 0.0 | 0.8 | −5.1 | 7.5 |
| Japan | −0.1 | 0.4 | 2.5 | −5.8 |
| South Asia | −0.1 | 0.1 | 0.2 | 0.3 |
| Korea | −0.2 | 0.9 | −5.9 | −2.2 |
| Singapore | −0.2 | 0.5 | 0.8 | −1.5 |
| Hong Kong | −0.4 | 0.8 | −0.1 | 0.2 |
| China | −2.3 | 0.6 | −4.2 | 1.5 |

ECFA = Economic Cooperation Framework Agreement; ASEAN = Association of Southeast Asian Nations.

*Source:* Model estimates.

Exports to China decline from trend, as an adjusting Taiwan moves faster up the value chain and takes a piece of US market share away, and US imports from China rise. If ASEAN+3 transpires and Taiwan joins, then Taiwan gets more of its imports from Asia and the US share grows less than half as much as in the ECFA-only case; US exports to China decline from the baseline and imports from China grow faster. The change in US trade with other Asian economies is minimal, but Asian integration in the ASEAN+3 scenario clearly displaces a considerable amount of US exports as well as diverting exports to the United States from Japan, Korea, and Singapore back into Asia.

## Broader Issues of Regional Leadership

Beyond the quantitative impact of the ECFA on the United States there are regional leadership implications for the United States as a result of China-Taiwan economic dynamics. The symbolic significance of Taiwan dismantling ostensible national security barriers to economic engagement with China is hard to exaggerate. Transcending unresolved political differences and liberalizing economic relations will create new vested interests and change behavior in the political sphere going forward. Taiwan does not intend to stop with the ECFA but rather seeks to build upon it to pursue further economic liberalization in the region. Beijing hinted obliquely at a willingness to stop frustrating that ambition prior to the

ECFA signing, and then did not object to Taiwan-Singapore trade talks announced shortly afterward. China aggressively pursues regional economic deepening in fora that do not include the United States. If the ECFA clears the way for Taiwan's inclusion in Asia's new regionalism, one of the largest missing pieces of an Asia-only bloc will be in place. China's embrace of ASEAN+1 was, after all, the main stated justification Taiwan had for starting cross-strait negotiations. Preliminary talks toward an ASEAN+3 FTA are already taking place.[9]

The progress toward regional integration highlighted by China-Taiwan economic deepening is even more notable in light of the hiatus in US action in this arena. The United States and South Korea negotiated an FTA (known as KORUS), but only in the weeks after the ECFA signing did US President Barack Obama commit to submitting it for quick ratification. The president lacks "fast track" trade promotion negotiating authority to pursue new agreements (without the threat of endless amendment in the Congress). ASEAN has been an important nexus of new economic arrangements in Asia, but until recently the United States was not involved in this process, in large part due to reluctance to engage with Burma, which is part of the group. The United States acceded to the ASEAN Treaty of Amity and Cooperation in July 2009,[10] opening the possibility of participation in the ASEAN-hosted East Asian Summit, and President Obama attended an ASEAN Summit in November 2009. These steps are politically important as a signal of US engagement with Southeast Asia, a region that has come to appreciate the positive role the United States plays in the region not just in economic terms but in geosecurity terms as well. There is far to go, however, before US economic relations with ASEAN have as much momentum as China-ASEAN relations.[11]

In late 2009, President Obama committed to involve the United States in the Trans-Pacific Strategic Economic Partnership Agreement (TPPA), which seeks to expand on an agreement among Chile and Singapore (with which the United States already has FTAs) and New Zealand and Brunei to craft a broader group with more comprehensive and binding coverage than many Asian agreements, and with an open architecture. The initial US announcement of involvement was somewhat ambiguous, and the lack of trade promotion negotiating authority creates a credibility gap, but

---

9. Han Qiao, "ASEAN+3 Financial Co-op Gains News Momentum," English-Xinhuanet. com, August 4, 2010. news.xinhuanet.com/english2010/indepth/2010-04/08/c_ 13242892. htm (accessed on September 15, 2010).

10. The Treaty of Amity and Cooperation is not a treaty under US legal interpretation, and will be implemented by the United States by executive agreement and not via Senate ratification.

11. In 2006, the United States had signed a Trade and Investment Framework Agreement with ASEAN, but that document only committed the parties to "consider ways to enhance trade and investment," which is as anodyne a commitment as imaginable.

the risk of the United States being left out of Asian trade deepening is fueling growing interest in the TPPA. Taiwan has indicated its desire to join the partnership once it expands to eight parties.[12] In June 2010, US Trade Representative Ron Kirk hosted a second round of TPPA negotiations, and described the undertaking in the larger context of US engagement with Asia and the US National Export Initiative.

In sum, the United States' reengagement in Asian economic liberalization has been modest, is in an early stage, and lacks the bureaucratic conditions at home to be credible at face value.[13] The effect of Taiwan-China liberalization is modest in direct economic terms, but has been more profound in symbolic terms. Taiwan is looking over the horizon at ongoing and far-reaching Asian integration, which with or without Taiwan's involvement would significantly impact the United States. To date the United States has not developed a strategy for being part of this process, but the ECFA has focused the attention of US policymakers on the need to do so. Exclusion from an Asia-wide trade pact could reduce US exports by tens of billions of dollars annually, thus reducing job creation by hundreds of thousands (Bergsten and Schott 2010).

The absence of US economic leadership in Asia carries costs beyond the trade and welfare effects described by models. In the ECFA, China and Taiwan agree to pursue mutual recognition of technical standards, joint industrial cooperation, and other objectives that will impact competition in the region. Regional caucuses have the potential to play an increasing role in standard setting, particularly given the weight of Asia in global growth in the decades ahead, and a central role in economic regime building will pay important—if hard to quantify—dividends. Similarly, disciplines on export credit practices, sanitary and phytosanitary regimes, cross-border investment reviews, and ultimately even monetary and currency agreements may be worked out in the fora that tackle trade integration. The region is moving quickly, and the momentum of this power shift could push aside long-enduring political and security impediments, as demonstrated by the Taiwan-China agreement.

Is it too speculative to argue that the ECFA marks a turning point? Some think so. First, some remain skeptical that the ECFA will be implemented, or are concerned that it might be abrogated in the future.[14] However, de-

---

12. "Taiwan Seeks to Join P4 Trade Group," *The China Post*, January 30, 2010. www.chinapost.com.tw/taiwan/t-business/2010/01/30/242892/Taiwan-seeks.htm (accessed on September 15, 2010).

13. In addition to the process issue of trade promotion authority, the political reality of the crowded legislative calendar and difficult domestic agenda make US trade policy less than trusted abroad.

14. See "Fourth Round of Informal Talks on ECFA Postponed," *Taiwan Journal*, November 1, 2009. http://taiwanjournal.nat.gov.tw/site/Tj/ct.asp?xItem=73949&ctNode=413 (accessed on September 15, 2010). Such reports have surfaced regularly since the prospect of the cross-strait pact arose.

spite domestic opposition, the turbulence of the financial crisis, arms sales tensions, and other distractions, preparations for and the signing of the cross-strait agreement played out very close to the schedule described by senior Taiwanese officials in early 2009. A second argument has been that the ECFA only formalizes the gradual trade opening that has already been taking place. But as discussed in chapter 2, China and Taiwan have negotiated an agreement that goes beyond trade to include investment, services, standards, dispute resolution, joint industrial coordination, and other economic matters that go far beyond the piecemeal opening to date. Third, some—especially from Taiwan's opposition DPP and conservative think tanks in the West (Scissors 2009)—argue that cross-strait liberalization is not as important as economic links for Taiwan with the rest of the world. Our analysis suggests that the cross-strait dimension of Taiwan's economic relations holds the lion's share of potential benefits, because it is the facet of Taiwan's trade that is not already normal. Furthermore, we see already that post-ECFA Taiwan will commence FTA-like consultations with other economies, as modeled in our scenarios. Singapore was the first. President Ma has expressed a priority interest in an undertaking with Japan as well.[15] The European Chamber of Commerce Taipei is calling for consultations on an EU-Taiwan trade enhancement process, and this is being supported by the European officials. The EU has already signed an FTA with South Korea, so a Taiwanese overture would build on European links in Asia already in place. In fact, the ECCT's chairman is citing the impending Korean advantage in the European market as the reason why Taiwan should urgently undertake discussions with Europe.

The prospect of Taiwan-China deepening, the catalytic effect of this process on Taiwan's inclusion in other agreements, and pan-Asian integration may together provide a wake-up call to pull American attention back into the Asian economic policy arena. As Rupert Hammond Chambers of the US-Taiwan Business Council has put it, "If the United States doesn't have a trade policy, it doesn't have an Asia policy."[16] The United States has contemplated an FTA with Taiwan in the past. For a variety of reasons, foremost that the benefits were too modest, not enough support could be mustered for such an agreement (Lardy and Rosen 2004). This was just as well for Taiwan, since such a negotiation would have distracted Taipei from the more important matter of cross-strait distortions, antagonized Beijing, and in the end run into the US-Korea FTA problem of sitting unratified due to domestic American politics. Instead, Taiwan looks set to get cross-strait economics on track and then turn to additional

---

15. "Ma Anticipates ECFA Inking in May," *Taiwan Today*, January 21, 2010. www.taiwan today.tw/ct.asp?xItem=92456&CtNode=414 (accessed on September 15, 2010).

16. Remarks at American Enterprise Institute conference on Free Trade Agreements in Asia: Implications for Taiwan and the United States, Washington, September 21, 2009. Available at http://www.aei.org/event/100131.

undertakings that, like the TPPA, could well include the United States. The US-Taiwan FTA concept that did not make sense as a first order of business (especially for Taiwan) could well make sense for both the United States and Taiwan now, assuming that Taiwan truly capitalizes on its new special relationship with the mainland to offer a unique domicile for managing Taiwanese commercial activity.

## Security Considerations

By dismantling most non-WTO-consistent limitations on economic engagement with China, and leapfrogging ahead to the WTO+ level of liberalization pursued by other Asian economies, Taiwan is shifting its grand strategy for achieving its security aim of prosperity while maintaining the freedom to decide its own preferences with regard to political relations with China. Our conclusions in the following chapter emphasize that the ECFA is a necessary, but not sufficient, step in the direction of that prosperity. But economic interaction creates the potential for external coercion. There is a voluminous literature on economic coercion as a tool of statecraft in general (Hufbauer, Schott, and Elliott 1985), and in the case of China-Taiwan relations in particular (Tanner 2007). The prospect of deeper Taiwanese economic relations with China raises concerns for those committed to shielding Taiwan from hostile intent not just in Taiwan but in the United States and elsewhere. This is especially true given the asymmetry in economic size. It would be reckless for economists to disregard these security considerations.

What security analysts sometimes fail to consider, however, is that Taiwan's reluctance to deepen economic relations with China certainly undermines long-term independence and welfare as well. Labor-intensive and scale-economy-dependent economic activities have been migrating from Taiwan to China for decades, and will continue to do so—and if not to China, then to other lower-cost regional centers. That is not surprising and cannot practically and affordably be stopped. What *is* questionable is whether these lower- rung activities will be replaced by sufficient higher-value activities dependent on knowledge, quality institutions, and innovation, for which Taiwan can sustain a comparative advantage and thus maintain its relative wealth in the face of China's economic advantages.

Taiwan is not the only place in Asia where US economic and security interests intersect. The United States has a military presence in South Korea and Japan, while it withdrew its forces stationed in Taiwan in 1979. Japan and Korea have normalized and rapidly deepened economic relations with China without directly impinging upon the US security presence. Beijing has not overtly pressed Seoul or Tokyo to diminish their security relationships with the United States as a condition for deepening economic engagement, and in fact has acknowledged the positive role the US military plays in the region as a stabilizing force. Taiwan is unique, however, in that Beijing fundamentally rejects the legitimacy of its independent status, while the United States is a guarantor of Taiwan's ability to resolve outstanding political issues "peacefully, with the assent of Taiwan's people, and without unilateral changes" (Kan 2009, 27). In his joint statement with President Hu Jintao in Beijing in November 2009, President Obama was definitive:

> We . . . applauded the steps that the People's Republic of China and Taiwan have already taken to relax tensions and build ties across the Taiwan Strait. Our own policy, based on the three U.S.-China communiqués and the Taiwan Relations Act, supports the further development of these ties—ties that are in the interest of both sides, as well as the broader region and the United States.[17]

At the same time, the United States is realistic about the potential for warming economic ties to be manipulated to a political or security end, and will be careful in its full endorsement. As a Taiwan analyst at the US Congressional Research Service put it:

> While U.S. policy favors improvements in Taiwan-China relations, it has been silent on what should be the speed, depth, and degree of cross-strait conciliation. Some observers worry that the KMT government may be overly responsive to economic imperatives and to pressures from influential Taiwan business interests that have substantial economic investments in China. They worry that the Ma government could reach a swift accommodation with Beijing [the ECFA] that may complicate U.S. regional interests. (Dumbaugh 2009, 21)

Clearly the United States must consider deepening China-Taiwan economic relations from the security perspective as well as viewing those relations through the economic lens. At one end of the security spectrum are narrow issues arising from economic integration, including specific policy concerns. At the other end there is the broader geostrategic significance of shifting Taiwan-China dynamics. US arms sales transcend this dichotomy: narrowly, there are concerns that cross-strait chumminess could compromise the weapons systems that the United States provides. For instance, more broadly, if the United States *does* scale down defense sales in response to a diminished Taiwan threat level, then not just the Taiwan Strait arena but the larger regional strategic matrix could be altered.[18] From the US perspective, the economic consequences of that could vastly overshadow the narrowly economic trade and investment consequences

---

17. "Joint Press Statement by President Obama and President Hu of China," White House press release, November 17, 2009, Beijing. www.whitehouse.gov/the-press-office/joint-press-statement-president-obama-and-president-hu-china (accessed on September 15, 2010).

18. For instance, advanced Taiwanese undersea monitoring capabilities are strategically important for "gatekeeping" China's east coast submarine operations, which in turn affects the strategic balance in North Asia. See Dutton (2009).

of China-Taiwan relations. And while the policy of the United States is to concern itself with Taiwan's interests, US interests are overarching, and it is unclear what Taiwan's cross-strait warming trend portends for those interests. As Nancy Tucker (2002, 21) put it in a prescient 2002 essay, "[t]he issue is, if Taiwan opted for unification with China without war, would this solve or exacerbate the US security dilemma in Asia."[19] The ECFA is not unification, far from it, but it steps in that direction economically and thus forces this larger question.

One issue at the narrow end of the spectrum is export control policy. Taiwan enjoys a different US export control regime status than China: the reality of US weapons sales to Taiwan is sufficient proof of that. Some observers react to the ECFA as though it entails complete integration of Taiwan into China's economy. That is not the case. It is useful to note that Hong Kong's separate status for US export-control licensing did not change after its reversion to Chinese rule,[20] and neither will Taiwan's distinct status as a result of the ECFA. No compromises over Taiwan's technology transfer controls in particular or its national security exceptions to economic liberalization in general are contemplated in the ECFA context. Taiwan will continue to exclude dual-use sectors of the economy from opening under the ECFA. And in any case, the United States is not significantly more permissive toward Taiwan than toward China, with the exception of systems under the control and responsibility of Taiwan's armed forces and Ministry of National Defense. The United States' broad spectrum of motivations of control is the same for Taiwan as it is for China.[21] The United States has been concerned about the potential for leakage of technology and know-how in Taiwan to Chinese interests for some time, as the list of major enforcement cases from the past decade shows.[22] Some US congressmen believe US export controls for China are already too permissive, and they are likely to see additional danger in Taiwan's opening to mainland investment under separate MOUs and in other steps toward

---

19. In answer to the question that was the title of her article—"If Taiwan Chooses Unification, Should the United States Care?"—Tucker concludes that China's opportunity to redeploy and pursue other goals would be enhanced (including displacement of US presence in littoral Asia), that the regional arms balance would be upset, and that US information collection capabilities would be diminished. But note that this is not the question we are asking here; here we look at the more limited scenario of cross-strait economic deepening.

20. In the case of Hong Kong, since the reversion the United States continues to treat Hong Kong SAR and China as separate destinations for export control purposes. See www.bis.doc.gov/licensing/hkongfaqs.htm.

21. See the US Department of Commerce Country Control List as of June 28, 2010. www.access.gpo.gov/bis/ear/pdf/738spir.pdf (accessed on September 15, 2010).

22. See the October 2009 update to the US Commerce Department's Bureau of Industry and Security's Major Cases List. www.bis.doc.gov/complianceandenforcement/majorcaselist/mcl102009.pdf (accessed on September 15, 2010).

economic deepening.[23] US policymakers and officials intent on maintaining defensive arms sales to Taiwan will be concerned that the ECFA and related undertakings do not prejudice views on Taiwan's firms as separate end-users from China's firms.

Cybersecurity is the fastest-growing national security concern of the United States, as indicated by the creation of a Cyber Command in the Defense Department in 2009, and both Taiwan (by virtue of its global lead in cyber component manufacturing) and China (by virtue of its reputation for provocative cyber behavior) are prominent US concerns in this domain. Cyber attacks deemed to originate from state-sponsored hackers in China, including the December 2009 attacks on Google, frequently are obscured by hijacking Taiwan-based computers for an initial point of attack on US systems. However, it is hard to see how deeper cross-strait economic relations would make Taiwan *more* vulnerable to Chinese penetration in the cyber domain, or in more traditional espionage terms, given the breathless description of penetrability seen in the limited amount of open-source commentary on this subject (US-China Economic and Security Review Commission 2009). China's penetration of critical Taiwan cyber infrastructure both as a target of interest and as a jumping-off point for attacks on third parties is destabilizing; but in practical terms it is not clear that cross-strait deepening changes the story. After all, Chinese hackers are alleged to be able to mount attacks directly into the United States with or without intermediary fronts.

Another concern for some in the United States is the involvement of Taiwan-based firms in US military-industry supply chains. The United States has long viewed with concern the migration of semiconductor fabrication foundries and capabilities offshore, and today there remain only limited domestic production facilities for these components in the United States. Semiconductors are ubiquitous in defense systems, and it is already exceedingly difficult to ensure that production chains are entirely uncompromised. Taiwan's semiconductor foundries are leaders in this industry, and many US defense technology specialists are concerned about the implications of China-Taiwan deepening for the reliability of supply in this area. The US Defense Advanced Research Projects Agency has undertaken a Trust in Integrated Circuits Program to address these issues.[24] The US Department of Defense is acutely concerned about the country's

---

23. See Rep. Edward J. Markey's (D-MA) January 29, 2008, letter to US Commerce Secretary Carlos Gutierrez, http://markey.house.gov/docs/defense/012908_veu_china.pdf (accessed on September 15, 2010); and the letter from Senators Jon Kyl (R-AZ) and Russ Feingold (D-WI) to the White House (February 2010), http://www.chinatradeextra.com/secure/ pdf14/wto2010_0547.pdf (subscription required to view).

24. Sally Adee, "The Hunt for the Kill Switch," *IEEE Spectrum,* May 2008, http://spectrum. ieee.org/semiconductors/design/the-hunt-for-the-kill-switch (accessed on September 15, 2008).

high-performance microchip supply and the risk of a supply disruption arising from China's influence (Defense Science Board Task Force 2005).

Taiwan's semiconductor industry has migrated capabilities to China for a decade, while less-advanced segments of the information technology industry moved to China more than two decades ago. By 2001, Taiwanese semiconductor firms, including UMC, had circumvented prohibitions and were operating in China. In 2002, there was conditional lifting of Taiwan's ban on outbound semiconductor industry investment in China. The sophistication of operations has continued to expand in step with the technology frontier since then.[25] In our discussions with Taiwan officials and industry leaders in this sector, we were told that economic negotiations with Beijing would not weaken Taiwanese policy with regard to technology transfer controls for semiconductors. This does not mean a standstill, however: independent of the ECFA process Taiwan continues to revise standards for outbound investment as capabilities advance, using the gap with Taiwan's most advanced capabilities as the benchmark, rather than the utility of older generations of technology to China.[26]

The United States is concerned not only with the supply of reliable components for its own systems, but the contribution that Taiwanese high-tech investment makes to China's indigenous capabilities and hence its potential as a military peer. These are serious considerations. However, it is difficult to see how putting Taiwan on a level playing field with the likes of Malaysia, the Philippines, and other ASEAN members will change the picture. Five percent of Taiwanese citizens—upwards of 1 million people—live in mainland China, and the higher the skill level the more mobile employees are. Mainland technical capabilities have converged dramatically with those of Taiwan, and it would require a major reversal of the current level of economic intercourse, not just foot-dragging on cross-strait liberalization, to have any chance of altering this trend.

Cross-strait deepening may affect US policy toward Taiwan and China in other narrow regards as well. US counterterrorism objectives and anti-money laundering and financial crime prevention efforts, as well as the US container shipping initiative, all depend on government-to-government cooperation, which has been limited or ad hoc between Taipei and Beijing, potentially opening loopholes. The amount of cross-strait coastal smuggling is indicative of poor coordination.[27] Seabed bathymetry data are in-

---

25. "China's Emerging Semiconductor Industry." Semiconductor Industry Association, October 2003, pp. 67–88. Available at http://www.sia-online.org/cs/papers_publications/press_release_detail?pressrelease.id=225.

26. Tim Culpan, "Taiwan Will Allow LCD, Chip Investments in China (Update2)," *Bloomberg Business Week*, February 10, 2010. www.businessweek.com/news/2010-02-10/taiwan-will-allow-lcd-chip-investments-in-china-update2-.html (accessed on September 15, 2010).

27. Mark J. Valencia, "Maritime Cooperation: Bridge to the Future?" *Taiwan Review*, March 1, 2010. http://taiwanreview.nat.gov.tw/ct.asp?xItem=93451&CtNode=1337&mp=1 (accessed on September 15, 2010).

creasingly being shared in the course of joint exploration and development of undersea resources between China's CNOOC and Taiwan's CPC oil companies (Guo, undated). The dual use of such information for submarine battlespace mapping is of concern to US strategists focused on the limited egress points from the Chinese coast to open waters in the vicinity of Taiwan (Dutton 2009). As noted in Tucker (2002), it was in this context that former Ambassador Jim Lilley described Taiwan as the "cork in China's bottle." Which brings us to the question of larger strategic concerns.

## Strategic Concerns

Beyond the narrow security laundry list lies the larger strategic question: does economic deepening hand Beijing the ability to overwhelm Taiwan with influence, or undermine Taiwan's inability to assert its own functional independence from China? The question is strategic for the United States because Washington would view a sudden change in Taiwan's political status quo as not just a local matter but a shock to the region. As stated in the Taiwan Relations Act (3301b), the United States will "consider any non-peaceful efforts to determine the future of Taiwan, including boycotts or embargoes, a threat to the peace and security of the Western Pacific region and of grave concern to the United States. . . ."

Will Beijing be able to dictate terms to Taiwan by virtue of its demand for Taiwan's output or provision of Taiwan's inputs? Table 2.4 in chapter 2 summarizes the aggregate answer to this question. In terms of exports, Taiwan is greater than 40 percent reliant on China today, and under a business-as-usual scenario will grow to be more than 50 percent reliant on the mainland. If Taiwan embraces the ECFA, Taiwan's reliance on China for its exports will surpass 60 percent. In terms of Taiwan's imports, the business-as-usual rise from 14 percent to nearly 20 percent in 2020 is significant, and overshadows the additional import dependence of up to 23 percent under the ECFA. (From China's perspective, exports and imports with Taiwan increase as well, of course, but the levels are asymmetrically small in national security terms.)

Our model thus validates the general perception of rising Taiwanese export dependence found in the security literature (Tanner 2007). However, note that a significant portion of these exports is destined for reexport from China to final destinations such as the United States and Europe, and therefore if China were to impede these Taiwanese exports to exert political pressure, (1) Chinese export competitiveness would be impaired and (2) these exports would tend to find their way into alternative production chains in competing manufacturing hubs such as Malaysia, South Korea, and, in the future, India. Given that final demand lies outside China, Beijing's ability to disrupt Taiwanese production in this way would be temporary and mitigated, and would entail a hit on China's employment and industrial value added (albeit concentrated among Taiwanese foreign-invested enterprises). It has even been suggested that increased economic dependence on China could reduce the chance of a military conflict across the strait, since Beijing will have that much more ability to deliver its influence in a nonmilitary manner.[28]

If Taiwan turned back on implementing the ECFA in order to limit its export dependence on China to 50 percent instead of 60 percent, would it be strategically better off? At these magnitudes of interdependence, it is hard to see how. At these export levels, Taiwan's leverage to resist pressure is more likely to depend on its technological achievements and unique, high-value productive capabilities. By resolving cross-strait abnormalities Taiwan maximizes its opportunity to achieve those objectives.

Strategically, it is helpful to note that the future is not a binary choice between the current irregular economic relationship between China and Taiwan, on the one hand, and the "Finlandization" of Taiwan to China or sliding toward political integration, on the other. Even in the most comprehensive economic deepening scenarios under consideration, Taiwan will maintain numerous exclusions to inward investment, trade, and labor flows; it will maintain its own currency, external tariffs, and economic and political institutions; and of course it will maintain its independent and China-skeptical military forces. Taiwan will be no more incorporated into China than Mexico or Canada are to the United States under NAFTA—less so, in fact.

## Peace Dividend?

We have considered whether there is a significant risk that deeper economic relations will lead to coercive action by China to press Taiwan toward political decisions. It is also worth considering that closer economic relations can contribute to upside effects in the political and security realms as well. The direct economic benefits to Taiwan from cross-strait deepening, and additional benefits if Taiwan can then join other liberalization schemes, could build confidence and amity between these two Chinese economies. While not appearing in the February 2010 US Quadrennial Defense Review, Taiwan is routinely defined as the highest-probability US-China flashpoint in security policy planning. For instance, the US Pacific Command's April 2009 strategy mentions only one tension point with China:

---

28. This point, which is redolent of the classic observation that parties with deeper economic relations are mutually vested in not going to war, was made by Scott L. Kastner in testimony to the US-China Economic and Security Review Commission, March 18, 2010. www.uscc. gov/hearings/2010hearings/written_testimonies/10_03_18_wrt/10_03_18_kastner_statement.pdf (accessed on September 15, 2010).

Through senior leadership engagement and focus on common cause issues, such as humanitarian assistance and disaster response, progress continues toward maturing the U.S.-China military-to-military relationship. Despite this progress, tension remains across the Taiwan Strait. (US Pacific Command 2009)

If the Taiwan flashpoint is a very significant element of the US Pacific security mission, then it is worth asking what reduction in defense expenditures would be possible in the event of that threat diminishing. Unfortunately, efforts to project "peace dividends" from conflict resolution have been notoriously inaccurate in the past.[29] In the case of Taiwan, such an estimate would be particularly difficult because of the range of US concerns about China independent of Taiwan per se. US defense budgeting is done by arm of service, not by region or flashpoint, and it is not possible to establish US Pacific Command costs based on open source information. Downgrading the security priority assigned to Taiwan could well increase the cost of other priorities, even if no other China-centered concerns arise.[30] The circumstances that mitigate Taiwan as a security risk could elevate US concerns about China's power projection in the region more generally, as argued by Tucker (2002). As National Intelligence Director John Negroponte told Congress in January 2007, "China's aspirations for great-power status, threat perceptions and security strategy would drive this modernization effort even if the Taiwan problem were resolved" (as quoted in Segal, forthcoming, 116).

## Conclusions

China-Taiwan economic relations are deepening under the ECFA and other arrangements, and this reality will generate significant economic and security consequences for the United States. This reflects a broader, regionwide deepening of economic relations. The narrow, direct impact on the United States is fairly modest, but the larger strategic significance is considerable. Once the ECFA initiative has run its course Taiwan may have a more integrated economic relationship with China than it has with the United States. The ECFA will add to regional integration momentum and underscore the relative anemia of US economic engagement with Asia. The economic and strategic projections will likely encourage the United States to bolster its engagement with Taiwan bilaterally, or perhaps through something like the TPPA, and on a pan-Asian basis where possible.

---

29. For a thoughtful discussion of the topic see Gupta et al. (2002).

30. See Krepinevich (2010) for an excellent description of the extended set of security concerns around China.

Neither US economic policymakers nor the security community have reacted in detail publicly as to the US national interest implications of the ECFA. Part of the reason for this is that it remains generally unclear to most observers what economic deepening will entail. Partly the silence is due to the difficultly of mustering a robust foreign policy response, given the logjam in Washington over domestic priorities and the backlog of economic agreements (such as KORUS) that still await implementation.

The change in Taiwan's grand strategy for addressing its security aims is too portentous to be met merely with subdued US comment. For one thing, the tack Taiwan is taking toward economic deepening with China, as opposed to the status quo, is the right one economically but is fraught with risk for the time being. It has precipitated an existential debate in Taiwan that could bring more independence-minded politicians back to power in the future, leading to renewed tensions involving the United States. If, on the other hand, it proceeds apace, it could showcase the displacement of the United States by China in Asian economic leadership. Either way, the situation invites thoughtful US consideration of both its narrow economic interests and its larger strategic interests.

# 5

# Conclusion

Taiwan and China each have compelling reasons to pursue a cross-strait deepening program that includes economic normalization and goes beyond it to match the degree of liberalization occurring in other regional agreements. Cross-strait economic relations have expanded at a fast pace for decades without a comprehensive bilateral agreement, but that approach is increasingly antiquated, especially from Taiwan's perspective. The MOUs negotiated in recent years have gotten more material. The ECFA signed on June 29, 2010, supplants that piecemeal approach with a hefty initial set of openings and a comprehensive roadmap for moving further. For Taiwan the agreement is key to maintaining parity with regional peers, while for China it is a step toward winning Taiwanese hearts and minds while turning the page on vestiges of the Cold War past. The United States was respectful of the complexity of the cross-strait discussions that led to the ECFA, and helpfully refrained from injecting its interests into the conversation. Since the signing, the United States has been supportive of these developments, since they generally promote a more peaceful and prosperous outlook for the two sides.

A number of policy conclusions relevant to this deepening can be drawn from the quantitative and qualitative economic analysis in the preceding chapters. While the ECFA and early harvest round of trade-opening commitments concluded in June 2010 provide a concrete starting point, the final shape of cross-strait economic relations will take years to negotiate. Negotiation of the main body of an FTA has yet to begin. Therefore these conclusions are relevant only to the current moment, and will need to be revisited frequently to reflect the fast-moving pace of developments to come. This final chapter offers concluding observations for Taiwan, China, and the United States, in turn.

# Taiwan

## The Economic Cooperation Framework Agreement—Just a Flat Field, Not a Cathedral

More comprehensive cross-strait economic liberalization is critical to maintain Taiwan's economic competitiveness in the years ahead. Proponents and opponents alike should recognize, however, that the ECFA is just a step toward a level playing field with regional competitors that have pushed beyond MFN status to a WTO+ relationship with China, as well as other economies concluding bilateral FTAs with China. Many of the economic competitiveness benefits Taiwan achieves in the ECFA process arise from dismantling its own unilateral non-WTO-compliant restrictions on trade with China, and thereby achieving a level playing field with the other 151 members of the global trade organization.

This bears repeating: *the ECFA means a level playing field only for Taiwan.* It contributes to significantly higher GDP in 2020 versus business as usual, but it does not necessarily improve Taiwan's comparative advantage vis-à-vis its competitors, all of which will also see gains from deepening economic intercourse with China.

While the lack of liberalized economic relations with the mainland is a definite negative for Taiwan, achieving parity with ASEAN does not by itself amount to an economic strategy to secure Taiwan's future prosperity. The ECFA, or even the ECFA plus ASEAN+3, is not the solution to Taiwan's long-term prosperity. Neither is an FTA with the United States. Rather, it is just a leveling of the playing field. The question is what Taiwan *does* on that playing field once it is leveled.

The economic gains our model projects for Taiwan are predicated on historical levels of productivity in Taiwanese industries. To fulfill these projections, Taiwan must sustain that productivity.[1] Whether to pursue parity with regional competitors through the ECFA is truly the easy question for Taiwan; what strategy for national competitiveness to build on the ECFA foundation is truly the hard question. We strongly recommend that Taiwan's leaders and citizens look beyond the question of matching ASEAN's terms of economic engagement with China through the ECFA and move urgently to the other challenges involved with nurturing Taiwan's future competitiveness.

A variety of national competitiveness initiatives have been tested in Taiwan over the past two decades. In the 1990s, Taiwan aspired to be an Asia-Pacific "regional operations center," taking advantage of its Chinese language, superior legal institutions, and highly skilled population to be a headquarters domicile for firms focused on the greater China region, in a

---

1. Productivity parameters are embedded in the macroeconomic data fed into the model; see the appendices for more detail.

manner similar to Hong Kong. But at the time, restrictions on travel, labor, and investment flows across the strait made this impossible, and up until now the prospect of future political difficulties has continued to hang over the relationship, making it more risky for international investors. The disadvantageous tariff treatment and other inferiorities arising from failure to match preferential arrangement terms would make these concerns still more acute.

Lately, Taiwan's national innovation institutions such as the Industrial Technology Research Institute (ITRI)—responsible for incubating some of Taiwan's greatest firms in the past—have emphasized a sectoral focus for Taiwan's competitiveness. The ITRI is focusing on information and communications, materials and nanotechnologies, biomedicine, advanced manufacturing, and energy/environment. However, these same sectors are an industrial policy focus in other economies as well, including China, Korea, Singapore, and Japan. The ITRI is concerned about the effect of ASEAN plus China on Taiwan's "network of competition," as it would create tariff disadvantages for some areas of communications, product trade, petrochemicals, and machine tools. More than tariffs, the ITRI is concerned about standards regimes for light emitting diodes (LEDs), batteries, appliances, communications devices, data storage, and other products, as well as verification and certification of testing labs and mutual recognition of pharmaceuticals.[2] The ECFA prescribes "joint industrial cooperation" with China, which is intended to draw the parties close together on technical industry coordination matters such as these. Taiwan recognizes that there may be a thin line, however, between advantageous industrial cooperation and joint industrial policy machinations that provoke complaints from third parties, including the United States.

## Cross-Strait versus Cross-Asia

It has been argued that the best thing about the ECFA is the prospect of Taiwan's inclusion in broader plurilateral liberalization beyond it. Politically, Taiwan's freedom to negotiate with others in the region may be important; in economic terms, this study suggests that the benefits to Taiwan lie in normalizing an abnormal cross-strait economic relationship more than further liberalizing other relationships. Taiwan interacts with the rest of the WTO membership on an MFN basis; it is the relationship with China that is distorted by policy interventions to block imports and investment, and hence liberalizing that relationship stands to deliver the greatest benefit. Not only is China the facet of Taiwan's external engagement that is distorted, but it is also where Taiwan stands to gain by far the greatest growth in the years ahead.

---

2. Authors' interviews with senior ITRI staff, April 2009.

Following the ECFA with inclusion in Asia-wide WTO+ liberalization does provide some economic benefits for Taiwan. In welfare terms, these are small compared to the cross-strait gains. Probably the greatest benefit accruing to Taiwan from inclusion in regional schemes would be the definitive evidence that Taiwan was "normal" and hence as attractive a place from which to serve the "Chinese" marketplace as any other. If these Asian regimes move into the role of setting standards and otherwise providing for the "soft tissue" of international trade, then having a seat in those regimes will become still more important for Taiwan, although this is a few years off.

Taiwan officials and others trying to be supportive of Taiwanese interests should continue to be careful on this issue. If Beijing really wants to demonstrate a desire to be accommodating of the economic aspirations of the Taiwanese people, it will make clear that having concluded an opening agreement with Taiwan itself, it has no objection to others doing so. This appears to be Beijing's intention, and what other economies in the region expect; and indeed Taiwan and Singapore have, as predicted, begun consultations to that end without eliciting complaints from Beijing. With the ECFA now in place, even if Taiwan proceeds to join future regionwide agreements its prosperity will still rely on a new competitiveness strategy to build on that opening, rather than on the liberalization per se. In the past, Taiwan had only to open a new area of external economic relations and private firms would rush to take advantage. At today's more advanced level of development, Taiwan must do more than just selectively get out of the way; government must proactively step in and deliver the leadership needed to revitalize the sense of future economic achievement.

## Prospects with the United States

In assessing the prospects for a US-Taiwan FTA six years ago, Lardy and Rosen (2004) concluded that liberalizing Taiwan's trade with the United States would not provide much benefit, given the relatively free nature of that relationship already. The authors called for cross-strait normalization instead.

The same economic analysis applies today. Taiwan will generate little immediate benefit from deepening trade ties with the United States because US-Taiwan trade is already predominantly free (and areas that are not, like apparel, would pull Taiwan in a backward direction). It would be a distraction for Taiwan to get fixated on the prospect of post-ECFA FTA negotiations with the United States. This is particularly true given a backlog on US trade policy action in Asia (and globally).

That said, as argued in the previous chapter, the momentum of ASEAN plus China followed by the ECFA may well serve as a wakeup call to the United States and impel its return to Asian economic liberalization. Post-

ECFA, Taiwan will have better market access in China than the United States does. There will be calls in the United States to pursue parity with the WTO+ border barriers being negotiated in Asia, and Taiwan should be prepared to discuss participation in Asian plurilateral agreements of interest to the United States. In addition, the logic of a US-Taiwan FTA is more compelling today than it was in the past, now that Taiwan has addressed cross-strait abnormalities and has a better prospect of playing a more important role as a Greater China operations center.

## Easy on the No's

Taiwan President Ma Ying-jeou's government declared "three no's" for the cross-strait economic negotiations: no sovereignty issues would be discussed, no labor opening would be entertained, and there would be no agriculture opening. This is a simple way to fix an idea in the public imagination, and the sovereignty point is straightforward. But such blanket exclusions may not be appropriate for areas of economic activity.

In the case of agriculture, Taiwan Council of Agriculture Chairman Chen Wu-hsiung made clear that the sector would not be included in talks. "Since the issues will not be discussed, the ECFA will have no impact on Taiwanese farmers at all," he said.[3] In our quantitative results, Taiwan's agriculture and food sectors are actually a mixed bag: we do see shrinkage in output in some food sectors under the ECFA scenario, but we see growth in others. This is despite the fact that we excluded agriculture and food from liberalization assumptions as agreed upon in the ECFA; effects arise due to general changes in GDP size and equilibrium effects despite their exclusion, and as a result of China's unilateral opening of some food sectors. Moreover, these sectors are impacted under the non-ECFA scenario as well: standing still or standing apart from opening processes is certainly no guarantee of higher output in the future.

Agriculture as it exists in Taiwan today, as in most high-tech economies, is not an area of obvious comparative advantage. And yet, faced with diminishing marginal productivity gains from traditional inputs and techniques, producing high-quality food efficiently and dependably is becoming a higher-tech industry all the time. There is a strong case to be made that Taiwanese farmers are in a position to gain from more open trade with China. There is in actuality already some amount of agriculture trade between the two, though not so much in terms of foodstuffs on the Taiwanese import side. China suffers from severe challenges in regulating and insuring a healthy, pollutant-free food chain, and the mainland market for higher-value organic food products is booming. Taiwan's food

---

3. "Agriculture Issues Not on ECFA Agenda," *Taiwan News,* January 4, 2010. www.etaiwan news.com/etn/news_content.php?id=1147128&lang=eng_news&cate_img=83.jpg&cate_rss=news_Politics_TAIWAN&pg=4 (accessed on September 15, 2010).

product standards are excellent, and "Made in Taiwan" is capable of attracting premium pricing and building a market in China vastly greater than the home market. Already, many higher-end food enterprises in eastern China are Taiwan invested and managed, and Taiwanese farmers can benefit from China's consumer market growth in the same way that farmers in New Zealand, Australia, Chile, and elsewhere have. In terms of concerns about reciprocal market access for grains and crops where scale is an issue, Taiwan is not obligated to forgo high-standards regimes in a cross-strait agreement.

In terms of labor markets, in agriculture, there has already been some modest flexibility: those few investments from China into Taiwan to date obviously require staffing by the investor, and with two-way investment opening already concluded under an MOU, this will expand. Moreover, there is some discussion of permitting higher-skilled labor from China to contribute to businesses in Taiwan, and also of creating bonded assembly zones where low-cost labor from China would be permitted in order to keep Taiwanese manufacturing in Taiwan. A flexible mindset on issues including labor can improve the outcomes for Taiwan.

# China

## Focus on the Economics

Officials in Beijing generally downplayed concerns about the details of the ECFA, instead focusing on key principles such as adherence to existing WTO commitments. This gave rise to the view in Taiwan that the undertaking is not essentially economic, which is unhelpful. The benefits to Taiwan arise more from dismantling protection at home than in China, and moderate pressure from Beijing not to exclude sensitive sectors (like agriculture) could be helpful to Taiwanese negotiators in the future as they confront domestic special vested interests if there is some requirement to do so. In trade negotiating parlance, the term *gaiatsu* has been borrowed from the Japanese to describe using pressure from abroad to justify needed changes at home. If such pressure is identified as having a legitimate marketplace basis, rather than a purely political basis, it could help reset Taiwanese perceptions about the essential purpose of the agreement.

## One Eye across the Pacific

Technically, China considers the ECFA an internal matter, not a matter of bilateral external affairs, much less an undertaking with trans-Pacific considerations. Practically, Beijing is mindful that US anxieties about closer cross-strait relations could flare up and complicate matters, potentially slowing momentum, if US sensitivities are neglected. The United States has been mildly supportive of cross-strait economic deepening to date. As former American Institute in Taiwan Director Stephen Young said in mid-2009, "[t]he expansion of economic ties is consistent with our goals of helping to foster Taiwan's security while avoiding unnecessary cross-strait friction. The policies also make Taiwan more attractive as a destination for U.S. investment."[4]

While the United States has not openly communicated detailed preferences with regard to cross-strait deepening at this point, China can best ensure continued US support for the process by ensuring that the ECFA is consistent with WTO standards for preferential trade agreements and by continuing to stand out of the way of Taiwan's participation in other economic liberalization regimes, whether bilateral or plurilateral. Given US priorities, this could include Taiwan's inclusion in future TPPA discussions. A US-Taiwan trade agreement was not a first-order priority for the United States in 2010, but as Taiwan deepens its connections to China this may evolve.

# The United States

### Economic Deepening in Taiwan's Interest Is Also in the Interest of the United States

The United States is better off with a prosperous Taiwan that can afford to chart its own future course. Pursuit of that prosperity requires that Taiwan liberalize its economic relations with China in step with its regional peers. Standing still is not an option for Taiwan while all the economies around it pursue more dynamic economic links with China. Therefore the United States should welcome a cross-strait economic agreement that supports Taiwan's economic interests without undermining other imperatives. While political and security concerns may arise, these are not more acute after cross-strait deepening than they are in the event of business as usual, and they should be addressed with appropriate safeguards rather than blanket Cold War prohibitions on Chinese exports and investment in Taiwan. On the other hand, there are specific terms in the ECFA, notably "joint industrial cooperation," that may be a source of concern. The United States should clarify that such objectives, and the ECFA as a whole, are WTO-consistent and procompetitive, rather than an invitation to collusion to take global market share.

---

4. "AIT Director Calls for End to Agricultural Trade Dispute," *Taiwan Today*, June 5, 2009. www.taiwantoday.tw/fp.asp?xItem=52148&CtNode=427 (accessed on September 15, 2010).

## Follow Suit Plurilaterally and Bilaterally

Resolving remaining economic distortions between Taiwan and China is critical to Taiwan's prosperity and can lessen the prospect of security tensions in the region if managed well. But the fact that even Taiwan and China have a forward-leaning trade policy agenda underscores the relative absence of the United States from Asian economic deepening. Five years ago, the notion that Taiwan could undertake an FTA with Beijing before doing so with Washington seemed fanciful. Now the first stage of that has come to pass. As has been pointed out, if the United States does not have a trade policy for Asia, it does not really have an Asia policy.

President Obama took steps to remedy this state of affairs in 2009, opening the way to deeper involvement with ASEAN and invigorating discussions of participation in the TPPA. The bilateral agreement with South Korea signed in 2007 will be submitted for ratification in 2010. Given the difficulty of making room for trade opening in general with a crowded policy agenda, and given the limited benefits possible in US-Taiwan trade deepening, Taiwan's involvement in a plurilateral undertaking seems like a first-best notion. However, as Taiwan parlays its ECFA opening into a position of new relevance to the greater China marketplace, the logic of a US-Taiwan FTA will likely grow.

For now, the United States should reopen the lapsed TIFA talks with Taiwan at an early opportunity. These discussions can facilitate US-Taiwan progress on resolving trade and market access disputes, further preliminary discussions on bilateral investment, and—importantly—assure consultations on the nature of the ECFA's joint industrial cooperation activities and other Taiwan-China initiatives that may raise concerns in Washington.

## Economic Policy Concerns

Our model suggests that China-Taiwan economic deepening will have only minor diversionary and other negative effects on the US economy. These diversions will generally reflect China's comparative advantage rather than unfair trade terms for the United States, and in many cases will accrue to US firms manufacturing in China. Nonetheless, the United States will want to take Taiwan's implementation of trade policy commitments all the more seriously in light of displacement of US exports (for instance in textiles, transport equipment, and machinery).

Taiwanese firms may enjoy operating benefits in China that exceed the MFN-level terms extended by China to other WTO partners. For instance, some requirements for Taiwanese financial institutions will be preferential. We are not aware of US firms likely to object to these outcomes, and a reluctance to complicate delicate regional policy dynamics may trump any US government objections. China is likely to argue that Taiwan will be treated differently because relations with the island are an internal matter, and, indeed, China already maintains a separate designation for firms from Taiwan, Hong Kong, and Macao under its regulatory system. Taiwan may well argue that its firms in many sectors, such as finance, have been in a holding pattern for years to gain full entry to China and should be able to waive time requirements imposed on other firms, such as three years of profitable operations before attaining the right to apply to take deposits in banking. The United States should prepare to respond to these arguments in case these issues arise in a sector of importance.

Finally, the United States must find the time in its busy schedule of domestic and international governmental affairs to consider the China-Taiwan situation in the long sweep of history. China is not politically static; it is evolving rapidly as a polity as well as an economy. The China we deal with today is much more liberal than the totalitarian communist entity we courted to hedge against Russian aspirations three decades ago. We should not lose our conviction that the middle-income China of the future will necessarily employ more politically accountable mechanisms to manage its affairs and balance its divergent social interests. Taiwan's young democracy may end up seeding the mainland with more progressive notions of citizenship if the cultural firewalls maintained across the strait are dismantled along with trade barriers. If this comes to pass, will the United States be remembered as a proponent of Chinese reconciliation, or as a self-interested obstructionist? The answer will profoundly affect American prospects in a future world in which China is a first-order power.

# Appendices

# Appendix A

# Specification of the Global Recursive Dynamic Computable General Equilibrium Model

The model is an extension of the computable general equilibrium (CGE) models used in China WTO accession studies by Wang (1997, 1999, 2003a, 2003b) with import-embodied technology transfer and trade-policy-induced TFP growth. It is part of a family of models used widely to analyze the impact of global trade liberalization and structural adjustment programs. The model focuses on the real side of the world economy and incorporates considerable detail on sectoral output and real trade flows, both bilateral and global. However, this structural detail is obtained at the cost of not explicitly modeling financial markets, interest rates, and inflation. The model is not designed to generate short-term macroeconomic forecasts. Rather, under exogenous assumptions on future world economic growth it generates the pattern of production and trade resulting from world economic adjustment to the shocks specified in the alternative policy scenarios using a recursive dynamic framework.

## Structure of the Model

The model has 20 fully endogenized regions and 32 production sectors in each region to represent the world economy.[1] There are six primary fac-

---

1. See table B.1 in appendix B for the correspondence between regions in the model, GTAP regions, and country names. See table B.2 for the correspondence between sectors in the model, GTAP, and International Standard Industrial Classifications (ISIC).

tors of production: agricultural land, natural resources, capital, agricultural labor, unskilled labor, and skilled labor. Unskilled labor has a basic education, while skilled labor has more advanced training. Agricultural labor has little or no education and works only in the farm sector. Natural resources and agricultural land are sector-specific, while capital, unskilled labor, and skilled labor are assumed to be mobile across sectors, but immobile across regions. All commodity and factor markets are assumed to clear through market prices. The details of intraperiod equilibrium structure and interperiod linkages are similar with what is described in Wang (2003a, 2003b).[2]

## Gains from Trade

Three types of gains from trade liberalization are captured by the model:

1. the gains from more efficient utilization of resources leading to a one-time permanent increase in GDP and social welfare;

2. more rapid physical capital accumulation from a "medium-run growth bonus" that compounds the efficiency gain from trade liberalization and leads to higher saving and investment; and

3. (through capital and intermediate goods) technology transfer among regions, which links sector-specific TFP growth with each region's imports of capital- and technology-intensive products.[3] Technology transfer is assumed to flow in one direction—from more-developed to less-developed regions.

## Savings and Capital Accumulation

Accumulation patterns for the capital stock in the model depend upon depreciation and gross real investment rates, which set exogenously based on forecasts from a world macroeconomic model.[4] However, household

---

2. A detailed algebraic specification of the model is in appendix B. The structures of production and consumption as well as the price system in the model are illustrated in figures B.1–B.3.

3. Empirical evidence suggests that there is strong positive feedback between trade expansion and productivity growth. Trade liberalization increases the prevalence of technology transfer as trade barriers are reduced. Firms in the liberalized regions will import more capital- and technology-intensive goods as both investment and intermediate inputs from abroad at cheaper prices. Those goods are usually embodied with advanced technology from other countries, thus stimulating productivity growth for all production factors.

4. The macroeconomic assumptions for this exercise are taken from Economist Intelligence Unit country forecasts.

savings, government surplus (deficit), and foreign capital inflows (foreign savings) are assumed to be perfect substitutes, and collectively constitute the source of gross investment in each region. This means that changes in trade balance, which directly affect foreign saving, are assumed to have only a partial effect on aggregate real investment in the region. Instead, they lead to an equilibrium adjustment in the domestic saving rate, which partially offsets the change in foreign saving.

Household saving decisions are endogenous in the model. They represent future consumption goods for the household sector with zero subsistence quantity (by assuming intertemporal separable preferences, extended linear expenditure system [ELES] demand). Government surplus (deficit) is the difference between the government's tax revenues and its expenditures, the latter fixed as a percentage of each region's GDP based on forecasts from the Economist Intelligence Unit (EIU).

Foreign capital inflows or outflows are determined by the accumulation of the balance of trade, which is also fixed as a percentage of GDP in each region based on the macro model's projections, except for the old 15 EU member countries (which are fixed as an international numeraire). The model does not include financial markets or portfolio investment. The trade balance is the only source of foreign savings (as an inflow or outflow). There is no explicit specification of FDI. However, FDI is partially captured in trade flows, because in order to convert FDI (other than mergers of existing companies in the same region) into production capital, certain technology and equipment will be purchased via international trade.

## Total Factor Productivity Growth

Economywide and sector-specific TFP growth variables exist for each region in the model. The economywide TFP variable is solved endogenously in the baseline calibration to match a prespecified path of real GDP growth in each region based on forecasts from the EIU. Then the economywide TFP variable is fixed when alternative scenarios are simulated; in such a case, the growth rate of real GDP and the sector-specific TFP variables that link productivity growth and imports are solved endogenously.

## Baseline Calibration

The model is calibrated around a 2004 world social accounting matrix (SAM) based on Version 7 of the GTAP database (Badri and Walmsley 2008). Details of this type of multiregional SAM and its construction from the GTAP database are described in Wang (1994). The model is implemented using the General Algebraic Modeling System and solved in levels.

Because the possible Taiwan-China agreement, like other FTAs in East Asia, will be phased in over a transition period, a baseline is established from 2005–20 using a reference growth path of the world economy with the implementation of already agreed-upon FTAs in East Asia without Taiwan's participation. This calibrated baseline will serve as a basis of comparison for scenarios in which Taiwan and other East Asian economies adopt different trade policy measures. The difference between these policy simulation scenarios and the baseline is our estimate of the potential gains and losses for Taiwan and other economies resulting from the trade policy measure in question.

Table A.1 summarizes the major macroeconomic assumptions and results from the baseline calibration. It uses the economywide TFP variable in each region as a residual and adjustment mechanism to match the prespecified real GDP growth rate under assumptions on the three macroeconomic variables (gross investment, government spending, and balance of trade) in the model. The baseline includes the termination of the Multi-Fiber Arrangement in 2005, the reimposition of quota restrictions for China's textile and wearing apparel exports to the EU-15 countries and the United States during 2006–08, and EU enlargement in 2007 to include the 12 new member countries. It also incorporates the impact of the recent world economic crisis. Gross investment, government expenditure, and balance of trade for 2005–20 are specified as percentages of GDP and are based on EIU forecasts. The extent of China's tariff reduction in its implementation of its WTO commitment is aggregated from the Harmonized Commodity Description and Coding System (HS) tariff schedules at the six-digit level based on China's final official offer (November 2001) and weighted by 2000 import data from the World Bank. Taiwan's tariff reduction in implementing its WTO commitment is based on Taiwan's official WTO offer downloaded from the WTO website. It is also aggregated from the six-digit HS tariff schedules and weighted by Taiwan's import data in 2001. All nontariff barriers of manufacturing products in both China and Taiwan are reduced by 10 percent each year from 2005 and stay at 50 percent in relation to the initial level after 2010.

Already agreed-upon FTAs in East Asia are implemented according to their established time schedule. Barriers to imports between China and ASEAN countries are assumed to be reduced according to the ASEAN plus China FTA and set to zero by 2010 (Vietnam by 2015). The sector structure of the protection reduction is based on what China and ASEAN countries reported to the WTO and aggregated from HS six-digit tariff lines. For all other already agreed-upon FTAs in East Asia, we assume there will be a 70 percent reduction in bilateral protection rates in the first year the agreement comes into force, then a reduction by 90 percent after five years of implementation and to zero in the final year of the implementation period. The East Asian FTAs included and the year of implementation are listed in table A.2. In all these FTAs, we assume three agricultural sectors are not included in the import protection reduction: rice, other grains, and livestock.

China's tariff collection is significantly below its nominal tariff level because of a large share of processing trade in total trade and extensive import duty exemptions. By 2006, about 48 percent of all imports in China were inputs used in production of exports and were exempted from tariffs.

Several studies have shown that failing to account for the presence of duty exemptions in China's trade regime leads to a serious overestimate of the impact of China's WTO entry at both aggregate and sectoral levels (Ianchovichina, Martin, and Fukase 2000; Lejour 2000). By using China's 2004 custom statistics, we incorporated China's processing trade and duty exemption pattern by sectors and by import sources into the baseline calibration, which scales down China's tariff level by routine-specific information. The initial protection rate at 2010 for each of the economies in our model is listed in table A.3, which is the import protection level after all above-mentioned adjustments.

## Simulations

We conducted the following six simulations to assess the policy impact of likely trade liberalization scenarios in the East Asia region:

1. China-Taiwan ECFA (Taiwan WTO+) with an early harvest program in 2011, which starts extending to all products except agriculture in 2013;

2. Taiwan joins ASEAN+1 (China) in 2013;

3. ASEAN+3 (China, Japan, and South Korea) is formed in 2013 with no policy response from Taiwan;

4. China-Taiwan ECFA as in (1) while the region moves to form ASEAN+3 in 2013;

5. Taiwan joins ASEAN+1 in 2013 while the region moves to form ASEAN+3 in 2013; and

6. Taiwan joins the newly formed ASEAN+3 in 2013.

As part of the ECFA, both China and Taiwan published a list of products to be included in the early harvest program. Under this program, listed products, specified at the eight-digit HS level, will follow an expedited liberalization schedule with zero tariffs by 2013. We can represent only aggregate sector-level tariffs and not individual products in our model. So tariff reduction for early harvest products was approximated by reducing a fraction of the aggregate sector tariff, the fraction being equal to early harvest products' share of imports in the sector.[5] The bilateral tariff reduction schedules for China and Taiwan under the ECFA are listed in table A.4.

For each of these policy simulation scenarios, we assume that participants reduce tariffs and nontariff barriers by 70 percent at the initial implementation year and to zero after five years, while maintaining their current levels of protection against imports from other regions (nonmember countries). All the assumptions and model parameters are exactly the same as the baseline except for the relevant policy changes. Hence, the difference between the policy simulations and the baseline is attributable to policy changes in the particular scenario only.

For each of the six scenarios, the CGE model generates results on the impact of policy actions on social welfare, terms of trade, volume of trade, output, consumption, real wages, and changes in prices and resource allocation. The difference in results generated by the six policy-response scenarios and the baseline scenario provides estimates of the impact of each of the six alternative policy options. However, these are outcomes from conditional projections rather than forecasts. In reality, actual trade and output patterns are affected by many more factors than just trade liberalization, such as domestic macroeconomic and income tax policy changes, which are not taken into account in our analysis.

---

5. The shares were calculated using 2009 trade data available at the eight-digit HS level from China Customs, http://english. customs.gov.cn. The implicit assumption is that the proportion of tariff cut for each individual product at the eight-digit HS level is the same within a GTAP goods-producing sector.

**Table A.1  Macroeconomic assumption for baseline calibration**

| | China | Taiwan | Hong Kong | Singapore | Korea | Japan | Australia | United States | EU-15 | EU-12 |
|---|---|---|---|---|---|---|---|---|---|---|
| **Average annual growth rate, 2010–20** (percent) | | | | | | | | | | |
| **Real GDP** | 6.5 | 3.9 | 3.0 | 4.0 | 4.3 | 0.8 | 2.9 | 2.5 | 1.9 | 3.1 |
| **Labor force** | 0.3 | 1.2 | 0.5 | 1.1 | 0.3 | -0.7 | 0.8 | 0.6 | 0 | -0.6 |
| **Skilled labor** | 3.5 | 1.6 | 1.9 | 1.4 | 1.8 | -0.5 | 1.0 | 0.8 | 0.2 | -0.1 |
| Total factor productivity | 2.6 | 1.5 | 1.1 | 1.0 | 2.6 | 0.8 | 0.6 | 1.6 | 1.3 | 2.1 |
| Capital stock | 9.4 | 5.4 | 2.2 | 4.1 | 3.7 | 1.4 | 3.7 | 2.1 | 1.5 | 3.2 |
| Real gross investment | 5.6 | 10.4 | 2.8 | 3.9 | 4.4 | 3.0 | 2.5 | 6.3 | 2.6 | 3.3 |
| Government spending | 8.3 | 1.7 | 1.3 | 0.4 | 1.2 | -1.9 | 3.0 | 2.9 | 0.9 | 1.7 |
| Real exports | 6.1 | 5.9 | 2.0 | 2.9 | 6.4 | 3.2 | 1.0 | 4.1 | 3.5 | 3.4 |
| Real imports | 5.8 | 5.4 | 4.0 | 4.5 | 4.5 | 2.0 | 4.3 | 2.6 | 2.2 | 2.9 |
| Household consumption | 7.4 | 1.3 | 4.8 | 8.8 | 4.6 | 0.7 | 3.6 | 1.5 | 1.6 | 3.4 |
| Total absorption | 6.8 | 3.8 | 4.1 | 6.3 | 4.0 | 0.7 | 3.2 | 2.5 | 1.6 | 3.1 |
| **Share of skilled labor** (percent) | | | | | | | | | | |
| 2010 | 15.0 | 28.7 | 29.2 | 41.4 | 19.8 | 28.5 | 38.3 | 34.8 | 32.7 | 27.3 |
| 2020 | 20.6 | 29.8 | 33.7 | 42.3 | 22.9 | 29.2 | 39.0 | 35.5 | 33.4 | 28.6 |
| **Gross investment as percent of GDP** | | | | | | | | | | |
| 2010 | 42.8 | 16.1 | 16.5 | 24.3 | 25.6 | 20.2 | 25.2 | 11.6 | 15.8 | 22.5 |
| 2020 | 39.3 | 29.7 | 16.1 | 24.0 | 26.1 | 24.9 | 24.3 | 16.6 | 17.0 | 22.9 |
| **Government spending as percent of GDP** | | | | | | | | | | |
| 2010 | 15.2 | 15.0 | 9.1 | 12.5 | 19.8 | 20.1 | 19.8 | 21.4 | 21.7 | 14.7 |
| 2020 | 17.9 | 12.1 | 7.7 | 8.8 | 14.8 | 15.2 | 20.1 | 22.2 | 19.7 | 12.8 |
| **Balance of trade as percent of GDP** | | | | | | | | | | |
| 2010 | 4.9 | 15.3 | 16.4 | 16.3 | -1.4 | -0.2 | -0.9 | -3.8 | 1.5 | -1.9 |
| 2020 | 1.8 | 17.0 | 7.7 | -4.8 | 1.3 | 1.1 | -4.6 | -2.8 | 3.6 | -1.7 |

(continued on next page)

**Table A.1  Macroeconomic assumption for baseline calibration** (*continued*)

| | Indonesia | Malaysia | Philippines | Thailand | Vietnam | Rest of East Asia | South Asia | Rest of the Americas | Rest of high-income countries | Rest of the world | World average |
|---|---|---|---|---|---|---|---|---|---|---|---|
| **Average annual growth rate, 2010–20** (percent) | | | | | | | | | | | |
| **Real GDP** | **4.9** | **4.5** | **5.7** | **4.4** | **4.8** | **10.7** | **6.4** | **3.5** | **2.3** | **4.2** | **2.9** |
| **Labor force** | **1.4** | **2.0** | **2.2** | **0.3** | **1.4** | **1.5** | **1.9** | **1.5** | **0.5** | **1.9** | **1.2** |
| **Skilled labor** | **4.1** | **4.3** | **4.3** | **2.1** | **3.6** | **4.8** | **4.1** | **3.4** | **0.7** | **4.3** | **2.0** |
| Total factor productivity | 1.2 | 2.0 | 3.0 | 3.6 | 1.2 | 6.4 | 1.7 | 0.7 | 0.6 | -0.1 | 1.5 |
| Capital stock | 6.2 | 3.4 | 4.1 | 1.8 | 6.8 | 7.9 | 8.9 | 3.7 | 2.8 | 5.5 | 3.2 |
| Real gross investment | 7.2 | 6.4 | 9.5 | 9.2 | 4.8 | 11.2 | 6.9 | 5.2 | 3.5 | 5.2 | 4.7 |
| Government spending | 2.8 | 1.8 | 3.2 | 4.3 | 6.0 | 11.9 | 8.0 | 2.3 | 2.0 | 4.2 | 2.4 |
| Real exports | 3.8 | 4.4 | 7.3 | 5.7 | 5.7 | 10.6 | 5.8 | 2.8 | 1.4 | 1.0 | 3.8 |
| Real imports | 5.3 | 4.8 | 6.4 | 5.2 | 5.1 | 9.0 | 6.2 | 4.2 | 2.7 | 5.4 | 3.9 |
| Household consumption | 4.8 | 5.0 | 5.3 | 1.5 | 3.6 | 8.9 | 6.3 | 3.4 | 2.1 | 4.5 | 2.5 |
| Total absorption | 5.3 | 4.8 | 5.8 | 4.3 | 4.2 | 10.0 | 6.7 | 3.6 | 2.4 | 4.6 | 2.9 |
| **Share of skilled labor** (percent) | | | | | | | | | | | |
| 2010 | **7.5** | **26.1** | **17.9** | **12.6** | **2.5** | **6.1** | **6.9** | **19.0** | **35.1** | **21.6** | **17.3** |
| 2020 | **9.8** | **32.7** | **21.9** | **14.9** | **3.0** | **8.4** | **8.6** | **23.0** | **35.8** | **27.3** | **20.7** |
| **Gross investment as percent of GDP** | | | | | | | | | | | |
| 2010 | **23.8** | **16.9** | **14.4** | **22.1** | **44.4** | **21.7** | **31.5** | **18.7** | **19.8** | **23.6** | |
| 2020 | **29.6** | **20.3** | **20.5** | **34.6** | **44.5** | **22.7** | **33.0** | **21.9** | **22.2** | **26.1** | |
| **Government spending as percent of GDP** | | | | | | | | | | | |
| 2010 | **9.1** | **15.8** | **10.5** | **14.1** | **6.0** | **10.4** | **11.0** | **14.9** | **19.6** | **18.1** | |
| 2020 | **7.5** | **12.2** | **8.3** | **14.0** | **6.7** | **11.7** | **12.8** | **13.3** | **19.0** | **18.1** | |
| **Balance of trade as percent of GDP** | | | | | | | | | | | |
| 2010 | **2.5** | **20.3** | **-1.0** | **7.0** | **-14.6** | **18.6** | **-5.8** | **-1.9** | **5.6** | **1.5** | |
| 2020 | **-2.3** | **19.2** | **-2.4** | **8.2** | **-9.0** | **23.5** | **-10.9** | **-2.5** | **5.0** | **-3.1** | |

Note: Data in boldface are set exogenously.

*Sources:* Real GDP growth rates are taken from the Economist Intelligence Unit; labor force projection is from the International Labor Organization; skilled labor growth rates for developed countries are based on years of schooling estimates from the World Bank, and rates for developing countries are based on projections of college enrollments made by the World Bank.

**Table A.2   Regional free trade agreements**

| Partner countries | Year of implementation |
|---|---|
| South Korea, Singapore | 2006 |
| South Korea, United States | 2011 |
| South Korea, ASEAN | 2007 |
| Japan, Singapore | 2007 |
| Japan, Malaysia | 2006 |
| Japan, Thailand | 2007 |
| Japan, Indonesia | 2008 |
| Japan, Philippines | 2008 |
| Japan, ASEAN | 2008 |
| China, Hong Kong | 2004 |
| China, Singapore | 2008 |
| China, ASEAN | 2005 |
| China, Australia | 2005 |
| Australia, ASEAN | 2010 |

ASEAN = Association of Southeast Asian Nations.

**Table A.3  Trade-weighted protection rate by sector and region, 2010**

| Sector | China | Taiwan | Hong Kong | Singapore | Korea | Japan | Australia | United States | EU-15 | EU-12 |
|---|---|---|---|---|---|---|---|---|---|---|
| Rice | 43.2 | 402.4 | 0 | 0 | 420.9 | 395.4 | 0 | 3.5 | 83.8 | 24.5 |
| Other grains | 38.7 | 1.5 | 0 | 0 | 3.9 | 51.8 | 0 | 0.1 | 12.7 | 14.1 |
| Vegetables and fruits | 11.2 | 25.6 | 0 | 0 | 80.2 | 6.8 | 0.9 | 0.5 | 14.7 | 6.9 |
| Nongrain crops | 7.3 | 1.7 | 0 | 0 | 54.0 | 1.3 | 0.1 | 7.4 | 4.4 | 1.8 |
| Livestock | 12.1 | 2.0 | 0 | 0 | 5.5 | 7.2 | 0 | 0.1 | 1.3 | 0.5 |
| Meat and dairy products | 10.5 | 28.2 | 0 | 0 | 31.3 | 53.4 | 0.5 | 5.0 | 29.8 | 6.4 |
| Sugar | 24.8 | 74.2 | 0 | 0 | 4.2 | 209.8 | 0 | 38.6 | 104.3 | 35.8 |
| Other processed food | 5.0 | 13.8 | 0 | 0 | 30.2 | 11.1 | 2.6 | 5.5 | 7.8 | 2.7 |
| Beverages and tobacco | 18.2 | 17.3 | 0 | 3 | 56.3 | 19.3 | 8.3 | 2.2 | 7.3 | 5.2 |
| Forest and fishery products | 1.2 | 12.4 | 0 | 0 | 8.5 | 2.2 | 0.2 | 0.1 | 2.0 | 1.7 |
| Oil and gas | 0.1 | 5.8 | 0 | 0 | 4.5 | 0 | 0 | 0.2 | 0 | 0.1 |
| Coal and other minerals | 0.6 | 0.1 | 0 | 0 | 1.2 | 0.1 | 0.1 | 0.1 | 0 | 0.2 |
| Textiles | 7.1 | 6.1 | 0 | 0 | 9.4 | 7.0 | 12.7 | 7.5 | 4.5 | 1.3 |
| Wearing apparel | 9.9 | 11.8 | 0 | 0 | 11.7 | 9.6 | 20.6 | 10.0 | 7.3 | 5.0 |
| Leather products | 4.8 | 4.2 | 0 | 0 | 8.0 | 12.6 | 9.5 | 11.8 | 5.2 | 2.7 |
| Other light manufactures | 8.2 | 2.4 | 0 | 0 | 8.7 | 0.9 | 3.6 | 1.1 | 1.2 | 0.9 |
| Wood and paper products | 2.7 | 1.6 | 0 | 0 | 3.2 | 1.0 | 3.5 | 0.2 | 0.2 | 0.2 |
| Petroleum and coal products | 6.3 | 5.4 | 0 | 0 | 5.1 | 2.0 | 0.6 | 1.3 | 1.3 | 0.7 |
| Chemical, rubber, and plastic products | 6.2 | 2.7 | 0 | 0 | 6.4 | 0.9 | 2.8 | 1.4 | 1.3 | 0.5 |
| Mineral products | 8.3 | 6.0 | 0 | 0 | 7.6 | 0.5 | 4.1 | 3.4 | 1.9 | 0.6 |
| Metal and metal products | 3.8 | 1.6 | 0 | 0 | 3.2 | 0.6 | 3.3 | 1.0 | 0.8 | 0.8 |
| Motor vehicles and parts | 16.1 | 23.4 | 0 | 0 | 8.0 | 0 | 8.5 | 1.1 | 3.2 | 0.7 |
| Other transport equipment | 2.8 | 1.6 | 0 | 0 | 2.0 | 0 | 0.8 | 0.5 | 1.1 | 0.6 |
| Electronic equipment | 1.3 | 0.2 | 0 | 0 | 1.1 | 0 | 0.8 | 0.3 | 1.3 | 0.5 |
| Machinery and equipment | 4.6 | 2.4 | 0 | 0 | 6.1 | 0.1 | 3.3 | 1.1 | 0.9 | 0.4 |

| Sector | Indonesia | Malaysia | Philippines | Thailand | Vietnam | Rest of East Asia | South Asia | Rest of the Americas | Rest of high-income countries | Rest of world |
|---|---|---|---|---|---|---|---|---|---|---|
| Rice | 16.4 | 0 | 49.8 | 22.9 | 19.0 | 3.4 | 20.6 | 13.9 | 3.4 | 14.9 |
| Other grains | 1.5 | 0 | 5.3 | 27.3 | 2.7 | 11.3 | 12.0 | 7.5 | 51.9 | 16.8 |
| Vegetables and fruits | 4.8 | 4.9 | 14.5 | 34.0 | 26.1 | 12.2 | 29.2 | 8.8 | 7.0 | 12.8 |
| Nongrain crops | 1.0 | 30.7 | 5.0 | 21.9 | 5.1 | 4.0 | 11.6 | 2.7 | 22.0 | 8.1 |
| Livestock | 2.2 | 0.4 | 8.0 | 3.8 | 3.3 | 7.2 | 11.4 | 4.1 | 14.7 | 6.0 |
| Meat and dairy products | 2.6 | 0.4 | 14.2 | 37.1 | 19.1 | 10.7 | 16.6 | 4.5 | 90.3 | 17.1 |
| Sugar | 34.0 | 0 | 26.1 | 23.5 | 9.3 | 14.7 | 54.3 | 13.1 | 11.5 | 16.1 |
| Other processed food | 4.6 | 2.6 | 4.3 | 29.5 | 14.7 | 9.6 | 52.9 | 10.3 | 18.3 | 12.8 |
| Beverages and tobacco | 32.1 | 215 | 6.5 | 53.3 | 65.8 | 32.2 | 113.4 | 18.2 | 15.6 | 37.0 |
| Forest and fishery products | 1.9 | 1.3 | 1.5 | 8.3 | 3.3 | 6.1 | 5.8 | 8.3 | 1.1 | 12.4 |
| Oil and gas | 0 | 2.5 | 3.0 | 0 | 2.0 | 0.1 | 9.6 | 3.2 | 0 | 0.5 |
| Coal and other minerals | 1.7 | 0.1 | 3.3 | 1.1 | 2.5 | 5.4 | 15.2 | 2.0 | 0 | 1.4 |
| Textiles | 7.8 | 13.3 | 6.3 | 19.8 | 30.7 | 14.1 | 16.8 | 8.3 | 3.9 | 13.8 |
| Wearing apparel | 10.1 | 16.5 | 14.2 | 35.4 | 44.8 | 24.9 | 17.4 | 14.2 | 6.8 | 17.1 |
| Leather products | 4.2 | 10.0 | 10.5 | 9.4 | 18.3 | 18.4 | 14.2 | 12.1 | 4.5 | 14.6 |
| Other light manufactures | 9.0 | 6.6 | 7.6 | 6.2 | 22.1 | 13.4 | 15.2 | 15.0 | 0.5 | 7.4 |
| Wood and paper products | 3.4 | 6.4 | 5.6 | 15.7 | 11.0 | 11.9 | 14.4 | 5.5 | 0.3 | 9.7 |
| Petroleum and coal products | 2.0 | 6.8 | 2.4 | 1.1 | 14.5 | 8.9 | 16.7 | 6.7 | 0.4 | 10.0 |
| Chemical, rubber, and plastic products | 4.3 | 4.0 | 4.7 | 10.7 | 4.3 | 6.1 | 13.7 | 5.3 | 0.4 | 7.0 |
| Mineral products | 5.0 | 10.6 | 6.5 | 13.3 | 15.7 | 11.1 | 17.9 | 8.6 | 0.5 | 10.9 |
| Metal and metal products | 4.9 | 6.0 | 3.9 | 7.6 | 4.5 | 8.9 | 15.4 | 5.2 | 0.2 | 7.5 |
| Motor vehicles and parts | 13.2 | 45.5 | 10.1 | 27.7 | 33.3 | 30.5 | 34.5 | 8.7 | 0.7 | 10.6 |
| Other transport equipment | 4.4 | 3.4 | 6.5 | 4.4 | 13.6 | 9.9 | 9.9 | 8.0 | 0.5 | 5.1 |
| Electronic equipment | 1.8 | 1.0 | 0.3 | 4.2 | 7.6 | 9.3 | 4.8 | 4.4 | 0 | 5.5 |
| Machinery and equipment | 3.3 | 4.4 | 3.2 | 7.5 | 6.4 | 11.1 | 13.2 | 6.0 | 0.3 | 6.4 |

*Source:* Global Trade Analysis Project Version 7 database; and authors' calculations.

159

**Table A.4  Percent reduction from 2010 tariff levels**

| | 2011 | 2012 | 2013 | 2014 | 2015 | 2016 | 2017 |
|---|---|---|---|---|---|---|---|
| **China's ECFA schedule** | | | | | | | |
| Rice | | | | | | | |
| Other grains | | | Sectors excluded from FTA | | | | |
| Fruits and vegetables | 5.8 | 11.7 | 75.3 | 81.4 | 87.6 | 93.8 | 100.0 |
| Nongrain crops | 0 | 0 | 70.0 | 77.5 | 85.0 | 92.5 | 100.0 |
| Livestock | | | Sector excluded from FTA | | | | |
| Meat and milk products | 0 | 0 | 70.0 | 77.5 | 85.0 | 92.5 | 100.0 |
| Sugar | 0 | 0 | 70.0 | 77.5 | 85.0 | 92.5 | 100.0 |
| Other processed food products | 4.8 | 9.5 | 72.9 | 79.6 | 86.4 | 93.2 | 100.0 |
| Tobacco and beverages | 0 | 0 | 70.0 | 77.5 | 85.0 | 92.5 | 100.0 |
| Forest and fishery products | 0 | 0 | 70.0 | 77.5 | 85.0 | 92.5 | 100.0 |
| Oil and gas | 0 | 0 | 70.0 | 77.5 | 85.0 | 92.5 | 100.0 |
| Coal and other mineral products | 0 | 0 | 70.0 | 77.5 | 85.0 | 92.5 | 100.0 |
| Textile | 33.8 | 67.7 | 90.3 | 92.7 | 95.2 | 97.6 | 100.0 |
| Wearing apparel | 34.3 | 68.6 | 90.6 | 92.9 | 95.3 | 97.6 | 100.0 |
| Leather and sporting goods | 1.7 | 3.4 | 71.5 | 78.6 | 85.7 | 92.9 | 100.0 |
| Other light manufactures | 14.5 | 29.0 | 78.7 | 84.0 | 89.4 | 94.7 | 100.0 |
| Wood and paper products | 0 | 0 | 70.0 | 77.5 | 85.0 | 92.5 | 100.0 |
| Petroleum, coal, and other mineral products | 33.5 | 67.0 | 90.1 | 92.6 | 95.0 | 97.5 | 100.0 |
| Chemical, rubber, and plastic products | 16.5 | 32.9 | 79.9 | 84.9 | 89.9 | 95.0 | 100.0 |
| Mineral products | 8.7 | 17.4 | 77.8 | 83.4 | 88.9 | 94.5 | 100.0 |
| Metal and metal products | 0 | 0 | 70.0 | 77.5 | 85.0 | 92.5 | 100.0 |
| Motor vehicles and parts | 30.8 | 61.5 | 88.5 | 91.3 | 94.2 | 97.1 | 100.0 |
| Transport equipment | 24.5 | 49.1 | 84.7 | 88.5 | 92.4 | 96.2 | 100.0 |
| Electronic equipment | 0.3 | 0.3 | 70.0 | 77.6 | 85.1 | 92.4 | 100.0 |
| Machinery and equipment | 5.8 | 11.6 | 73.5 | 80.1 | 86.7 | 93.4 | 100.0 |
| **Taiwan's ECFA schedule** | | | | | | | |
| Rice | | | | | | | |
| Other grains | | | | | | | |
| Fruits and vegetables | | | Sectors excluded from FTA | | | | |
| Nongrain crops | | | | | | | |
| Livestock | | | | | | | |
| Meat and milk products | 0 | 0 | 70.0 | 77.5 | 85.0 | 92.5 | 100.0 |
| Sugar | 0 | 0 | 70.0 | 77.5 | 85.0 | 92.5 | 100.0 |
| Other processed food products | 0 | 0 | 70.0 | 77.5 | 85.0 | 92.5 | 100.0 |
| Tobacco and beverages | 0 | 0 | 70.0 | 77.5 | 85.0 | 92.5 | 100.0 |
| Forest and fishery products | 0 | 0 | 70.0 | 77.5 | 85.0 | 92.5 | 100.0 |
| Oil and gas | 0 | 0 | 70.0 | 77.5 | 85.0 | 92.5 | 100.0 |
| Coal and other mineral products | 0 | 0 | 70.0 | 77.5 | 85.0 | 92.5 | 100.0 |
| Textiles | 12.5 | 25.0 | 77.5 | 83.1 | 88.8 | 94.4 | 100.0 |
| Wearing apparel | 0 | 0 | 70.0 | 77.5 | 85.0 | 92.5 | 100.0 |
| Leather and sporting goods | 0 | 0 | 70.0 | 77.5 | 85.0 | 92.5 | 100.0 |
| Other light manufactures | 10.7 | 21.0 | 76.3 | 82.3 | 88.0 | 94.0 | 100.0 |
| Wood and paper products | 0 | 0 | 70.0 | 77.5 | 85.0 | 92.5 | 100.0 |
| Petroleum, coal, and other mineral products | 26.7 | 53.5 | 86.0 | 89.5 | 93.0 | 96.5 | 100.0 |
| Chemical, rubber, and plastic products | 12.1 | 24.1 | 77.2 | 83.0 | 88.8 | 94.2 | 100.0 |

**Table A.4    Percent reduction from 2010 tariff levels** *(continued)*

|  | 2011 | 2012 | 2013 | 2014 | 2015 | 2016 | 2017 |
|---|---|---|---|---|---|---|---|
| **Taiwan's ECFA schedule** | | | | | | | |
| Mineral products | 3.8 | 7.8 | 72.3 | 79.2 | 86.2 | 93.1 | 100.0 |
| Metal and metal products | 0 | 0 | 70.0 | 77.5 | 85.0 | 92.5 | 100.0 |
| Motor vehicles and parts | 0 | 0 | 70.0 | 77.5 | 85.0 | 92.5 | 100.0 |
| Transport equipment | 49.9 | 100.0 | 100.0 | 100.0 | 100.0 | 100.0 | 100.0 |
| Electronic equipment | 2.4 | 2.4 | 70.7 | 78.0 | 85.4 | 92.7 | 100.0 |
| Machinery and equipment | 13.9 | 28.1 | 78.5 | 83.8 | 89.1 | 94.7 | 100.0 |

ECFA = Economic Cooperation Framework Agreement; FTA = free trade agreement.

*Source:* Authors' calculations.

# Appendix B

# Algebraic Specification of the Model

This appendix provides a detailed mathematical specification of the 20-region, 32-sector recursive dynamic computable general equilibrium (CGE) model for world production and trade used in this study (see tables B.1 and B.2). The structures of production and consumption as well as the price system in the model are illustrated in figures B.1 to B.3.

## Notation

- Regions are defined in set $R$ and indexed by $r$ or $s$
- Sectors are defined in set $I$ and indexed by $i$ or $j$
- Agricultural sectors are defined as a subset of $I$: $IAG(I)$
- Natural-resource-based sectors are defined as a subset of $I$: $RES(I)$
- Primary factors are defined in set $F$ and indexed by $f$.

## Conventions

An uppercase English letter indicates variables, unless they have a bar on top, in which case that variable is always set exogenously. A Greek letter or lowercase English letter refers to parameters, which need to be calibrated or supplied from exogenous sources. When multiple subscripts of a variable or parameter come from the same set, the first one represents the region or sector supplying goods; the next represents the region or sector purchasing goods (see tables B.3 and B.4).

## Price Equations

Equations 1–11 are price equations in the model. Equations 1 and 2 define the relationship between border (world) prices and internal prices, while equations 3–8 define price indices for aggregate imported goods, Armington goods, composite value added, and the firm's output with and without production taxes, respectively. In equations 3–7, the price indices are the unit cost functions, while in equation 8 they are unit revenue functions, all of which are dual to the corresponding unit quantity aggregator functions. For example, equation 7 is the result of cost minimization by the representative firm in each sector with respect to its aggregate factor and inputs, subject to a constant elasticity of substitution (CES) production function. Since CES functions are used as the building blocks of the basic model, and this quantity aggregator function is homogeneous of degree 1, the total costs can be written as total quantity multiplied by unit cost (Varian 1984, 28). This implies that the average cost, under cost minimization, is independent of the number of units produced or purchased. Thus, the unit cost function also stands for the price of the composed commodity. Equation 5 defines the unit price for aggregate inputs, which is the input-output (IO) coefficient weighted sum of all the value of its contents. Equation 9 states that the domestic consumer price is the Armington goods price plus sales taxes. Equation 10 specifies an economy-wide consumer price index, which is used as the price of household savings. Equation 11 defines the numeraire in the model.

$$PWM_{isr} = (1 + trs_{isr}) \times PWE_{isr} \tag{1}$$

$$PWE_{isr} = (1 + te_{isr}) \times (\frac{1}{ER_r}) \times PE_{ir} \tag{2}$$

$$PM_{ir} = \frac{1}{\mu_{ir}} \times \{ \sum_{s \in R} \xi_{irs}^{\sigma t_i} \times [(1 + tm_{irs} + tn_{irs}) \times ER_r \times PWM_{irs}]^{1 - \sigma t_i} \}^{\frac{1}{1 - \sigma t_i}} \tag{3}$$

$$PX_{ir} = \frac{1}{\Gamma_{ir}} \times \{ \sum \alpha_{ir}^{\sigma m_i} \times PD_{ir}^{1 - \sigma m_i} + (1 - \alpha_{ir})^{\sigma m_i} \times PM_{ir}^{1 - \sigma m_i} \}^{\frac{1}{1 - \sigma m_i}} \tag{4}$$

$$PN_{jr} = \sum_{i \in I} io_{ijr} \times PX_{ir} \tag{5}$$

$$PV_{ir} = \frac{1}{\Lambda_{ir} \times tfp_r \times ITFP_{ir}} \times \{ \sum_{f \in F} \delta_{fir}^{\sigma v_i} \times PF_{fr}^{1 - \sigma v_i} \}^{\frac{1}{1 - \sigma v_i}} \tag{6}$$

$$PP_{ir} = \frac{1}{A_{ir}} \times \{\lambda_{ir}^{\sigma p_i} \times PN_{ir}^{1-\sigma p_i} + (1-\lambda_{ir})^{\sigma p_i} \times PV_{ir}^{1-\sigma p_i}\}^{\frac{1}{1-\sigma p_i}} \qquad (7)$$

$$P_{ir} = \frac{1}{\chi_{ir}} \times \{\kappa_{ir}^{\sigma e_i} \times PD_{ir}^{1-\sigma e_i} + (1-\kappa_{ir})^{\sigma e_i} \times PE_{ir}^{1-\sigma e_i}\}^{\frac{1}{1-\sigma e_i}} \qquad (8)$$

$$PC_{ir} = (1+tc_{ir}) \times PX_{ir} \qquad (9)$$

$$CPI_r = \frac{\sum_{i \in I} PC_{ir} \times C_{ir}}{\sum_{i \in I} PCO_{ir} \times C_{ir}} \qquad (10)$$

$$PID_r = \prod_{i \in I} PC_{ir}^{\beta_{ir}} \times CPI_r^{mps_r} \qquad (11)$$

## Factor Demand and Firms' Supply Equations

Equations 12 and 13 specify the demand functions for aggregate factor and intermediate inputs, while equation 14 gives demand functions of each primary factor. They equal unit demand function multiplied by the quantities of total output, and the unit demand functions are obtained by taking partial derivatives of the unit cost functions (equations 6 and 7) with respect to the relevant factor prices, according to Shephard's lemma.

$$NX_{ir} = (\frac{1}{A_{ir}})^{1-\sigma p_i} \times (\lambda_{ir} \times \frac{PP_{ir}}{PN_{ir}})^{\sigma p_i} \times Q_{ir} \qquad (12)$$

$$VA_{ir} = (\frac{1}{A_{ir}})^{1-\sigma p_i} \times [(1-\lambda_{ir}) \times \frac{PP_{ir}}{PV_{ir}}]^{\sigma p_i} \times Q_{ir} \qquad (13)$$

$$DF_{fir} = (\frac{1}{\Lambda_{ir} \times tfp_r \times ITFP_{ir}})^{1-\sigma v_i} \times (\delta_{fir} \times \frac{PV_{ir}}{PF_{fr}})^{\sigma v_i} \times VA_{ir} \qquad \sum_{f \in F} \delta_{fir} = 1 \quad (14)$$

Equations 15–18 are the domestic and export supply functions corresponding to the constant elasticity of transformation (CET) function commonly used in today's CGE models. They are derived from revenue maximization, subject to the CET function, in a way similar to the derivation of factor demand functions. Equation 19 aggregates exports by the representative firm in each region, which implies that producers only differentiate output sold in domestic and foreign markets, but do not differentiate exports by destination (foreign markets are perfect substitutes). Equations 15–18 can be partially or entirely turned off in the model; in such case, $PD_{ir} = PE_{ir} = P_{ir}$ will be enforced and exports and domestic sales become perfect substitutes in the model.

$$DX_{sv,r} = (\frac{1}{\chi_{sv,r}})^{1-\sigma e_{sv}} \times (\kappa_{sv,r} \times \frac{P_{sv,r}}{PD_{sv,r}})^{\sigma e_{sv}} \times (Q_{sv,r} - TRQS_r)$$

$$\text{for } s \neq sv \tag{15}$$

$$DX_{ir} = (\frac{1}{\chi_{ir}})^{1-\sigma e_i} \times (\kappa_{ir} \times \frac{P_{ir}}{PD_{ir}})^{\sigma e_{sv}} \times Q_{ir} \tag{16}$$

$$EX_{sv,r} = (\frac{1}{\chi_{sv,r}})^{1-\sigma e_{sv}} \times \{(1-\kappa_{sv,r}) \times \frac{P_{sv,r}}{PE_{sv,r}}\}^{\sigma e_{sv}} \times (Q_{sv,r} - TRQS_r)$$

$$\text{for } s \neq sv \tag{17}$$

$$EX_{ir} = (\frac{1}{\chi_{ir}})^{1-\sigma e_i} \times \{(1-\kappa_{ir}) \times \frac{P_{ir}}{PE_{ir}}\}^{\sigma e_i} \times Q_{ir} \tag{18}$$

$$EX_{ir} = \frac{1}{PE_{ir}} \times \sum_{s \in R} \frac{ER_r}{(1+te_{irs})} \times PWE_{irs} \times X_{irs} \tag{19}$$

## Trade and Final Demand Equations

Trade and final demand equations are listed in equations 20–26. Equation 20 is the consumer demand function, which is the ELES derived from maximizing a Stone-Geary utility function subject to household disposable income, which is specified in equation 31. Equation 21 defines household supernumerary income, which is disposal income less total expenditure on the subsistence minimum. Equations 22 and 23 give government and investment demands. Equations 24–26 are demand functions for domestic goods, aggregate imported goods, and imported goods by source, respectively. They describe the cost-minimizing choice of domestic and import purchases, as well as import sources. They are derived from corresponding cost functions according to Shephard's lemma in a way similar to the derivation of factor demand functions (taking partial derivatives of the cost function with respect to the relevant component prices). Because of the linear homogeneity of the CES function, the cost function that is dual to the commodity aggregator can be represented by its unit cost function (equations 3 and 4) multiplied by total quantity demanded.

$$C_{ir} = \gamma_{ir} + \frac{\beta_{ir}}{PC_{ir}} \times SY_r \tag{20}$$

$$SY_r = HDI_r - \sum_{j \in I} PC_{jr} \times \gamma_{jr} \tag{21}$$

$$GC_{ir} = \frac{\theta_{ir}}{PC_{ir}} \times GSP_r \tag{22}$$

$$ID_{ir} = \frac{kio_{ir}}{PC_{ir}} \times INV_r \tag{23}$$

$$DX_{ir} = (\frac{1}{\Gamma_{ir}})^{1-\sigma m_i} \times (\alpha_{ir} \times \frac{PX_{ir}}{PD_{ir}})^{\sigma m_i} \times TX_{ir} \tag{24}$$

$$MX_{ir} = (\frac{1}{\Gamma_{ir}})^{1-\sigma m_i} \times \{(1-\alpha_{ir}) \times \frac{PX_{ir}}{PM_{ir}}\}^{\sigma m_i} \times TX_{ir} \tag{25}$$

$$X_{isr} = (\frac{1}{\mu_{ir}})^{1-\sigma t_i} \times \{\xi_{isr} \times (\frac{PM_{ir}}{(1+tm_{isr}+tn_{irs}) \times ER_r \times PWM_{isr}})^{\sigma t_i} \times MX_{ir} \quad \sum_{s \in R} \xi_{isr} = 1 \tag{26}$$

$$\text{for } s \neq r$$

## International Shipping Equations

Equations 27–30 describe the international shipping industry in the model. Equations 27 and 28 describe the supply side of the international shipping industry. Equation 27 states that at equilibrium, the returns from shipping activity must cover its cost. Like other industries in the model, it also earns zero profit. Equation 28 describes the demand for each region's services sector exports to the international shipping industry, which is generated by the assumed Cobb-Douglas technology in this industry. The next two equations (29 and 30), refer to the demand side of the international shipping industry. The demand for shipping services associated with commodity $i$ in region $r$ is generated by a fixed-proportion input requirement (Leontief) coefficient $trs_{isr}$, which is routine/commodity specific (equation 29). In equilibrium, the total demand of shipping service must equal its total supply (equation 30).

$$TRQ = \frac{1}{PTR} \times \sum_{r \in R} \frac{P_{sv,r}}{ER_r} \times TRQS_r \tag{27}$$

$$TRQ = \sum_{r \in R} \sum_{i \in I} TRQD_{ir} \tag{28}$$

$$TRQS_r = \frac{\tau_r \times ER_r}{P_{sv,r}} \times PTR \times TRQ \tag{29}$$

$$TRQD_{ir} = \frac{1}{PRT} \times (\sum_{s \in R} trs_{isr} \times PWE_{isr} \times X_{isr}) \tag{30}$$

## Income and Saving Equations

Equations 31–39 are income and saving equations in the model. Equations 31 and 32 define household disposal income and savings. Equations 33–37 determine government revenue from production taxes, consumption taxes, tariffs, and export taxes (its negative equals a subsidy), respectively, while equations 38–39 define government transfers to household and the balance of trade (foreign savings) in each region.

$$HDI_r = \sum_{f \in F} PF_{fr} \times \overline{FS_{fr}} - dk_r \times \overline{FS_{KAr}} + GTRANS_r \tag{31}$$

$$GR_r = PTAX_r + CTAX_r + TARRIF_r + ETAX_r \tag{32}$$

$$SAV_r = \frac{HDI_r \times \sum_{i \in I} PC_{ir} \times C_{ir}}{CPI_r} \tag{33}$$

$$PTAX_r = \sum_{i \in I} tp_{ir} \times P_{ir} \times Q_{ir} \tag{34}$$

$$CTAX_r = \sum_{i \in I} tc_{ir} \times PX_{ir} (C_{ir} + GC_{ir} + ID_{ir}) \tag{35}$$

$$TARRIF_r = \sum_{s \in R} \sum_{i \in I} (tm_{isr} + tn_{irs}) \times ER_r \times PWM_{isr} \times X_{isr} \tag{36}$$

$$ETAX_s = \sum_{r \in R} \sum_{i \in I} te_{isr} \times PE_{is} \times X_{isr} \tag{37}$$

$$GTRANS_r = GR_r - GSP_r - GSVA_r \tag{38}$$

$$BOT_r = \sum_{s \in R} \sum_{i \in I} PWE_{irs} X_{irs} + \frac{P_{sv,r}}{ER_r} \times TRQS_r - \sum_{s \in R} \sum_{i \in I} PWM_{isr} \times X_{isr} \tag{39}$$

## General Equilibrium Conditions

Equations 40–43 define general equilibrium conditions of the model, which are system constraints that the model economy must satisfy. For every sector in each region, the supply of the composite goods must equal total demand (equation 40), which is the sum of household consumption ($C_{ir}$), government purchases ($GC_{ir}$), investment ($ID_{ir}$), and the firm's intermediate demand. Similarly, the demand for each factor in every region must equal the exogenously fixed supply (equation 41). In this dual formulation, output in each region is determined by demand. Sectoral equilibrium is determined in equation 42, unit output price equals average cost, which is also the zero profit condition. Equation 43 describes the macroeconomic equilibrium identity in each region, which is also the budget constraint for the investor. Since all agents in each region (households, governments, investors, and firms) satisfy their respective budget constraints, it is well known that the sum of the excess demand for all goods is zero; that is, Walras's law holds for each region. Therefore, there is a functional dependence among the equations of the model. One equation is redundant in each region and thus can be dropped.

$$TX_{ir} = C_{ir} + GC_{ir} + ID_{ir} + \sum_{j \in I} io_{ijr} \times NX_{jr} \tag{40}$$

$$\sum_{i \in I} DF_{fir} = \overline{FS_{fr}} \tag{41}$$

$$P_{ir} = \frac{PN_{ir} \times NX_{ir} + PV_{ir} \times VA_{ir} + tp_{ir} \times P_{ir} \times Q_{ir}}{Q_{ir}} \tag{42}$$

$$INV_r = dr_r \times \overline{FS_{k,r}} + CPI_r \times (SAV_r + GSAV_r) - ER_r \times BOT_r \tag{43}$$

There are 52,402 equations and 52,582 variables in each of the intraperiod blocks of the model. Since the 120 factor endowment variables ($FS_r$) are determined by the initial stock and interperiod linkage equations, three additional sets of variables (60) have to be set exogenously as macro closures in order to make the model fully determinate. They are chosen from following variables for alternative closures: (1) gross investment or government transfer ($INV_r$ or $GTRANS_r$); (2) balance of trade or exchange rate ($BOT_r$ or $ER_r$); and (3) government spending or surplus (deficit) ($GSP_r$ or $GSAV_r$).

## Interperiod and Trade-Productivity Linkages

Equations 44–48 define the recursive structure of the five types of factor endowments (natural resources are sector specific and held constant, and they can be modified if more reliable data become available in the modeled economy). For instance, capital stock in each region at period $t$ equals the last period's capital stock plus the region's gross investment minus depreciation. Unskilled labor equals last period's employment multiplied by population growth rate, plus rural-urban migration, $MIG_{rt}$, minus the increase of skilled labor $SK_{rt}$ (set exogenously).

$$FS_{KAr,t} = (1 - dk_r) \times FS_{KAr,t-1} + INV_{rt} \tag{44}$$

$$FS_{SLr,t} = (1 + n_{rt}) \times FS_{SLr,t-1} + ds_r \times \overline{VSK_{rt}} \tag{45}$$

$$FS_{ULr,t} = (1 + n_{rt}) \times FS_{ULr,t-1} + MIG_{rt} - ds_r \times \overline{VSK_{rt}} \tag{46}$$

$$FS_{RLr,t} = (1 + n_{rt}) \times FS_{RLr,t-1} - MIG_{rt} \tag{47}$$

$$FS_{LDr,t} = (1 - dl_t) \times FS_{LDr,t-1} \tag{48}$$

Equation 49 links import-embodied technology transfer (via imports of capital goods and intermediate inputs) and TFP. Where $X0_{jsr}$ is the base year real trade flows, $IM$ is a subset of $I$, including those products embodied with advanced technology. It operates through share parameter and elasticities. An elasticity ($ip_{ir}$) of 0.1 implies that a 10 percent increase in real imports of capital- and technology-intensive goods would result in no more than a 1 percent increase in TFP in that sector, depending on the share of intermediate inputs in the sector's total imports. As pointed out by Lewis, Robinson, and Wang (1995), while there is fairly widespread agreement that linkage between imports of intermediate inputs and productivity gains do exist, there is less evidence of the size of the feedback. In our simulation exercises, the elasticities used for developed countries are at least less than half the values used for the developing countries.

$$ITFP_{ir} = 1 + ims_{ir} \times \left\{ \frac{NX_{ir}}{NX_{ir} + VA_{ir}} \times \left[ \frac{\sum\limits_{j \in IM} \sum\limits_{s \in R} x_{jsr}}{\sum\limits_{j \in IM} \sum\limits_{s \in R} xo_{jsr}} \right]^{\sigma ip_{ir}} + \frac{VX_{ir}}{NX_{ir} + VA_{ir}} - 1 \right\} \tag{49}$$

**Table B.1    Model regions, Global Trade Analysis Project (GTAP) region codes, and country name concordance**

| Model regions | Country name | GTAP region code |
|---|---|---|
| China | China | CHN |
| Taiwan | Taiwan | TWN |
| Hong Kong | Hong Kong | HKG |
| Indonesia | Indonesia | IDN |
| Japan | Japan | JPN |
| Korea | Korea, Republic of | KOR |
| Malaysia | Malaysia | MYS |
| Philippines | Philippines | PHL |
| Singapore | Singapore | SGP |
| Thailand | Thailand | THA |
| United States | United States of America | USA |
| Vietnam | Vietnam | VNM |
| Rest of East Asia | Cambodia | KHM |
| | Lao People's Democratic Republic | LAO |
| | Myanmar | MMR |
| | Macau | XEA |
| | Mongolia | |
| | Korea, Democratic People's Republic of | |
| | Brunei Darussalam | XSE |
| | Timor Leste | |
| Australia and New Zealand | Australia | AUS |
| | New Zealand | NZL |
| South Asia | Bangladesh | BGD |
| | India | IND |
| | Sri Lanka | LKA |
| | Pakistan | PAK |
| | Afghanistan | XSA |
| | Bhutan | |
| | Maldives | |
| | Nepal | |
| EU-12 | Bulgaria | BGR |
| | Cyprus | CYP |
| | Czech Republic | CZE |
| | Estonia | EST |
| | Hungary | HUN |
| | Lithuania | LTU |
| | Latvia | LVA |
| | Malta | MLT |
| | Poland | POL |
| | Romania | ROM |
| | Slovakia | SVK |
| | Slovenia | SVN |
| EU-15 | Austria | AUT |
| | Belgium | BEL |
| | Germany | DEU |
| | Denmark | DNK |
| | Spain | ESP |

*(continued on next page)*

**Table B.1   Model regions, Global Trade Analysis Project (GTAP) region codes, and country name concordance** *(continued)*

| Model regions | Country name | GTAP region code |
|---|---|---|
| | Finland | FIN |
| | France | FRA |
| | United Kingdom | GBR |
| | Greece | GRC |
| | Ireland | IRL |
| | Italy | ITA |
| | Luxembourg | LUX |
| | Netherlands | NLD |
| | Portugal | PRT |
| | Sweden | SWE |
| Rest of the Americas | Argentina | ARG |
| | Bolivia | BOL |
| | Brazil | BRA |
| | Chile | CHL |
| | Colombia | COL |
| | Costa Rica | CRI |
| | Ecuador | ECU |
| | Guatemala | GTM |
| | Mexico | MEX |
| | Nicaragua | NIC |
| | Panama | PAN |
| | Peru | PER |
| | Paraguay | PRY |
| | Uruguay | URY |
| | Venezuela | VEN |
| | Belize | XCA |
| | Honduras | |
| | El Salvador | |
| | Aruba | XCB |
| | Anguilla | |
| | Netherlands Antilles | |
| | Antigua and Barbuda | |
| | Bahamas | |
| | Barbados | |
| | Cuba | |
| | Cayman Islands | |
| | Dominica | |
| | Dominican Republic | |
| | Guadeloupe | |
| | Grenada | |
| | Haiti | |
| | Jamaica | |
| | Saint Kitts and Nevis | |
| | Saint Lucia | |
| | Montserrat | |
| | Martinique | |
| | Puerto Rico | |

**Table B.1** **Model regions, Global Trade Analysis Project (GTAP) region codes, and country name concordance** (*continued*)

| Model regions | Country name | GTAP region code |
|---|---|---|
| | Turks and Caicos | |
| | Trinidad and Tobago | |
| | Saint Vincent and the Grenadines | |
| | Virgin Islands, British | |
| | Virgin Islands, US | |
| | Bermuda | XNA |
| | Greenland | |
| | Saint Pierre and Miquelon | |
| | Falkland Islands (Malvinas) | XSM |
| | French Guiana | |
| | Guyana | |
| | Suriname | |
| Rest of high-income countries | Canada | CAN |
| | Switzerland | CHE |
| | Norway | NOR |
| | Iceland | XEF |
| | Liechtenstein | |
| Rest of the world | Albania | ALB |
| | Armenia | ARM |
| | Azerbaijan | AZE |
| | Belarus | BLR |
| | Botswana | BWA |
| | Egypt | EGY |
| | Ethiopia | ETH |
| | Georgia | GEO |
| | Croatia | HRV |
| | Iran, Islamic Republic of | IRN |
| | Kazakhstan | KAZ |
| | Kyrgyzstan | KGZ |
| | Morocco | MAR |
| | Madagascar | MDG |
| | Mozambique | MOZ |
| | Mauritius | MUS |
| | Malawi | MWI |
| | Nigeria | NGA |
| | Russian Federation | RUS |
| | Senegal | SEN |
| | Tunisia | TUN |
| | Turkey | TUR |
| | Tanzania, United Republic of | TZA |
| | Uganda | UGA |
| | Ukraine | UKR |
| | Angola | XAC |
| | Congo, Democratic Republic of the | |
| | Central African Republic | XCF |
| | Cameroon | |
| | Congo | |

(continued on next page)

## Table B.1 Model regions, Global Trade Analysis Project (GTAP) region codes, and country name concordance *(continued)*

| Model regions | Country name | GTAP region code |
|---|---|---|
| | Gabon | |
| | Equatorial Guinea | |
| | São Tomé and Príncipe | |
| | Chad | |
| | Burundi | XEC |
| | Comoros | |
| | Djibouti | |
| | Eritrea | |
| | Kenya | |
| | Mayotte | |
| | Reunion | |
| | Rwanda | |
| | Sudan | |
| | Somalia | |
| | Seychelles | |
| | Moldova, Republic of | XEE |
| | Andorra | XER |
| | Bosnia and Herzegovina | |
| | Faroe Islands | |
| | Gibraltar | |
| | Monaco | |
| | Macedonia, Former Yugoslav Republic of | |
| | Serbia and Montenegro | |
| | San Marino | |
| | Algeria | XNF |
| | Libyan Arab Jamahiriya | |
| | American Samoa | XOC |
| | Cook Islands | |
| | Fiji | |
| | Guam | |
| | Kiribati | |
| | Marshall Islands | |
| | Micronesia, Federated States of | |
| | Northern Mariana Islands | |
| | New Caledonia | |
| | Norfolk Island | |
| | Niue | |
| | Nauru | |
| | Palau | |
| | Papua New Guinea | |
| | French Polynesia | |
| | Solomon Islands | |
| | Tokelau | |
| | Tonga | |
| | Tuvalu | |
| | Vanuatu | |
| | Wallis and Futuna | |

| Model regions | Country name | GTAP region code |
|---|---|---|
| | Samoa | |
| | Lesotho | XSC |
| | Namibia | |
| | Swaziland | |
| | Tajikistan | XSU |
| | Turkmenistan | |
| | Uzbekistan | |
| | Benin | XWF |
| | Burkina Faso | |
| | Côte d'Ivoire | |
| | Cape Verde | |
| | Ghana | |
| | Guinea | |
| | Gambia | |
| | Guinea-Bissau | |
| | Liberia | |
| | Mali | |
| | Mauritania | |
| | Niger | |
| | Saint Helena | |
| | Sierra Leone | |
| | Togo | |
| | United Arab Emirates | XWS |
| | Bahrain | |
| | Iraq | |
| | Israel | |
| | Jordan | |
| | Kuwait | |
| | Lebanon | |
| | Oman | |
| | Palestinian Territory Occupied | |
| | Qatar | |
| | Saudi Arabia | |
| | Syrian Arab Republic | |
| | Yemen | |
| | South Africa | ZAF |
| | Zambia | ZMB |
| | Zimbabwe | ZWE |

**Table B.2  Model sectors, GTAP sectors, and ISIC/CPC concordance**

| Model sectors | GTAP sectors | ISIC revision 3/CPC code |
|---|---|---|
| Rice | 1. Paddy rice 18. Processed rice | 0113, 0114 |
| Other grains | 2. Wheat 3. Cereal, grains nec | 0111, 0112, 0115, 0116, 0119 |
| Vegetables and fruits | 4. Vegetables, fruit, nuts | 012, 013 |
| Nongrain crops | 5. Oil seeds 6. Sugarcane, sugarbeet 7. Plant-based fibers 8. Crops nec | 014, 018, 0192, 015, 016, 017, 0191, 193, 0194, 0199 |
| Livestock | 9. Bovine cattle, sheep, and goats, horses 10. Animal products nec 11. Raw milk 12. Wool, silk-worm cocoons | 0211, 0299, 0212, 0292, 0293, 0294, 0295, 0297, 0298, 0291, 0296 |
| Meat and dairy products | 19. Bovine meat products 20. Meat products nec | 21111, 21112, 21115, 21116, 21117, 21118, 21119, 2161, 21113, 21114, 2112, 2113, 2114, 2162 |
| Sugar | 24. Sugar | 235 |
| Other processed food | 21. Vegetable oils and fats 22. Dairy products, 25. Food products nec | 2163, 2164, 2165, 2166, 2167, 2168, 2169, 217, 218, 22, 212 |
| Beverages and tobacco | 26. Beverages and tobacco products | 24, 25 |
| Forest and fishery products | 13. Forestry 14. Fishing | 02 Forestry, logging and related service activities; 015 Hunting, trapping and game propagation including related service activities; 05 Fishing, operation of fish hatcheries and fish farms; service activities incidental to fishing |
| Oil and gas | 16. Oil 17. Gas | 111 Extraction of crude petroleum and natural gas; 112 Service activities incidental to oil and gas extraction excluding surveying |

| | | |
|---|---|---|
| Coal and other minerals | 15. Coal 18. Minerals nec | 101 Mining and agglomeration of hard coal; 102 Mining and agglomeration of lignite; 103 Mining and agglomeration of peat; 12 Mining of uranium and thorium ores; 13 Mining of metal ores; 14 Other mining and quarrying |
| Textiles | 27. Textiles | 17 Manufacture of textiles; 243 Manufacture of man-made fibers |
| Wearing apparel | 28. Wearing apparel | 18 Manufacture of wearing apparel; dressing and dyeing of fur |
| Leather products | 29. Leather products | 19 Tanning and dressing of leather; manufacture of luggage, handbags, saddlery, harness and footwear |
| Manufacturers | 42. Manufactures nec | 36 Manufacturing nec |
| Wood and paper products | 30. Wood products; 31. Paper products, publishing | 20 Manufacture of wood and of products of wood and cork, except furniture; manufacture of articles of straw and plaiting materials; 361 Manufacture of furniture; 21 Manufacture of paper and paper products; 2211 Publishing of books, brochures, musical books and other publications; 2212 Publishing of newspapers, journals and periodicals; 2219 Other publishing (photos, engravings, postcards, timetables, forms, posters, art reproductions, etc.); 222 Printing and service activities related to printing |
| Petroleum and coal products | 32. Petroleum, coal products | 231 Manufacture of coke oven products; 232 Manufacture of refined petroleum products |
| Chemical, rubber, and plastic products | 33. Chemical, rubber, plastic products | 233 Processing of nuclear fuel; 241 Manufacture of basic chemicals; 242 Manufacture of other chemical products; 25 Manufacture of rubber and plastic products |
| Mineral products | 34. Mineral products nec | 26 Manufacture of other nonmetallic mineral products |

*(continued on next page)*

**Table B.2   Model sectors, GTAP sectors, and ISIC/CPC concordance** *(continued)*

| Model sectors | GTAP sectors | ISIC revision 3/CPC code |
|---|---|---|
| Metals and metal products | 35. Ferrous metals 36. Metals nec 37. Metal products | 271 Manufacture of basic iron and steel; 2731 Casting of iron and steel; 272 Manufacture of basic precious and nonferrous metals; 2732 Casting of nonferrous metals; 28 Manufacture of fabricated metal products, except machinery and equipment |
| Motor vehicles and parts | 38. Motor vehicles and parts | 34 Manufacture of motor vehicles, trailers and semitrailers |
| Other transport equipment | 39. Transport equipment nec | 35 Manufacture of other transport equipment |
| Electronic equipment | 40. Electronic equipment | 30 Manufacture of office, accounting and computing machinery; 32 Manufacture of radio, television and communication equipment and apparatus |
| Machinery and equipment | 41. Machinery and equipment nec | 2213 Publishing of recorded media; 223 Reproduction of recorded media; 29 Manufacture of machinery and equipment ; 31 Manufacture of electrical machinery and apparatus nec; 33 Manufacture of medical, precision and optical instruments, watches and clocks |
| Trade and transportation | 47. Trade 48. Other transportation 48. Water transportation 49. Air transportation | 521 Nonspecialized retail trade in stores; 522 Retail sale of food, beverages and tobacco in specialized stores; 523 Other retail trade of new goods in specialized stores; 524 Retail sale of secondhand goods in stores; 525 Retail trade not in stores; 60 Land transport; transport via pipelines; 61 Water transport; 62 Air transport; 51 Wholesale trade and commission trade, except of motor vehicles and motorcycles |
| Finance and insurance | 52. Financial services nec 53. Insurance | 65 Financial intermediation, except insurance and pension funding; 66 Insurance and pension funding, except compulsory social security; 67 Activities auxiliary to financial intermediation; |

| | | |
|---|---|---|
| Business services | 54. Business services nec | 70 Real estate activities; 711 Renting of transport equipment; 526 Repair of personal & household goods; 712 Renting of other machinery and equipment; 713 Renting of personal & household goods nec; 72 Computer & related activities; 74 Other business activities |
| Communication | 51. Communication | 64 Post and telecommunications |
| Construction | 46. Construction | 45 Construction |
| Recreational and other services | 55. Recreational and other services | 55 Hotels and restaurants; 63 Supporting and auxiliary transport activities; activities of travel agencies; 92 Recreational, cultural and sporting activities; 93 Other service activities; 95 Private households with employed persons |
| Utilities and other nontradable services | 43. Electricity 44. Gas manufacture, distribution 45. Water 56. Public administration and defense, education, health 57. Dwellings | 401 Production, collection and distribution of electricity; 402 Manufacture of gas; distribution of gaseous fuels through mains; 403 Steam and hot water supply; 41 Collection, purification and distribution of water; 90 Sewage and refuse disposal, sanitation and similar activities; 73 Research and development; 75 Public administration and defense compulsory social security; 80 Education; 85 Health and social work; 91 Activities of membership organizations nec; 99 Extraterritorial organizations and bodies |

GTAP = Global Trade Analysis Project; ISIC/CPC = International Standard Industrial Classification/Central Product Classification; nec = not elsewhere classified.

**Figure B.1   Structure of production**

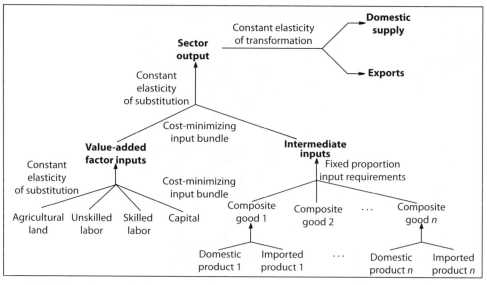

... = additional goods or products

**Figure B.2   Structure of demand**

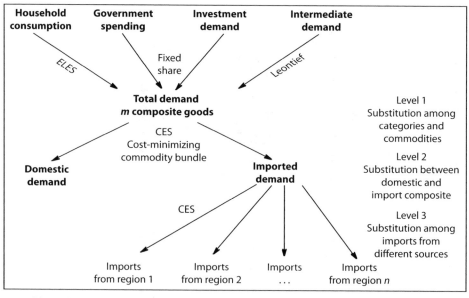

... = additional goods or products; CES = constant elasticity of substitutions; ELES = extended linear expenditure system

Note: Leontief refers to Leontief production technology, which assumes no substitution among different intermediate inputs.

**Figure B.3  The price system**

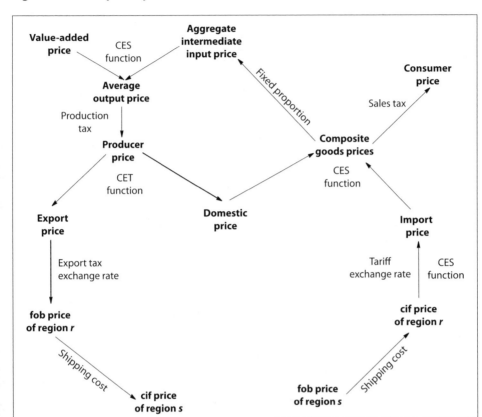

CES = constant elasticity of substitution; CET = constant elasticity of transformation; cif = cost, insurance, and freight; fob = free on board

## Table B.3    Definitions of variables

| Variable | Definition | Number of variables |
|---|---|---|
| $PWE_{isr}$ | World fob price for goods from region $s$ to region $r$ | $I \times R(R-1)$ (12,160) |
| $PWM_{isr}$ | World cif price for goods from region $s$ to region $r$ | $I \times R(R-1)$ (12,160) |
| $PM_{ir}$ | Price of aggregate imported goods in region $r$ | $I \times R$ (640) |
| $PX_{ir}$ | Price of composite goods in region $r$ | $I \times R$ (640) |
| $PD_{ir}$ | Price of domestic products sold at domestic market in region $r$ | $I \times R$ (640) |
| $PE_{ir}$ | Price of domestic goods for export in region $r$ | $I \times R$ (640) |
| $PC_{ir}$ | Domestic consumer price in region $r$ | $I \times R$ (640) |
| $PP_{ir}$ | Average output price before production tax in region $r$ | $I \times R$ (640) |
| $P_{ir}$ | Average output price after production tax in region $r$ | $I \times R$ (640) |
| $PF_{fr}$ | Factor price in region $r$ | $F \times R$ (120) |
| $PV_{ir}$ | Price of value added in region $r$ | $I \times R$ (640) |
| $PN_{ir}$ | Price of aggregate intermediate inputs in region $r$ | $I \times R$ (640) |
| $CPI_r$ | Price of savings in region $r$ (consumer price index) | $R$ (20) |
| $ER_r$ | Exchange rate of region $r$ | $R$ (20) |
| $PID_r$ | Price index in region $r$ | $R$ (20) |
| $Q_{ir}$ | Sector output in region $r$ | $I \times R$ (640) |
| $VA_{ir}$ | Variable sector production cost in region $r$ | $I \times R$ (640) |
| $NX_{ir}$ | Aggregate sector intermediate input in region $r$ | $I \times R$ (640) |
| $DF_{fir}$ | Sector factor demand in region $r$ | $(F-3) \times I \times R + (IAG + RES) \times R$ (2,080) |
| $DX_{ir}$ | Sector domestic sales in region $r$ | $I \times R$ (640) |
| $EX_{ir}$ | Domestic goods for export in region $r$ | $I \times R$ (640) |
| $C_{ir}$ | Household consumption in region $r$ | $I \times R$ (640) |
| $GC_{ir}$ | Government spending in region $r$ | $I \times R$ (640) |
| $ID_{ir}$ | Investment demand in region $r$ | $I \times R$ (640) |
| $TX_{ir}$ | Composite goods demand (supply) in region $r$ | $I \times R$ (640) |
| $MX_{ir}$ | Sector composite goods imports in region $r$ | $I \times R$ (640) |
| $X_{isr}$ | Trade flows from region $s$ to region $r$ | $I \times R(R-1)$ (12,160) |
| $TRQ$ | Total international transportation supply | 1 |
| $PTR$ | Price of international shipping service | 1 |
| $TRQD_{ir}$ | International shipping demand by region $r$ | $I \times R$ (640) |
| $TRQS_r$ | International shipping service supply by region $r$ | $R$ (20) |
| $HDI_r$ | Household disposable income in region $r$ | $R$ (20) |
| $SY_r$ | Household supernumerary income in region $r$ | $R$ (20) |
| $GR_r$ | Total government revenue in region $r$ | $R$ (20) |
| $GSP_r$ | Total government spending in region $r$ | $R$ (20) |
| $TARRIF_r$ | Total tariff revenue in region $r$ | $R$ (20) |
| $ETAX_r$ | Total export tax revenue (subsidy expenditure) in region $r$ | $R$ (20) |
| $PTAX_r$ | Total production tax revenue in region $r$ | $R$ (20) |
| $CTAX_r$ | Total consumer sale tax in region $r$ | $R$ (20) |
| $SAV_r$ | Household saving in region $r$ | $R$ (20) |
| $GSAV_r$ | Government saving (deficit) in region $r$ | $R$ (20) |
| $GTRNS_r$ | Government transfer in region $r$ | $R$ (20) |
| $BOT_r$ | Balance of trade in region $r$ (net capital inflow) | $R$ (20) |
| $INV_r$ | Gross investment by region $r$ | $R$ (20) |
| $ITFP_{ir}$ | Import-embodied total factor productivity shifter by sector in region $r$ | $I \times R$ (640) |
| $FS_{fr}$ | Factor endowment by region $r$ | $F \times R$ (160) |
| | Total number of variables: | |
| | $17 \times R + (2 \times F + IAG + RES) \times R + 21 \times I \times R + 3 \times I \times R(R-1) + (F-3) \times I \times R + 2$ (52,582) | |

fob = free on board; cif = cost, insurance, and freight.

## Table B.4    Definitions of parameters

| Parameter | Definition |
|---|---|
| $te_{isr}$ | Sector export tax (subsidy) rate for goods to region $r$ from region $s$ |
| $tm_{isr}$ | Sector tariff rate for goods from region $s$ in region $r$ |
| $tn_{isr}$ | Sector nontariff barrier for goods from region $s$ in region $r$ |
| $tp_{ir}$ | Sector indirect tax rate in region $r$ |
| $tc_{ir}$ | Consumer sales tax rate in region $r$ |
| $trc_{isr}$ | International transportation cost margin as percent value of fob |
| $io_{ijr}$ | Input/output coefficients for region $r$ |
| $kio_{ir}$ | Sector share of total investment in region $r$ |
| $dk_r$ | Depreciation rate of capital stock in region $r$ |
| $\tau_r$ | Regional share of international shipping service supply |
| $\Gamma_{ir}$ | Unit coefficients in first-level Armington aggregation function |
| $\mu_{ir}$ | Unit coefficients in second-level Armington aggregation function of region $r$ |
| $\alpha_{ir}$ | Share parameters in the first-level Armington aggregation function of region $r$ |
| $\xi_{ir}$ | Share parameters in the second-level Armington aggregation function of region $r$ |
| $\sigma m_i$ | Substitution elasticities between domestic and import goods |
| $\sigma t_i$ | Substitution elasticities among import goods from different regions |
| $\chi_{ir}$ | Unit coefficients in CET function of region $r$ |
| $\kappa_{lr}$ | Share parameters in CET function of region $r$ |
| $\sigma e_i$ | Elasticities of transformation between domestic sales and exports |
| $A_{ir}$ | Unit parameter in aggregate cost function |
| $\lambda_{lr}$ | Intermediate input share in aggregate cost function |
| $\sigma p_{ir}$ | Elasticities of substitution between aggregate factor and intermediate input |
| $\Lambda_{ir}$ | Unit parameter in value-added function |
| $\delta_{fir}$ | Factor share in value-added function |
| $\sigma v_{ir}$ | Elasticities of substitution among primary factors in value added |
| $\gamma_{ir}$ | Sector minimum subsistence requirements for private households in region $r$ |
| $\beta_{ir}$ | Marginal propensity to consume for private households in region $r$ |
| $Mps_r$ | Marginal propensity to save for private households in region $r$ |
| $\theta_{ir}$ | Sector share of government spending in region $r$ |
| $Tfp_r$ | General total factor productivity shifter in region $r$ |
| $Ims_{ir}$ | Share of intermediate inputs in sector's total imports |
| $\sigma ip_{ir}$ | Elasticity between intermediate goods import growth with total factor productivity growth |
| $dl_r$ | Land depletion rate in region $r$ |
| $Ds_r$ | Share of additional tertiary education stock that goes to skilled labor force at each period |
| $t\varphi_r$ | Parameter that controls the speed of wage convergence between agriculture and unskilled labor |
| $N_{rt}$ | Population growth rate in region $r$ at period $t$ |
| $Wdf_r$ | Wage ratio of agricultural labor and unskilled labor in region $r$ at base year |

fob = free on board; CET = constant elasticity of transformation.

# References

Badri, Narayanan G., and Terrie L. Walmsley, eds. 2008. *Global Trade, Assistance, and Production: The GTAP 7 Data Base.* Center for Global Trade Analysis, Purdue University.

Bergsten, C. Fred, and Jeffrey J. Schott. 2010. Paper submitted to the US Trade Representative in Support of a Trans-Pacific Partnership Agreement. Peterson Institute for International Economics. Mimeo (January 25). www.piie.com/publications/papers/paper.cfm?ResearchID=1482 (accessed on September 15, 2010).

Bush, Richard. 2005. *Untying the Knot: Making Peace in the Taiwan Strait.* Washington: Brookings Institution Press.

Chen, Lee-in. 2010. A Study on Economic Consequences for the Cross Strait Sea and Air Transport Link. Council for Economic Planning and Development, Taiwan (February). http://www.cepd.gov.tw/m1.aspx?sNo=0013005&ex=3&ic=0000152

Chen, Lee-in. 2004. Current Situation and the Impact Assessment of Taiwan's Investment in China. *Review of Taiwan Economics* (Ministry of Economic Affairs, December).

Cheung, Yin-Wong, Menzie D. Chinn, and Eiji Fujii. 2007. *The Economic Integration of Greater China.* Hong Kong: Hong Kong University Press.

Defense Science Board Task Force. 2005. High Performance Microchip Supply. Report to the Office of the Secretary of Defense (February). www.cra.org/govaffairs/images/2005-02-HPMS_Report_Final.pdf (accessed on September 15, 2010).

Dumbaugh, Kerry. 2009. *Taiwan-U.S. Relations: Developments and Policy Implications.* Congressional Research Service Report for Congress (November 2). www.fas.org/sgp/crs/row/R40493.pdf (accessed on September 15, 2010).

Dutton, Peter. 2009. *Scouting, Signaling, and Gatekeeping: Chinese Naval Operations in Japanese Waters and the International Law Implications.* China Maritime Studies No. 2 (February). Newport RI: US Naval War College. www.usnwc.edu/Research—Gaming/China-Maritime-Studies-Institute/Publications/documents/CMS2_Dutton.aspx (accessed on September 15, 2010).

ECCT (European Chamber of Commerce Taipei). 2008 EU-Taiwan Trade Enhancement Study (October). www.ecct.com.tw/index.php?option=com_content&task=view&id=249&Itemid=168 (accessed on September 15, 2010).

ECCT (European Chamber of Commerce Taipei). 2009–10. Retail and Distribution 2009–10 Position Paper. www.ecct.com.tw/index.php?option=com_content&task=view&id=28&Item id=48 (accessed on September 15, 2010).

Ferrantino, Michael J., and Zhi Wang. 2008. Accounting for Discrepancies in Bilateral Trade: The Case of China, Hong Kong, and the United States. *China Economic Review* 19 (September): 502–20.

Frost, Ellen. 2008. *Asia's New Regionalism*. Boulder, CO: Lynne Rienner Publishers, Inc.

Guo, Zhao Li. Undated. Seabed Petroleum in the East China Sea: Geological Prospects and the Search for Cooperation. China National Offshore Oil Corporation. Mimeo. www.wilsoncenter.org/topics/docs/Zhao_Li_Guo.pdf (accessed on September 15, 2010).

Gupta, Sanjeev, Benedict Clements, Rina Bhattacharya, and Shamit Chakravarti. 2002. The Elusive Peace Dividend. *Finance and Development* 39, no. 4. www.imf.org/external/pubs/ft/fandd/2002/12/gupta.htm (accessed on September 15, 2010).

He, Jianwu, and Louis Kuijs. 2007. Rebalancing China's Economy—Modeling a Policy Package. World Bank China Research Paper No. 7 (September). Washington: World Bank.

Hsueh, Li-min, An-loh Lin, and Su-wan Wang. 2003. The Growth and Potential of Taiwan's Foreign Trade in Services. In *Trade in Services in the Asia Pacific Region*, NBER East Asia Seminar on Economics, volume 11. Cambridge, MA: National Bureau of Economic Research.

Hufbauer Gary, Jeffrey J. Schott, and Kimberly Ann Elliott. 1985. *Economic Sanctions Reconsidered*. Washington: Institute for International Economics.

Hufbauer Gary, Jeffrey J. Schott, Kimberly Ann Elliott and Barbara Oegg. 2007. *Economic Sanctions Reconsidered: 3rd Edition*. Washington: The Peterson Institute for International Economics.

Hufbauer, Gary, et al. 2008. *Maghreb Regional and Global Integration: A Dream to Be Fulfilled*. Washington: Peterson Institute for International Economics. http://www.iie.com/publications/briefs/maghreb.pdf.

Ianchovichina E. I., Martin W., Fukase E. 2000. *Assessing the Implications of Merchandise Trade Liberalization in China's Accession to the WTO*. Washington: World Bank.

Kan, Shirley A. 2009. China/Taiwan: Evolution of the "One China" Policy—Key Statements from Washington, Beijing, and Taipei. Congressional Research Service Report for Congress (August 17). www.fas.org/sgp/crs/row/RL30341.pdf (accessed on September 15, 2010).

Kawai, Masahiro, and Ganeshan Wignaraja. 2008. *Regionalism as an Engine of Multilateralism: A Case for a Single East Asian FTA*. ADB Working Paper Series on Regional Economic Integration No. 14 (February). Manila: Asian Development Bank. Available at www.adb.org/Documents/Papers/Regional-Economic-Integration/WP14-East-Asian-FTA.pdf (accessed on September 15, 2010).

Koopman, Robert, Zhi Wang, and Shang-Jin Wei. 2008. *How Much of Chinese Exports Is Really Made in China. Assessing Domestic Value-added When Processing Trade Is Pervasive*. NBER Working Paper No.14109. Cambridge, MA: National Bureau of Economic Research.

Krepinevich, Andrew F. 2010. *Why AirSea Battle?* Center for Strategic and Budgetary Assessments. www.csbaonline.org/.../R.20100219.Why_AirSea_Battle.pdf (accessed on September 15, 2010).

Lardy, Nicholas, and Daniel H. Rosen. 2004. Prospects for a US-Taiwan Trade Agreement. Washington: Institute for International Economics.

Lejour, A. 2000. *China and the WTO; the Impact on China and the World Economy*. Paper presented at the third annual conference of Global Economic Analysis, Monash University, http://www.monash.edu.au/policy/conf/3Lejour.pdf.

Lewis, Jeffrey D., Sherman Robinson, and Zhi Wang. 1995. Beyond the Uruguay Round: The Implication of an Asian Free Trade Area. *China Economic Review—An International Journal* 7: 35–90.

Noland, Marcus, Li-Gang Liu, Sherman Robinson, and Zhi Wang. 1998. *Global Economic Effects of the Asian Currency Devaluations*. Policy Analysis Series No. 56. Washington: Institute for International Economics.

Romberg, Alan D. 2009. Cross-Strait Relations: Weathering the Storm. *China Leadership Monitor* 30 (fall). http://media.hoover.org/documents/CLM30AR.pdf (accessed on September 15, 2010).

Rosen, Daniel H. 1998. *Behind the Open Door: Foreign Enterprises in the Chinese Marketplace.* Washington: Institute for International Economics.

Rosen, Daniel H., and Thilo Hanemann. 2009. *China's Changing Outbound Foreign Direct Investment Profile: Drivers and Policy Implications.* PIIE Policy Brief 09-14 (June). Washington: Peterson Institute for International Economics.

Scissors, Derek. 2009. Taiwan's Economy Needs More Than Cooperation with China. Heritage Foundation WebMemo (November 9). www.heritage.org/Research/Asiaandthe Pacific/wm2691.cfm (accessed on September 15, 2010).

Securities and Futures Commission. 2008. Hong Kong Consolidates Its Role as a Fundraising Platform for the Greater China Region with Increased Listing of Taiwanese Companies. HK SFC Research Paper No. 40 (May). Hong Kong Securities and Futures Commission.

Segal, Adam. Forthcoming. *Advantage: How American Innovation Can Overcome the Asian Challenge.* New York: W.W. Norton.

Setser, Brad W., and Pandey, Arpana. May 2009. *China's $1.5 Trillion Bet: Understanding China's External Portfolio.* Working Paper 6. Council on Foreign Relations Press. http://www.cfr.org/publication/18149/chinas_15_trillion_bet.html.

Shear, David B. 2010. China-Taiwan: Recent Economic, Political and Military Developments Across the Strait and Implications for the United States." Testimony of David B. Shear, Deputy Assistant Secretary, Bureau of East Asian and Pacific Affairs, US-China Economic and Security Review Commission, March 18, 2010.

Shen, Chung-Hua, and Wang, Lee-Rong. 2004. The Economics of the "Three Links." In *Sources of Conflict and Cooperation in the Taiwan Strait.* July 2006. New Jersey: World Scientific Pub. http://ebooks.worldscinet.com/ISBN/9789812707314/9789812707314_0004.html.

Tanner, Murray Scot. 2007. *Chinese Economic Coercion Against Taiwan: A Tricky Weapon to Use.* Santa Monica, CA: The Rand Corporation.

Tucker, Nancy. 2002. If Taiwan Chooses Unification, Should the United States Care? *Washington Quarterly* 25, no. 3: 15–28.

Tung, Chen-yuan. 2010. The East Asian Economic Integration Regime and Taiwan. *Asian Perspective* 34, no. 2: 83–112.

US-China Economic and Security Review Commission. 2009. Report on the Capability of the People's Republic of China to Conduct Cyber Warfare and Computer Network Exploitation (McLean, VA: Northrop Grumman, October 9). www.uscc.gov/research papers/2009/NorthropGrumman_PRC_Cyber_Paper_FINAL_Approved%20 Report_16Oct2009.pdf (accessed on September 15, 2010).

US Pacific Command. 2009. Strategy: Partnership, Readiness, Presence (April 2). www.pacom.mil/web/PACOM_Resources/pdf/PACOM%20STRATEGY%2002Apr09.pdf (accessed on September 15, 2010).

Varian, Hal R. 1984. *Microeconomic Analysis,* second edition. New York: W.W. Norton & Company.

Wang, Zhi. 1994. *The Impact of Economic Integration Among Taiwan, Hong Kong and China—A Computable General Equilibrium Analysis,* Department of Applied Economics, PhD Dissertation. University of Minnesota.

Wang, Zhi. 1997. China and Taiwan Access to the World Trade Organization: Implications for U.S. Agriculture and Trade. *Agricultural Economics* 17, no. 4: 239–64.

Wang, Zhi. 1999. Impact of China's WTO Entry on Labor Intensive Export Market—A Recursive Dynamic CGE Analysis. *The World Economy* 22, no. 3: 379–405.

Wang, Zhi. 2003a. Impact of China's WTO Accession on the Patterns of World Trade. *Journal of Policy Modeling* 20, no. 1: 1–41.

Wang, Zhi. 2003b. WTO Accession, "Greater China" Free Trade Area and Economic Integration across the Taiwan Strait. *China Economic Review* 14, no. 3: 316–49.

Wang, Zhi, and G. Edward Schuh. 2000. The Impact of Economic Integration among Taiwan, Hong Kong and China: A Computable General Equilibrium Analysis. *Pacific Economic Review* 5, no. 2 (Special Issue on Hong Kong Reversion to China): 229–62.

Wang, Zhi, and G. Edward Schuh. 2002. The Emergence of a "Greater China" and Its Impact on World Trade—A Computable General Equilibrium Analysis. *Journal of Comparative Economics* 30, no. 3: 531–66.

WTO (World Trade Organization). 2006. WTO Trade Policy Review Body. WT/TPR/M/165/Rev.1 (October 10).

# Index

Australia and New Zealand Closer
    Economic Relations Trade Agreement
    (ANZCERTA), 66f
auto industry
    early-harvest agreement and, 86
    Taiwan phasing out of quota
    restrictions, 121–22

balance of payments of Taiwan, 20, 31
balance of services trade
    of China, 24f
    of Taiwan, 22f
ban on goods from China
    impact on Taiwanese households, 55
    Taiwan extensions on, 18
banking
    Chinese investment, 26
    opening market access, 90
Bay of Bengal Initiative for Multi-Sectoral
    Technical and Economic Cooperation
    Free Trade Agreement (BIMSTEC
    FTA), 66f
bilateral trade deficits of China, 10
Board of Foreign Trade (Taiwan). See
    Mainland Affairs Council and Board
    of Foreign Trade (Taiwan)
bonded assembly zones, 142
Brunei, TPPA and, 124
business travel, 43–44

capital flight, by Taiwan businesses, 56
Caribbean
    offshore financial centers, 115
    tax havens, 29
Central America–United
    States–Dominican Republic Free
    Trade Area (CAFTA-DR), 66f
Central Bank of China, 31
    estimate of tax haven flows to China,
    29n
CGE model. See computable general
    equilibrium (CGE) model
charter air services, Taiwan agreement on
    expanding, 39
Chen-Chiang talks, 92–93
Chi Mei Corporation, 13n
Chiang Chen talks, 90
Chile, TPPA and, 124
China
    absorption change, 2010–20, 78f
    banks, 90
    comparative advantage, 49
    and cyber attacks, 130

efforts to prevent agreements by
    Taiwan, 106
estimate of Taiwan citizen residency, 44
future consumer market, 33f
gross domestic product (GDP), 5
impact of Taiwan's regional trade, 100
Ministry of Commerce (MOFCOM),
    23–24, 39
Ministry of Commerce (MOFCOM),
    web resources, 57n
output changes by sectors, 2020, 94t
per capita GDP in 2009, 5n
population size vs. Taiwan, 41
portfolio assets, 41
real absorption changes, 74
and Taiwan, legitimacy of
    independence, 128
US investment in, 115
view of FTA, 58n
view of Taiwan, 1
China agreements
    agreement on open ports, 17
    ECFA schedule, 160t
    restrictions on Taiwanese commerce, 19
China AMC, 26, 42
China direct investment
    by Taiwan, 27–36
    by Taiwan, regional breakdown by
    manufacturing sectors, 37f
    by Taiwan, regional breakdown by
    services sectors, 37f
    in Taiwan, 26, 36–40
    in Taiwan, approved, 40f
    in US, 115, 116
China International Fund Management,
    26, 42
China Investment Corporation, 41
China-Singapore FTA, 86n
China State Council, economic
    development plan for "Western
    Taiwan Straits," 93
China State Council's Taiwan Affairs
    Office, 58
China stock exchanges, relaxed quotas on
    Taiwan investment, 41
China trade
    balance by region, 11f
    balance of services trade, 24f
    bilateral trade deficits, 10
    dependence between Taiwan and, 72,
    73t
    export and import changes, 72f
    highest value Taiwan exports to, 83–84t

East Asia Free Trade Agreement (EAFTA), 66f
ECFA. *See* Economic Cooperation Framework Agreement
Economic Cooperation Council, 61
Economic Cooperation Framework Agreement (ECFA), 1, 6, 51, 62–63
  aggregate impact on US trade, 120–23, 121t
  comprehensive analysis preparation, 68
  and early harvest, 86, 95
  gains for economies in Asia, 109
  impact, 137
  potential impact on Taiwan GDP, 99–100
  projected benefits, 95
  scenarios for Taiwan's participation beyond, 98t
  simulation of results, 69
  structural adjustment, 87
  and Taiwan, 138–39
  Taiwan economic participation limited to, 67t
  and US, 117–23, 121, 122t
  US business interests and product coverage, 114
economic integration arrangements, 57
economic policy
  analyzing impact of change, 52
  reforms, 16
education, Taiwan development, 20
El Salvador, Taiwan FTA with, 98
electrical components, 32
electrical machinery
  as China export, 12
  as Taiwan import, 14
electronics, 32, 83–84t, 87–89
  comparative disadvantage, 82
  percent change in production, 2020, 103–105t
  US sector, 120, 121
engineering, Taiwan development, 20
environmental services, Taiwan development, 20
ethylene glycol, 79
European Chamber of Commerce Taipei, 114, 126
European Union (EU), 54, 152
  and China's total services trade, 24
  FTA with South Korea, 126
  FTA with Taiwan, 60
export control policy, 129
export processing zones, in China, 27

exports
  China and Taiwan changes, 2012–2020, 72f
  China to Taiwan, 7
  electrical machinery from China, 12
  fob prices for valuation, $7n$
  highest value, from Taiwan not to China, 85t
  highest value, from Taiwan to China, 83–84t
  Taiwan estimates to China, 9b
  Taiwan to China, 7
  US agriculture, 121
  valuation in fob prices, $7n$
extended linear expenditure system (ELES) demand, 151

FDI. *See* foreign direct investment
financial crimes prevention, 131
financial services industry
  China restrictions on Taiwan, 19–20
  Early harvest agreement and, 86
  in Taiwan, 20, 90
  US comparative advantage, 115
Financial Supervisory Commission (Taiwan), 42
First Sino bank (Shanghai), 90
flat-screen television producers, operating profit margins, $82n$
flows of people, 42–46
food, 32. *See also* agriculture sector
foreign direct investment
  by China, in Taiwan, 36–40
  dimensions of Taiwanese outward, 30t
  between Taiwan and China, 6, 26, 27–36
  by Taiwan, average size in China, 35f
  by Taiwan, growth in China by industry, 35f
  by Taiwan, in China by province, 36f
  by Taiwan, in China, regional breakdown by manufacturing sectors, 37f
  by Taiwan, in China, regional breakdown by services sectors, 37f
  by Taiwan, in Chinese industries, 34f
foreign securities, Taiwan investors shift to, 56
free trade agreements (FTAs), 1,
  in China, 57
  in East Asia, 152
  inclusions, 54
  and investment flow changes, 92
  negotiations, 137

policy changes as long-run, 75
regional, 157*t*
WTO rules, 53–54
Fubon Bank, 91
Fujian Cement, 59
Fujian Expressway, 59
Fujian province, 59
  direct shipping between, 17
  investments in, 33
  sectoral outcomes, 93

*gaiatsu*, 142
GCDT Property, 59
General Algebraic Modeling System, 151
Germany, 25
GFJY Porcelain, 59
global financial crisis, 43
global manufacturing value chains,
    China's role, 12
global market, impact on Taiwan exports, 14
Global Trade Analysis Project (GTAP)
    database, 73, 75
  region codes, 171–75*t*
  sectors, 176–79*t*
globalization, 5
gross domestic consumption, vs. GDP, 74
gross domestic product (GDP), 99–100
  aggregate economic impact of ECFA on
    US, 117–18
  change for other economies with
    Taiwan limitations, 107*t*
  change for other economies with
    Taiwan participation in regional
    agreements, 108*t*
  change projections, 68–70
  vs. gross domestic consumption, 74
  Hong Kong and Singapore reduction, 106
  Taiwan change over baseline, 70*f*
Guangdong
  investments in, 33
  and Taiwan export estimates to China, 9*b*
Guatemala, Taiwan FTA with, 98

hackers, Chinese, 130
Hon Hai Precision, 13*n*
Honduras, Taiwan FTA with, 98
Hong Kong, 129*n*
  Census and Statistics Department, 9*n*
  China and Taiwan FTA effect, 58–59
  China designation for firms from, 145
  and China's total services trade, 24
  Closer Economic Partnership
    Agreement, 110

economic side effects of China-Taiwan
    liberalization, 109
  GDP reduction, 106
  GDP with Taiwan limited to ECFA, 107*t*
  GDP with Taiwan participation in
    regional agreements, 108*t*
  as major transshipment location, 7, 17, 55
  negative effects from cross-strait
    liberalization, 109–11
  offshore financial centers, 115
  passenger travel through, 44
  status for US export-control licensing, 129
  and Taiwan export estimates to China, 9*b*
  Taiwan investment reports, 29
Hsinchu Technology Park, 5
Hu Jintao, 128
hub-and-spoke frameworks, between
    ASEAN, Japan and South Korea, 69*n*

IMF (International Monetary Fund), 5*n*
Indonesia, GDP with Taiwan limited to
    ECFA, 107*t*
Industrial Technology Research Institute
    (Taiwan), 59, 139
information and media, Taiwan
    development, 20
information technology, 23, 32, 111
  work visas for Chinese professionals, 45
Information Technology Agreement
    (WTO), 16, 79, 111
institutionalized mechanism, for
    managing economic relationships, 61
insurance services, 23
intellectual property rights, 23
interdependence, 5
International Monetary Fund (IMF), 5*n*
international pressure, for domestic
    change, 142
Inventec Corp., 13*n*
investment flows, 75
  from China, Taiwan ban on, 55–56
investment growth, 92–93

Japan, 9
  in ASEAN-China accord, 57
  and China's total services trade, 24
  effect of possible FTA extension by
    China, 69–70
  framework agreement between ASEAN
    and, 65*n*
  GDP with Taiwan limited to ECFA, 107*t*
  GDP with Taiwan participation in
    regional agreements, 108*t*

# Other Publications from the Peterson Institute for International Economics

* = out of print

## POLICY ANALYSES IN INTERNATIONAL ECONOMICS Series

Completing the Uruguay Round: A Results-Oriented Approach to the GATT Trade Negotiations* Jeffrey J. Schott, ed.
*September 1990* ISBN 0-88132-130-3
Economic Sanctions Reconsidered (2 volumes)
Economic Sanctions Reconsidered: Supplemental Case Histories
Gary Clyde Hufbauer, Jeffrey J. Schott, and Kimberly Ann Elliott
*1985, 2d ed. Dec. 1990* ISBN cloth 0-88132-115-X
ISBN paper 0-88132-105-2
Economic Sanctions Reconsidered: History and Current Policy Gary Clyde Hufbauer, Jeffrey J. Schott, and Kimberly Ann Elliott
*December 1990* ISBN cloth 0-88132-140-0
ISBN paper 0-88132-136-2
Pacific Basin Developing Countries: Prospects for the Future* Marcus Noland
*January 1991* ISBN cloth 0-88132-141-9
ISBN paper 0-88132-081-1
Currency Convertibility in Eastern Europe*
John Williamson, ed.
*October 1991* ISBN 0-88132-128-1
International Adjustment and Financing: The Lessons of 1985-1991* C. Fred Bergsten, ed.
*January 1992* ISBN 0-88132-112-5
North American Free Trade: Issues and Recommendations* Gary Clyde Hufbauer and Jeffrey J. Schott
*April 1992* ISBN 0-88132-120-6
Narrowing the U.S. Current Account Deficit*
Alan J. Lenz
*June 1992* ISBN 0-88132-103-6
The Economics of Global Warming
William R. Cline
*June 1992* ISBN 0-88132-132-X
US Taxation of International Income: Blueprint for Reform Gary Clyde Hufbauer, assisted by Joanna M. van Rooij
*October 1992* ISBN 0-88132-134-6
Who's Bashing Whom? Trade Conflict in High-Technology Industries Laura D'Andrea Tyson
*November 1992* ISBN 0-88132-106-0
Korea in the World Economy* Il SaKong
*January 1993* ISBN 0-88132-183-4
Pacific Dynamism and the International Economic System* C. Fred Bergsten and Marcus Noland, eds.
*May 1993* ISBN 0-88132-196-6
Economic Consequences of Soviet Disintegration* John Williamson, ed.
*May 1993* ISBN 0-88132-190-7
Reconcilable Differences? United States-Japan Economic Conflict* C. Fred Bergsten and Marcus Noland
*June 1993* ISBN 0-88132-129-X
Does Foreign Exchange Intervention Work?
Kathryn M. Dominguez and Jeffrey A. Frankel
*September 1993* ISBN 0-88132-104-4
Sizing Up U.S. Export Disincentives*
J. David Richardson
*September 1993* ISBN 0-88132-107-9

NAFTA: An Assessment
Gary Clyde Hufbauer and Jeffrey J. Schott, *rev. ed.*
*October 1993* ISBN 0-88132-199-0
Adjusting to Volatile Energy Prices
Philip K. Verleger, Jr.
*November 1993* ISBN 0-88132-069-2
The Political Economy of Policy Reform
John Williamson, ed.
*January 1994* ISBN 0-88132-195-8
Measuring the Costs of Protection in the United States Gary Clyde Hufbauer and Kimberly Ann Elliott
*January 1994* ISBN 0-88132-108-7
The Dynamics of Korean Economic Development* Cho Soon
*March 1994* ISBN 0-88132-162-1
Reviving the European Union*
C. Randall Henning, Eduard Hochreiter, and Gary Clyde Hufbauer, eds.
*April 1994* ISBN 0-88132-208-3
China in the World Economy
Nicholas R. Lardy
*April 1994* ISBN 0-88132-200-8
Greening the GATT: Trade, Environment, and the Future Daniel C. Esty
*July 1994* ISBN 0-88132-205-9
Western Hemisphere Economic Integration*
Gary Clyde Hufbauer and Jeffrey J. Schott
*July 1994* ISBN 0-88132-159-1
Currencies and Politics in the United States, Germany, and Japan C. Randall Henning
*September 1994* ISBN 0-88132-127-3
Estimating Equilibrium Exchange Rates
John Williamson, ed.
*September 1994* ISBN 0-88132-076-5
Managing the World Economy: Fifty Years after Bretton Woods Peter B. Kenen, ed.
*September 1994* ISBN 0-88132-212-1
Reciprocity and Retaliation in U.S. Trade Policy Thomas O. Bayard and Kimberly Ann Elliott
*September 1994* ISBN 0-88132-084-6
The Uruuay Round: An Assessment*
Jeffrey J. Schott, assisted by Johanna Buurman
*November 1994* ISBN 0-88132-206-7
Measuring the Costs of Protection in Japan*
Yoko Sazanami, Shujiro Urata, and Hiroki Kawai
*January 1995* ISBN 0-88132-211-3
Foreign Direct Investment in the United States, 3d ed. Edward M. Graham and Paul R. Krugman
*January 1995* ISBN 0-88132-204-0
The Political Economy of Korea-United States Cooperation* C. Fred Bergsten and Il SaKong, eds.
*February 1995* ISBN 0-88132-213-X
International Debt Reexamined*
William R. Cline
*February 1995* ISBN 0-88132-083-8
American Trade Politics, 3d ed. I. M. Destler
*April 1995* ISBN 0-88132-215-6

Managing Official Export Credits: The Quest for a Global Regime*          John E. Ray
*July 1995*          ISBN 0-88132-207-5
Asia Pacific Fusion: Japan's Role in APEC*
Yoichi Funabashi
*October 1995*          ISBN 0-88132-224-5
Korea-United States Cooperation in the New World Order*          C. Fred Bergsten and Il SaKong, eds.
*February 1996*          ISBN 0-88132-226-1
Why Exports Really Matter!*
          ISBN 0-88132-221-0
Why Exports Matter More!*  ISBN 0-88132-229-6
J. David Richardson and Karin Rindal
*July 1995; February 1996*
Global Corporations and National Governments          Edward M. Graham
*May 1996*          ISBN 0-88132-111-7
Global Economic Leadership and the Group of Seven          C. Fred Bergsten and C. Randall Henning
*May 1996*          ISBN 0-88132-218-0
The Trading System after the Uruguay Round*
John Whalley and Colleen Hamilton
*July 1996*          ISBN 0-88132-131-1
Private Capital Flows to Emerging Markets after the Mexican Crisis*  Guillermo A. Calvo, Morris Goldstein, and Eduard Hochreiter
*September 1996*          ISBN 0-88132-232-6
The Crawling Band as an Exchange Rate Regime: Lessons from Chile, Colombia, and Israel          John Williamson
*September 1996*          ISBN 0-88132-231-8
Flying High: Liberalizing Civil Aviation in the Asia Pacific*          Gary Clyde Hufbauer and Christopher Findlay
*November 1996*          ISBN 0-88132-227-X
Measuring the Costs of Visible Protection in Korea*          Namdoo Kim
*November 1996*          ISBN 0-88132-236-9
The World Trading System: Challenges Ahead
Jeffrey J. Schott
*December 1996*          ISBN 0-88132-235-0
Has Globalization Gone Too Far?  Dani Rodrik
*March 1997*          ISBN paper 0-88132-241-5
Korea-United States Economic Relationship*
C. Fred Bergsten and Il SaKong, eds.
*March 1997*          ISBN 0-88132-240-7
Summitry in the Americas: A Progress Report
Richard E. Feinberg
*April 1997*          ISBN 0-88132-242-3
Corruption and the Global Economy
Kimberly Ann Elliott
*June 1997*          ISBN 0-88132-233-4
Regional Trading Blocs in the World Economic System          Jeffrey A. Frankel
*October 1997*          ISBN 0-88132-202-4
Sustaining the Asia Pacific Miracle: Environmental Protection and Economic Integration          Andre Dua and Daniel C. Esty
*October 1997*          ISBN 0-88132-250-4

Trade and Income Distribution
William R. Cline
*November 1997*          ISBN 0-88132-216-4
Global Competition Policy
Edward M. Graham and J. David Richardson
*December 1997*          ISBN 0-88132-166-4
Unfinished Business: Telecommunications after the Uruguay Round
Gary Clyde Hufbauer and Erika Wada
*December 1997*          ISBN 0-88132-257-1
Financial Services Liberalization in the WTO
Wendy Dobson and Pierre Jacquet
*June 1998*          ISBN 0-88132-254-7
Restoring Japan's Economic Growth
Adam S. Posen
*September 1998*          ISBN 0-88132-262-8
Measuring the Costs of Protection in China
Zhang Shuguang, Zhang Yansheng, and Wan Zhongxin
*November 1998*          ISBN 0-88132-247-4
Foreign Direct Investment and Development: The New Policy Agenda for Developing Countries and Economies in Transition
Theodore H. Moran
*December 1998*          ISBN 0-88132-258-X
Behind the Open Door: Foreign Enterprises in the Chinese Marketplace          Daniel H. Rosen
*January 1999*          ISBN 0-88132-263-6
Toward A New International Financial Architecture: A Practical Post-Asia Agenda
Barry Eichengreen
*February 1999*          ISBN 0-88132-270-9
Is the U.S. Trade Deficit Sustainable?
Catherine L. Mann
*September 1999*          ISBN 0-88132-265-2
Safeguarding Prosperity in a Global Financial System: The Future International Financial Architecture, Independent Task Force Report Sponsored by the Council on Foreign Relations
Morris Goldstein, Project Director
*October 1999*          ISBN 0-88132-287-3
Avoiding the Apocalypse: The Future of the Two Koreas          Marcus Noland
*June 2000*          ISBN 0-88132-278-4
Assessing Financial Vulnerability: An Early Warning System for Emerging Markets
Morris Goldstein, Graciela Kaminsky, and Carmen Reinhart
*June 2000*          ISBN 0-88132-237-7
Global Electronic Commerce: A Policy Primer
Catherine L. Mann, Sue E. Eckert, and Sarah Cleeland Knight
*July 2000*          ISBN 0-88132-274-1
The WTO after Seattle          Jeffrey J. Schott, ed.
*July 2000*          ISBN 0-88132-290-3
Intellectual Property Rights in the Global Economy          Keith E. Maskus
*August 2000*          ISBN 0-88132-282-2
The Political Economy of the Asian Financial Crisis          Stephan Haggard
*August 2000*          ISBN 0-88132-283-0
Transforming Foreign Aid: United States Assistance in the 21st Century   Carol Lancaster
*August 2000*          ISBN 0-88132-291-1

Fighting the Wrong Enemy: Antiglobal
Activists and Multinational Enterprises
Edward M. Graham
*September 2000*          ISBN 0-88132-272-5

Globalization and the Perceptions of American
Workers          Kenneth Scheve and
Matthew J. Slaughter
*March 2001*          ISBN 0-88132-295-4

World Capital Markets: Challenge to the G-10
Wendy Dobson and Gary Clyde Hufbauer,
assisted by Hyun Koo Cho
*May 2001*          ISBN 0-88132-301-2

Prospects for Free Trade in the Americas
Jeffrey J. Schott
*August 2001*          ISBN 0-88132-275-X

Toward a North American Community:
Lessons from the Old World for the New
Robert A. Pastor
*August 2001*          ISBN 0-88132-328-4

Measuring the Costs of Protection in Europe:
European Commercial Policy in the 2000s
Patrick A. Messerlin
*September 2001*          ISBN 0-88132-273-3

Job Loss from Imports: Measuring the Costs
Lori G. Kletzer
*September 2001*          ISBN 0-88132-296-2

No More Bashing: Building a New Japan–
United States Economic Relationship
C. Fred Bergsten, Takatoshi Ito, and Marcus
Noland
*October 2001*          ISBN 0-88132-286-5

Why Global Commitment Really Matters!
Howard Lewis III and J. David Richardson
*October 2001*          ISBN 0-88132-298-9

Leadership Selection in the Major Multilaterals
Miles Kahler
*November 2001*          ISBN 0-88132-335-7

The International Financial Architecture:
What's New? What's Missing?     Peter B. Kenen
*November 2001*          ISBN 0-88132-297-0

Delivering on Debt Relief: From IMF Gold to a
New Aid Architecture     John Williamson and
Nancy Birdsall, with Brian Deese
*April 2002*          ISBN 0-88132-331-4

Imagine There's No Country: Poverty,
Inequality, and Growth in the Era of
Globalization          Surjit S. Bhalla
*September 2002*          ISBN 0-88132-348-9

Reforming Korea's Industrial Conglomerates
Edward M. Graham
*January 2003*          ISBN 0-88132-337-3

Industrial Policy in an Era of Globalization:
Lessons from Asia          Marcus Noland and
Howard Pack
*March 2003*          ISBN 0-88132-350-0

Reintegrating India with the World Economy
T. N. Srinivasan and Suresh D. Tendulkar
*March 2003*          ISBN 0-88132-280-6

After the Washington Consensus: Restarting
Growth and Reform in Latin America
Pedro-Pablo Kuczynski and John Williamson, eds.
*March 2003*          ISBN 0-88132-347-0

The Decline of US Labor Unions and the Role
of Trade          Robert E. Baldwin
*June 2003*          ISBN 0-88132-341-1

Can Labor Standards Improve under
Globalization?          Kimberly Ann Elliott and
Richard B. Freeman
*June 2003*          ISBN 0-88132-332-2

Crimes and Punishments? Retaliation under
the WTO          Robert Z. Lawrence
*October 2003*          ISBN 0-88132-359-4

Inflation Targeting in the World Economy
Edwin M. Truman
*October 2003*          ISBN 0-88132-345-4

Foreign Direct Investment and Tax
Competition          John H. Mutti
*November 2003*          ISBN 0-88132-352-7

Has Globalization Gone Far Enough? The
Costs of Fragmented Markets
Scott C. Bradford and Robert Z. Lawrence
*February 2004*          ISBN 0-88132-349-7

Food Regulation and Trade: Toward a Safe and
Open Global System          Tim Josling,
Donna Roberts, and David Orden
*March 2004*          ISBN 0-88132-346-2

Controlling Currency Mismatches in Emerging
Markets          Morris Goldstein and Philip Turner
*April 2004*          ISBN 0-88132-360-8

Free Trade Agreements: US Strategies and
Priorities          Jeffrey J. Schott, ed.
*April 2004*          ISBN 0-88132-361-6

Trade Policy and Global Poverty
William R. Cline
*June 2004*          ISBN 0-88132-365-9

Bailouts or Bail-ins? Responding to Financial
Crises in Emerging Economies
Nouriel Roubini and Brad Setser
*August 2004*          ISBN 0-88132-371-3

Transforming the European Economy
Martin Neil Baily and Jacob Funk Kirkegaard
*September 2004*          ISBN 0-88132-343-8

Chasing Dirty Money: The Fight Against
Money Laundering          Peter Reuter and
Edwin M. Truman
*November 2004*          ISBN 0-88132-370-5

The United States and the World Economy:
Foreign Economic Policy for the Next Decade
C. Fred Bergsten
*January 2005*          ISBN 0-88132-380-2

Does Foreign Direct Investment Promote
Development?          Theodore H. Moran,
Edward M. Graham, and Magnus Blomström,
eds.
*April 2005*          ISBN 0-88132-381-0

American Trade Politics, 4th ed.     I. M. Destler
*June 2005*          ISBN 0-88132-382-9

Why Does Immigration Divide America?
Public Finance and Political Opposition to
Open Borders          Gordon H. Hanson
*August 2005*          ISBN 0-88132-400-0

Reforming the US Corporate Tax
Gary Clyde Hufbauer and Paul L. E. Grieco
*September 2005*          ISBN 0-88132-384-5

WORKS IN PROGRESS

China's Energy Evolution: The Consequences
of Powering Growth at Home and Abroad
Daniel H. Rosen and Trevor Houser
Global Identity Theft: Economic and Policy
Implications              Catherine L. Mann
Globalized Venture Capital: Implications
for US Entrepreneurship and Innovation
Catherine L. Mann
Forging a Grand Bargain: Expanding Trade and
Raising Worker Prosperity        Lori G. Kletzer,
J. David Richardson, and Howard F. Rosen
Why Reform a Rich Country? Germany and the
Future of Capitalism            Adam S. Posen
Global Forces, American Faces: US Economic
Globalization at the Grass Roots
J. David Richardson
The Impact of Global Services Outsourcing on
American Firms and Workers J. Bradford Jensen
Policy Reform in Rich Countries
John Williamson, ed.
Banking System Fragility in Emerging
Economies    Morris Goldstein and Philip Turner
Witness to Transformation: Refugee Insights
into North Korea              Stephan Haggard and
Marcus Noland
Aligning NAFTA with Climate Change
Objectives        Jeffrey J. Schott, Meera Fickling,
and Tanya Lat
Private Rights and Public Problems: The
Global Economics of Intellectual Property in
the 21st Century                Keith Maskus
The Positive Agenda for Climate Change and
Trade      Trevor Houser, Jacob Funk Kirkegaard,
and Rob Bradley
Stable Prices, Unstable Currencies: The Weak
Link between Exchange Rates and Inflation
and What It Means for Economic Policy
Joseph E. Gagnon
How Latvia Came through the Financial Crisis
Anders Åslund and Valdis Dombrovskis
Foreign Direct Investment and Development:
Launching a Second Generation of Policy
Research, Avoiding the Mistakes of the First,
and Reevaluating Policies for Developed and
Developing Countries.        Theodore H. Moran
The Impact of Global Services Outsourcing on
American Firms and Workers
J. Bradford Jensen
Carbon Abatement Costs and Climate Change
Finance                    William R. Cline

## DISTRIBUTORS OUTSIDE THE UNITED STATES

**Australia, New Zealand,
and Papua New Guinea**
D. A. Information Services
648 Whitehorse Road
Mitcham, Victoria 3132, Australia
Tel: 61-3-9210-7777
Fax: 61-3-9210-7788
Email: service@dadirect.com.au
www.dadirect.com.au

**India, Bangladesh, Nepal, and Sri Lanka**
Viva Books Private Limited
Mr. Vinod Vasishtha
4737/23 Ansari Road
Daryaganj, New Delhi 110002
India
Tel: 91-11-4224-2200
Fax: 91-11-4224-2240
Email: viva@vivagroupindia.net
www.vivagroupindia.com

**Mexico, Central America, South America,
and Puerto Rico**
US PubRep, Inc.
311 Dean Drive
Rockville, MD 20851
Tel:  301-838-9276
Fax: 301-838-9278
Email: c.falk@ieee.org

**Asia** (*Brunei, Burma, Cambodia, China,
Hong Kong, Indonesia, Korea, Laos, Malaysia,
Philippines, Singapore, Taiwan, Thailand,
and Vietnam*)
East-West Export Books (EWEB)
University of Hawaii Press
2840 Kolowalu Street
Honolulu, Hawaii 96822-1888
Tel: 808-956-8830
Fax: 808-988-6052
Email: eweb@hawaii.edu

**Canada**
Renouf Bookstore
5369 Canotek Road, Unit 1
Ottawa, Ontario KlJ 9J3, Canada
Tel: 613-745-2665
Fax: 613-745-7660
www.renoufbooks.com

**Japan**
United Publishers Services Ltd.
1-32-5, Higashi-shinagawa
Shinagawa-ku, Tokyo 140-0002
Japan
Tel:  81-3-5479-7251
Fax:  81-3-5479-7307
Email: purchasing@ups.co.jp
*For trade accounts only. Individuals will find
Institute books in leading Tokyo bookstores.*

**Middle East**
MERIC
2 Bahgat Ali Street, El Masry Towers
Tower D, Apt. 24
Zamalek, Cairo
Egypt
Tel. 20-2-7633824
Fax: 20-2-7369355
Email: mahmoud_fouda@mericonline.com
www.mericonline.com

**United Kingdom, Europe**
(*including Russia and Turkey*)**, Africa,
and Israel**
The Eurospan Group
c/o Turpin Distribution
Pegasus Drive
Stratton Business Park
Biggleswade, Bedfordshire
SG18 8TQ
United Kingdom
Tel: 44 (0) 1767-604972
Fax: 44 (0) 1767-601640
Email: eurospan@turpin-distribution.com
www.eurospangroup.com/bookstore

**Visit our website at:
www.piie.com
E-mail orders to:
petersonmail@presswarehouse.com**